The Technology Criterion in Patent Law

A controversial but indispensable requirement

Reinier B. Bakels

The Technology Criterion in Patent Law

A controversial but indispensable requirement

Reinier B. Bakels

The Technology Criterion in Patent Law
A controversial but indispensable requirement

Reinier B. Bakels

ISBN: 978-90-5850-862-1

This book is an updated version of a PhD thesis written under supervision of professor Anselm Kamperman Sanders, and defended at Maastricht University on 25 April 2008.

Design: Ditty Vos for Wolf Legal Publishers

Published by:
Wolf Legal Publishers (WLP)
PO Box 313
5060 AH Oisterwijk
The Netherlands
E-Mail: info@wolfpublishers.nl
www.wolfpublishers.com

TABLE OF CONTENTS

Preface

Patenting allegedly non-technical subject-matter like software and business methods is controversial both from a political and a legal perspective. Political opinions about patents in these fields vary from "indispensable" to "disastrous". Lawyers complain about opaque rules that would violate statutes.

US law allows patents on non-technical subject-matter, but it excludes "abstract ideas", an exclusion that leads to remarkably similar controversies, again both at the political and the legal level.

Coincidentally, in 2010 both the Enlarged Board of Appeal of the European Patent Office and the U.S. Supreme Court addressed these problems, but unfortunately both failed to provide the clarification one had hoped for.

For all these reasons, the technology criterion in patent law is an almost ideal topic for a PhD research project, an exciting intellectual challenge at the same time fulfilling a topical social need.

Many people inspired me for this study. I would like to acknowledge a number of people here who have been of particular interest to this research project.

Firstly I would like to mention the professor who allowed me to defend this study as an academic dissertation, *Anselm Kamperman Sanders* of Maastricht University. This university, and Anselm in particular, are very internationally oriented. While not an expert in the specific topic of this study, Anselm gave me some essential directions, although as an external PhD candidate I did most of my research independently, in Anselms opinion perhaps *too* independently.

Also I like to mention *Feer Verkade*, former professor at Leiden University. When I asked him for an original topic for my master thesis, in view of my past in the world of information technology, he immediately answered: software patents. "Is there something with these patents?" was my naive question. In the years that followed a whole new world opened to me. Feer, and his later successor *Dirk Visser* also taught me how amusing legal arguing can be. In particular in this field patent law is an inexhaustible source of often utterly funny fallacies.

Certainly I want to mention professor *Reto Hilty*, who allowed me to work for some time at the *Max-Planck-Institut für Immaterialgüter- und Wettbewerbsrecht* in Munich. That also gave me the opportunity to attend lectures at the *Ludwig-Maximilians-Universität* in the same city by patent law Nestor professor *Joseph Straus*.

Law is a social science. Therefore, I am fortunate that I had the opportunity to play a role in the social debate about patent policy, and in particular about the proposal for a European Directive on the patentability of "computer-implemented inventions". Because I came in touch with lobbyists who read the report about this topic I wrote for the European Parliament under supervision of professor *Bernt Hugenholtz* at the Institute for Information Law of the University of Amsterdam, again a whole new world opened for me, this time the political world in Brussels, Strasbourg and The Hague. Furthermore, as a member of the *Commissie Giskes* I had the opportunity to contribute to an advice for the then Deputy Minister of Economic Affairs, *Carien van Gennip*.

While I support patent critics, and software patent critics in particular, I do not necessarily share all their perceptions. It remains a challenge to devise rules that limit the domain of patent law in a just and certain manner. This is by all means a challenge for academic research.

When I did my research I had the privilege – just like *Isaac Newton* over three centuries ago – to stand on the shoulders of giants. In particular I was inspired by two people who preceded me as PhD candidates. Firstly I mention dr. *Ralph Nack*, who motivated me to pay particular attention to American patent law. In his comparative analysis of an immense amount of case law I discovered a recurring theme, that inspired me to conceive the idea of an additional "dimension" in patent law, that I elaborated into the "vertical" technology concept in this study. And I would like to mention dr. *Justine Pila* of Oxford University, who published a number of articles in connection of her PhD research about the invention concept that were essential for my understanding of the history of the technology requirement in European patent law. Finally, I mention patent agents *Axel Horns* and *Arnoud Engelfriet*, who clarified to me what a "software patent" really is. In any case, it is not a patent for software.

I hope that the reader will be just as fascinated by the subject of this study as I am.

I. Introduction

I.1. Problem

Proponents of a broad patent law are convinced that firms will not invest in research and development unless those investments are protected, by patents. So a country wishing to innovate should offer as much patent protection as possible. However, in Europe patents were always only granted for *technology*. The question whether innovation outside the realm of technology may suffer from this limitation is usually responded to by a reference to the tradition only to grant patents for technology. But a tradition by itself is no reason.

Whoever tries to find a rational answer is inevitably faced by the question what should be considered "technology" in this context. At first sight, it does not seem a problem that the "technology" concept is hard to grasp in words. Isn't this another case of "I know it when I see it"?[1] No, it is not that simple. Intuition fails for the very subject-matter that is not always considered sufficiently technical to be patentable: computer software. Perhaps for a mechanical engineer all software is non-technical, and those who feel that software consists of algorithms, and that algorithms are mathematical, and that mathematics is no technology will agree with that. But for a software engineer, as well as a clumsy end-user cursing the unmanageable "technology" of his word processor software, software is definitely technical, not to mention the legal scholars who argue that software is too technical to be protected by copyright.

Courts too struggle with the problem how to assess whether patent applications are sufficiently technical. Inconsistent decisions hurt legal certainty, and lead to dissatisfaction for those who believe that the limits are drawn too wide, or rather too narrow. Courts feel forced again and again to develop new assessment criteria, not

---

[1] U.S. Supreme Court 22 June 1964, no. 11, 378 *U.S.* 184, 197, 84 *S.Ct.* 1676, 1683 (*Jacobellis v. Ohio*).

because policy perceptions are changing, but because so far none of the attempts has been successful to devise acceptable, manageable and consistent rules in this field. There are even complaints that the European Patent Office outright violates the European Patent Convention in the assessment of the technical content of patent applications.

In 2002, the European Committee made a proposal for a Directive for "computer-implemented inventions"[2] to improve unity and clarity, in essence by codifying certain EPO case law. The proposal, presented as a harmonisation measure, was perceived as a highly controversial policy change,[3] and three years later it was rejected by the European Parliament with an overwhelming majority. While politics failed to bring clarity, the EPO President in 2008 made another attempt to get clarity about the limits of software patentability by invoking the EPO Enlarged Board of Appeal.[4] But this Board attributed the alleged inconsistencies in EPO case law to a normal development of law, and considered itself incompetent to respond to the request to set general rules for software patentability, unconnected to a specific case.

At first sight, the situation in the United States is completely different because American courts categorically reject a *technological arts test*. In this respect, there is no rapprochement, rather an increasing divergence: while recently the technology requirement as an age-old rule of customary law has been codified in Europe,[5] the U.S. Supreme Court recently confirmed that in principle there are no objections against patenting business methods, the typical non-technical inventions. Still American patent law is not unlimited either: it

---

[2] Proposal for a Directive of the European Parliament and of the Council on the patentability of computer-implemented inventions, Brussels, 20 February 2002.

[3] *See for instance* Müller 2006.

[4] She referred to the special competence attributed to the EPO President by Art. 112(1b) EPC.

[5] As we will discuss later, it is debatable whether the modified EPC should really be interpreted to that effect. *See* p. 29.

excludes "abstract ideas" for ages, and the interpretation of this exclusion leads to difficulties very similar to the difficulties with the interpretation of the technology requirement in Europe. Starting from Supreme Court decisions, in the course of the years lower courts developed various interpretations, but they never lived very long, and lately the U.S. Supreme Court rejected the recent "machine or transformation test", without giving a concrete alternative.

In sum, on both sides of the Atlantic, a solution seems farther away than ever: nobody really knows the precise boundaries of the domain of patent law.[6]

I.2. Research question

At first sight, the research question could be: how should the technology criterion in patent law be interpreted? What is "technology" in patent law? Now that the technology criterion has been codified in the EPC,[7] the law of treaties requires the term to be understood in its "ordinary" meaning[8] – but we noted already that this meaning is ambiguous.

If language is ambiguous, it may be helpful to investigate the purpose of a criterion.[9] Is there a rational reason why patents should only be granted for technology? Why would a legislator allow only patents for technology? Are the Americans wrong by allowing patents for non-technical subject-matter, or is this a policy choice that can be defended as well? Are business method patents fundamentally wrong, or was the problem rather that the American patent office initially had insufficient experience for a proper assessment of patent applications for these methods?

---

[6] *See also* Bakels 2010.

[7] *See* note 5.

[8] That is even prescribed by the law of treaties. Art. 31(1) Vienna Convention on the Law of Treaties (hereinafter VCLT).

[9] *See* Wank 1985.

The technology criterion is an age-old German tradition,[10] that was adopted by the European patent Office. In these jurisdictions, the technology criterion is not presented as a policy choice, but as a *"self-evident"*, *inherent* limitation of patent law. If the technology criterion is unclear, it is impossible to decide whether that is true. Therefore this statement will be considered a given, as the starting point to determine the meaning of the technology concept in this context. In this approach, we only decide in retrospect whether this meaning corresponds to one of the many meanings of this concept in common parlance.

Thus we arrive at the following problem statement:

What are the inherent boundaries of the patent law domain, and are they related to "technology", in any meaning?

The answer to this question allows the legal rules to be interpreted that are apparently associated with the inherent boundaries of patent law.

We focus on *inherent* boundaries. That is a limitation insofar that there may be policy reasons for further limitations, and that *relative* criteria of novelty and non-obviousness are left out of consideration. Still we emphasise that subject-matter outside the inherent boundaries is inherently unpatentable, even if it is very inventive, or the result of huge research investments.

If the second part of the research question is answered in the affirmative, then American patent law too is logically limited to technology – albeit that one of the many other meanings of the "technology" may apply than the kind of interpretation usually given to this concept in Europe. If we manage to find that meaning, that knowledge may be used to substantiate the exclusion of "abstract ideas" in American patent law.

---

[10] RG 12 January 1933, 38 *GRUR* 1933, p. 289-292 (290), at II.A (*Multiplikationstabelle*). "RG" stands for "Reichsgericht", the German supreme court from 1879-1945.

I.3. Method

Essentially this study is an *analysis,* followed by a *synthesis.*

The *analysis* of positive law looks for common patterns in the perceptions in course of the years over several jurisdictions about the assessment of the technical content of patent applications. This analysis of statutory and case law can be designated as *inductive,* as it strives to arrive at general conclusions from specific observations. Induction can not prove anything. We can only conclude that *as far as we know* no truly satisfactory solution has been found for this problem, and that it is unlikely that it will ever be found in the chosen direction, due to incorrect presumptions.

For that reason, we will subsequently investigate whether we can find how the technology requirement should be interpreted by *deduction,* merely from the observation that this requirement is seen as an inherent boundary by those who subscribe to it.[11]

It is impossible to prove the correctness of our findings like in mathematics, or to test them with observations like natural scientists do. Actually "correctness" is not a criterion at all. The proposal we develop should primarily be assessed for consistency. And we will investigate whether our interpretation of the technology concept could serve as a common denominator for the assessment of subject-matter not always considered technical by the EPO.[12]

In essence, we develop a *model.* Unlike for instance in general private law or criminal law, the development of models in patent law is still in its infancy. Models look for the essence, leaving out all details that are irrelevant in the given context. They are the indispensable basis for an intelligible analysis of complex facts, and to articulate the basic conflicts of interest that eventually are the core of law.

Some believe that it is outright impossible to define patent law concepts like "technology", "invention" and "patentable subject-

---

[11] Section I.2, "Research question", p. 3.

[12] This is the subject-matter listed in art. 52(2) EPC.

matter".[13] Others argue that strict definitions are undesirable, because they would make it harder to adapt to new developments. But for legal certainty precise definitions are indispensable. Vague definitions are harder to interpret, and one should acknowledge that these concepts are applied every day routinely for the assessment of numerous patent applications by patent offices, who have less time than courts. If the rules are unclear, patent offices will naturally stay on the safe side. That will cause patents to be granted that should not have been granted. Unclear rules will erode.

The *dominium* concept can be applied to 21st century *gadgets* the Romans not even dreamt of. We will develop a model of similar timeless abstractions in patent law.

I.4. Positioning and limitation

Basically legal topics may be addressed both by studying legislation and case law as it applies and applied in the past (in a "positivist" manner),[14] and by investigating what law might be desirable (in a "normative" manner). We will pursue both approaches, and yet another one.

In our investigation of statutes and case law we will concentrate on the shortcomings of present interpretations, in view of possible improvements. There already is an abundance of literature on the application of present law that shows practitioners what subject-matter can be patentable,[15] and in particular under what conditions

---

[13] *The British often refer to*: High Court of Australia 16 December 1959, *RPC* 1961, p. 134-147 (142, line 32-34), 102 *CLR* 252, 271 (*N.R.D.C.*).

[14] Note that the legal "positivism" concept is used in different meanings.

[15] *See for instance* Stobbs 2008; European Patent Office 2007; Melullis 2002; Nack 2002. Last mentioned writer gives an overview of patentable subject-matter in the United States too. All these sources give numerous further references. Also the guidelines for the examiners of patent offices should be mentioned. While these guidelines formally don't have force of law, they strive to give a comprehensive overview of the state of the law. EPO

software and business methods are deemed sufficiently technical for patent.[16]

In the quest for *desirable* law one may try to grasp the *ontology* of the invention concept. An example is the debate whether patents should only be granted for physically tangible subject-matter.[17] Alternatively, one may try to find what rules lead to an optimum economic result. This is still a major challenge for economists. For instance, attempts to establish the usefulness of software patents consistently failed due to the diversity of these patents.[18] If thus no arguments are found for a categorical acceptance or rejection of these patents, is the technology content – whatever that means – perhaps an appropriate *policy lever*?[19] Meanwhile one should keep in mind that legislative change may be hard to implement in the foreseeable future, if only because patent law is entrenched by various international treaties. If a clean slate approach leads to a concrete proposal at all, another question is whether it is feasible in practice, or merely academic.

Hence we ventured yet another approach: we analysed the system of patent law strictly following present legislation, but we left present case law out of consideration. Thus we find an interpretation that follows present legislation more strictly than present case law, and at the same time avoids the pitfalls of that case law. Such a radical departure from present case law may be a bold proposal, but actually it is inevitable, in view of paradoxes found in present interpretations.

Examination Guidelines 2010, Part C Chapter IV; USPTO 2007, § 2106, 'Patent Subject-matter Eligibility', p. 5.

[16] *See for instance* Bakels & Hugenholtz 2002, Sedlmaier 2004, Winischhofer 2000. Zirn 2004 also discusses the situation in the United Kingdom, France, Austria, Switzerland, the United States, Japan and Russia. For a concise historical overview of the possibilities to obtain patents for software-inventions in the United States *see* Fellas 1999. Standard works also discuss the technology requirement in other areas: Melullis 2002, Art. 52, Rn. 60-79 and Kraßer 2009, p. 142-186.

[17] Pila 2010a, p. 7-8.

[18] *See* Bakels & Hugenholtz 2002.

[19] *See* Burk & Lemley 2009.

Current practice of patent law is dominated by an ingenious wordplay. That would still be appropriate if that would lead to consistent results, but actually there are strong complaints about poor consistency.[20] A better understanding of the system of patent law gives more convincing rational arguments.

As we noted in the beginning of this chapter, patenting subject-matter with a disputed technical contents is politically controversial as well. The political opinions about software and business method patents vary from "indispensable" to "disastrous". However, this book is not a political pamphlet. This study tries to adopt a neutral point of view as much as possible. Our purpose is to find *rational* arguments that may convince reasonable opponents of certain positions too. Patent law practice tends to be dominated by people who *believe* in patents, but obviously in patent law a rational balance must be found, just like in other fields of law.

I.5. Readers' guide

This study in essence consists of three parts: an *analysis* of positive law, a *synthesis* of an alternative approach, and a *verification* whether the alternative approach provides satisfactory results.

In chapter II, 'Positive law' we discuss and analyse pertinent law as it applied and applies in the past and presently in various jurisdictions.[21] We will concentrate on three aspects of the traditional technology requirement. Firstly, we will discuss the statutory basis for granting patents only for technology, next we review definitions of "technology" used in patent law, and finally we discuss in which respect an invention must be "technical" in order to be patentable. Here we will run into a paradox that explains the persistent uncertainty about the interpretation of the technology criterion more than precarious political perceptions.

---

[20] *See* Chapter II, 'Positive law', p. 11.

[21] Please note that the "positive law" concept has a very different meaning in U.S. law.

Hence in chapter III, "Towards a better technology criterion" we will try another tack. Starting from the idea that "technology" is the natural realm of patent law, we will investigate the inherent boundaries of the patent law domain. That leads to an entirely new insight in the technology requirement, which can be used to arrive at a better interpretation of the problematic rules associated with inherent boundaries of patent law.

The last chapter before the conclusion, chapter IV: 'The application of the "vertical" technology criterion' is devoted to the "verification" of the answer to the research question. Here we will investigate whether the "vertical" technical content test we developed in the previous chapter is not just appropriate but also sufficient for the interpretation of the present exclusions, notably for the subject-matter listed in Art. 52(2) EPC.

Finally, we will see that the application of the "vertical" technology criterion for the interpretation or the "abstract ideas" exclusion in American corresponds with interpretations developed in the United States from the nineteenth century (that are still considered relevant precedents). Contrary to common wisdom, American patent law never protected "anything under the sun made by man",[22] and 19th century precedents show the direction.

I.6. Notes

The research for this study was completed early 2012. Only occasionally information of a later date has been incorporated. That applies in particular to the *Mayo v. Prometheus* decision of the U.S. Supreme Court in March 2012. Internet URLs have been re-checked mid-2012.

This study is oriented at an international audience. Wherever possible – preferably official – English translations of citations in other languages have been added, but in particular for the reader who has a command of the German language we have not restricted ourselves

---

[22] *See* p. 51.

in referring to the abundance of relevant literature and case law that is only available in German.

II. Positive law

II.1. Introduction

II.1.1. Purpose of this chapter

In this chapter, we discuss pertinent law as it applied and applies in the past and presently in various jurisdictions.[23]

Even more important than the question what makes a patent application sufficiently technical is the question why there are still no clear, satisfactory rules to make the assessment. In the United States, the assessment whether an idea is too abstract to be patented is a similar problem. Is this one of those legal dilemma's that never will be solved because there are contrary interests weighed differently by different people, or is there a misconception that may be resolved?

Obviously the central question is, what is understood by "technology" in the patent law context. Does it follow common parlance, if that is unambiguous at all? Or is it a specific legal concept, used "teleologically" for a certain purpose? If so, what purpose?

The question about the meaning of the technology concept is preceded by the question, why – at least in Europe – patents are only granted for technology. It is assumed that this rule is codified now that the European Patent Convention since late 2007 provides that patents are granted "in all fields of technology", but this interpretation is debatable, because the literal text says something else. Also the rejection of a technology requirement in American patent law is discussed here.

The third question is how patent applications should be assessed that are considered *partially* technical. Intuitively, the technical part should

[23] As noted before, the "positive law" concept has a very different meaning in U.S. law.

be novel, but a principal rule of patent law requires applications to be assessed as a whole. How could this paradox be resolved?

This chapter has been structured in view of the purpose to find similarities. Hence the discussion is organised according to the three above themes. For each of those themes, case law in a number of jurisdictions is compared, and for each of the jurisdictions the development in course of time is discussed.

Despite major differences between the European and the American legal culture, and hardly less differences between the legal cultures in the countries that dominate European patent law, Germany and the United Kingdom, similarities are striking.

II.1.2. Choice of the jurisdictions

In our comparative investigation we will first focus on worldwide treaties. Next we will investigate European and American patent law.

In Europe, the grant of patents is primarily regulated by the European Patent Convention, executed by the European Patent Office. The Boards of Appeal of the EPO have jurisdiction in conflicts related to this grant process.[24] Once a patent has finally been granted by the EPO,[25] it can not be revoked by the EPO.[26]

From that moment, a European patent is almost equivalent to a national patent in the EPO member states.[27] Consequently, a patent application approved by the EPO still may be invalidated by courts in one or more member states, if they find that the patent should not

[24] EPO Boards of Appeal, Art. 21 EPC, EPO Enlarged Board of Appeal, Art. 22 EPC.

[25] After expiration of the opposition term, or after any oppositions have been completed. Art. 99-105 EPC.

[26] A European patent can be limited or revoked after grant by its proprietor though. Art. 105 EPC.

[27] Art. 64 EPC. Nowadays it is assumed that the applicant has designated all member states, unless the applicant explicitly withdraws a designation for a member state. Art. 79 EPC.

have been granted, for instance if they decide that the application was insufficiently technical.[28] Therefore the case law of the member states of the European Patent Organisation[29] is interesting too. It is also relevant because there is still the possibility to obtain patents from national patent offices, such as the *UK Intellectual Property Office*.[30]

The number of court cases on the technology requirement in patent law varies greatly by EPO member state.[31] For instance, in the Netherlands never a case about the patentability of software was submitted to an independent court. Only the former Board of Appeal of the Dutch Patent Office[32] has made some decisions on such patents, the last time over twenty-five years ago, under the previous Dutch Patent Act, that was not yet adapted to the EPC. Nevertheless those decisions have historical interest, and they caught international attention at the time by their "progressive" views on the technology requirement.

---

[28] Art. 138 EPC limits the grounds for revocation by national courts. These include all provisions about substantive requirements for patentability (Art. 52-57 EPC).

[29] The European Patent Organisation encompasses the European Patent Office and its Administrative Council, comprised of member state representatives. Art 4(2) EPC.

[30] http://www.ipo.gov.uk Until April 2007, this office was called the *UK Patent and Trademark Office*.

[31] From 1 October 2010 the European Patent Organisation has 38 members. *EPO Member States*, http://www.epo.org/about-us/organisation/member-states.html.

[32] The former Board of Appeal of the Dutch Patent Office, regulated in Art. 14 and 15 ROW 1910, was an administrative appeal body, not an independent court in the sense of Art. 116 Gw in conjunction with Art. 2 Wet R.O. This Board had no function anymore under the new Dutch patent act adopted in 1995, and has been withdrawn in September when the old Patent Act was withdrawn (which remained in force in parallel to new patent act for patents granted under the old act that had not expired when the new act went into force in 1995). "ROW" stands for "Rijksoctrooiwet", the patent act for The Netherlands and its overseas territories (as indicated by the prefix "Rijks"). The current version dates from 1995, the previous one from 1910.

Other European countries investigated in this chapter are Germany[33] and the United Kingdom. Unlike Germany, the United Kingdom has no tradition to grant only patents for "technology". But since this country became a member of the European Patent Organisation[34] the British too must decide whether patent applications comply with the provisions that are associated with the technical character requirement.[35] We choose our words carefully, because the British still have their own perceptions on the technology requirement.

As announced, we will also pay attention to the developments in the United States, not so much because in the US patents are granted too for non-technical subject-matter, like business methods, but because American courts struggle with the interpretation of the exclusion of "abstract ideas" with problems similar to the problems European courts encounter with the interpretation of the technology requirement. While from our European perspective the United States in this chapter is discussed last (under each of the main themes), we encourage the reader not to skip the relevant paragraphs.[36]

---

[33] To be precise: we will discuss the case law of the courts of the German Federal Republic, and occasionally about German case law predating the establishment of the German Federal Republic in 1949, in particular of the *Reichsgericht,* the Supreme Court of the German Reich. The history of these courts is summarised in http://www.bundesgerichtshof.de/SharedDocs/Downloads/DE/DerBGH/broschuereBGHAktuell.pdf?__blob=publicationFile. To our knowledge there is no relevant case law of the Supreme Court (*Oberste Gericht)* of the former "German Democratic Republic", which may be related to the fact that patents play a different role in a communist system.

[34] The United Kingdom is a founding member of the European Patent Organisation (since 7 October 1977).

[35] Section 1 UK Patents Act, corresponding to Art. 52 EPC.

[36] Section II.2.6, p. 48, section II.3.5, p. 82 and section II.4.4, p. 119.

II.1.3. European harmonisation

While the idea of a European patent system[37] implies a need to strive for a uniform interpretation,[38] formally this system is an autonomous legal system standing side by side to the patent law systems in the member states.[39] Although the EPC limits the grounds for revocation of a "European" patent by a member state,[40] an obligation to follow EPO case law is not inferred from that.[41] EPO Boards of Appeal decisions will only be followed if they are substantially convincing. That even applies to EPO Enlarged Board of Appeal decisions, although this Board may have more authority when judges from member states participate as "external members".[42]

While generally the EPO and the member states, and the member states among themselves are entitled to foster different opinions on the validity of a particular "European" patent, there is one exception: a European Directive may enforce a uniform interpretation in certain fields for those member states of the European Patent Organisation that are EU members as well.[43] Then the European Court of Justice

---

37 See the Preamble to the European Patent Convention.

38 There is no centralised European court for this phase as yet. For decades attempts have been made to establish such a court, without concrete results so far. *See* Luginbühl 2011 for newer developments.

39 Jestaedt 2002, Art. 1, Rn. 4-6.

40 Art. 138(1) EPC.

41 Rogge 2002, Art. 138, Rn. 40.

42 Art. 11(5) EPC. The possibility to appoint external members in EPO Boards of Appeal has been curtailed by the latest revision of the EPC, which becomes apparent from the replacement of Art. 160 EPC 1973 by this new provision. The underlying reason is that the EPO nowadays is supposed to be sufficiently experienced to depend no longer on external experts.

43 All EU member states are members of the European Patent Organisation. The following members of the European Patent Organisation are not EU members: Iceland, Liechtenstein, the Former Yugoslav Republic of Macedonia, Monaco, Norway, San Marino, Serbia, Switzerland and Turkey.

has the final say. Presently there is only such a Directive for biotechnological inventions.[44]

Although international law otherwise does not oblige member states of the European Patent Organisation to follow the European Patent Office or each other, high courts in member states have repeatedly indicated that courts should consider relevant decisions made elsewhere in this field.[45]

The U.K Patents Act even contains a provision on uniform interpretation:[46]

> Whereas by a resolution made on the signature of the Community Patent Convention the governments of the member states of the European Economic Community resolved to adjust their laws relating to patents so as (among other things) to bring those laws into conformity with the corresponding provisions of the European Patent Convention, the Community Patent Convention and the Patent Co-operation Treaty, it is hereby declared that the following provisions of this Act, that is to say, sections 1(1) to (4), 2 to 6, 14(3), (5) and (6), 37(5), 54, 60, 69, 72(1) and (2), 74(4), 82, 83, 100 and 125, <u>are so framed as to have, as nearly as practicable, the same effects in the United Kingdom as the corresponding provisions of the European Patent Convention</u>, the Community Patent Convention and the Patent Co-operation Treaty have in the territories to which those Conventions apply.

The *House of Lords* has established that EPO decisions "are not strictly binding upon courts in the United Kingdom but they are of great persuasive authority".[47] This statement should be seen in the context of the British "common law" system of binding precedents: it is allowed to deviate from EPO decisions if there are good reasons.

---

[44] Directive 98/44/EC of the European Parliament and of the Council of 6 July 1998 on the legal protection of biotechnological inventions (*OJEC* 1998, L 213).

[45] *See in general*: Brinkhof 2009; Luginbühl 2011.

[46] Section 130(7) UK Patents Act. Emphasis added.

[47] House of Lords 26 October 1995, *RPC* 1996, p. 76, *BMLR* 1997, p. 201, at 12. (*Merrell Dow v. Norton*).

The highest German court has decided that German courts should observe in their judgements decisions in similar cases made by the EPO and other member states of the European Patent Organisation, and that they are only allowed to deviate with a proper motivation.[48]

While courts usually subscribe to the desirability of uniform interpretation of European patent law, that does not mean that they agree on the technology criterion. As in other differences in patent law,[49] the British are opposed to the Germans, and the EPO that follows a German tradition.

In 2002 the European Commission and the European Council submitted a proposal for a Directive for "computer implemented inventions",[50] in essence with the purpose to force British courts to follow the interpretation developed by the EPO Boards of Appeal.[51] Suggesting that the sole purpose was harmonisation, the proposal actually involved a politically controversial broadening of software patentability, in particular for the United Kingdom. After numerous amendments a chaos developed that might have led to a reduction of software patentability just as well, so the initial proponents turned against the proposal as well, and eventually it was rejected by the European Parliament with an overwhelming majority.[52]

Nonetheless, in the years that followed the British courts tried to follow EPO case law more closely. Those attempts met difficulties however because the British found EPO interpretations to be

---

[48] BGH 15 April 2010, no. Xa ZB 10/09, 112 *GRUR* 2010, p. 950-952 (951-52), at 13-14 (*Walzenformgebungsmaschine*). "BGH" stands for "Bundesgerichtshof", the German Federal Supreme Court, established in 1950.

[49] Think of the controversy about the determination of the extent of protection, as laid down in Art. 69 EPC and the associated Protocol.

[50] Proposal for a Directive of the European Parliament and of the Council on the patentability of computer-implemented inventions, Brussels, 20 February 2002.

[51] For a general introduction to this Directive Proposal see e.g. Kraßer 2004, p. 166-171.

[52] Müller 2006, p. 332.

inconsistent. Eventually a British court suggested[53] that the President of the EPO should use his authority[54] to invoke the EPO Enlarged Board of Appeal[55] for clarification of the rules on software patentability. The then French EPO President rejected the suggestion,[56] but his British successor in 2008 eventually submitted a number of questions to the EBA on this problem (albeit other questions than suggested by the British court).[57] However, the EBA noted that it is not authorised to clarify abstract points of law unrelated to a specific case,[58] and it considered the alleged inconsistencies as a normal consequence of the development of law in a continental-European legal system that does not recognise binding precedents, unlike Anglo-Saxon legal systems.[59] The EBA gave to understand that there would be rather a task for the legislator.[60] Whether the submitted questions – different from the questions proposed by the British court – would have allowed to find a structural solution is doubtful though, because they implicitly confirmed presuppositions that are the very reason for the inconsistencies that were found.[61]

---

[53] Court of Appeal 27 October 2006, no. 2006 EWCA Civ 1371, 2006 All ER (D) 346 (Oct), at 25, 75 (*Aerotel*).

[54] Art. 112(1b) EPC. Whether this authority really applies here is controversial.

[55] Hereinafter: EBA. Art 22 EPC.

[56] President of the EPO's letter to Jacob LJ, http://www.ipo.gov.uk/pro-types/pro-patent/p-law/p-pn/p-pn-subjectmatter/p-pn-subjectmatter-letter.htm.

[57] "Referral by the President of the European Patent Office to the Enlarged Board of Appeal dated 23 October 2008 regarding divergent decisions of two boards of appeal", 32 *OJ* 2009, p. 142-166.

[58] EBA 12 May 2010, no. G 3/08, 34 *OJ* 2011, p. 10-59, at 7.2.4 and 7.2.5 (*Patentability of programs for computers*).

[59] *Id.* at 7.3.

[60] *Id.* at 7.2.7: "When judiciary-driven legal development meets its limits, it is time for the legislator to take over."

[61] *See* Bakels 2009.

As we will see in this chapter, as yet no one has found a satisfactory interpretation of Art. 52 EPC that does not suffer from contradictions. It remains to be seen who will resolve this stalemate eventually. After the failure of the above Directive Proposal, no EU politician will burn his fingers on another proposal for the foreseeable future. If the EBA is reluctant to cut the knot, would a future European patent court[62] be willing to do so?[63] Or will it simply follow the dominant EPO approach, rooted in a German tradition? This prospect may be a reason for the UK not to support the long-expected European patent court. Incidentally, this study will show that neither the EPO nor the UK approach are correct.

II.1.4. Terminology

For simplicity, we will refer to the patent law of the European Patent Organisation under the European Patent Convention as "European" patent law, although that organisation is not part of the European Union, and while there is an Eurasian Patent Organisation[64] having several Eastern European countries as member states, so that *the* European patent law actually does not exist. Reversely, Turkey is also an EPO member state, a country located almost entirely in Asia, so in turn "European" patent law (in our terminology) applies not exclusively in Europe.

While the European Patent Convention is an international treaty, we will refer to its provisions by the generic designation "statutory" if that fosters simplicity, for instance if the substantive provisions for patentability in various jurisdictions are compared.

Whether the Boards of Appeal of the EPO can be considered "courts" is controversial.[65] In any case, the people on these Boards are

---

[62] *See* Luginbühl 2011.

[63] Pila 2011, p. 226.

[64] Евразийская патентная организация http://www.eapo.org. Member states include (partially) European states like the Russian Federation, Belarus and Moldova.

[65] An EPC change is considered in order to strengthen the autonomy of these Boards. 'Autonomy of the boards of appeal', http://www.epo.org/

designated as *members* rather than *judges*. Nonetheless, for simplicity sake we will also refer to the decisions of these boards as case law, and "case law of the EPO" in particular, because these Boards are part of the European Patent Office.[66] Note that the EPO Board of Appeal decisions do not constitute "case law" in the strict Anglo-Saxon meaning of the term, because they are not binding as precedents.[67]

Court decisions are designated in different ways in different jurisdictions. In Dutch, a difference is made between "vonnissen", "arresten" en "beschikkingen", dependent on the type of court. Americans refer to "opinions". Here we preferably use the more neutral designation "decision", following the German example.[68]

In European terminology, the legal "invention" concept implies a judgement: not every patent application relates to an invention. The corresponding American concept is "patentable subject-matter".[69] The American invention concept is not just interpreted differently, it means something essentially different: it corresponds more or less to what is referred to as "patent application" in Europe. No application is ever rejected in the U.S. for not relating to an invention. The American "invention" concept includes discoveries,[70] while in the European perception a "discovery as such" is no invention.[71] So these terminological differences have nothing to do with different perceptions on the law.

---

law-practice/legislative-initiatives/autonomy.html. Implicitly this initiative confirms that these Boards currently are not truly independent courts.

[66] Art. 15(f) EPC.

[67] TBA 15 November 2006, no. T 154/04, 31 *OJ* 2008, p. 46-79 (58), at 2 (*Method of estimating product distribution/DUNS*). "TBA" stands for "technical board of appeal", Art. 21 EPC. Remarkably, these Boards are part of the European Patent Office: Art. 15(f) EPC.

[68] The German word for "decision" is "Entscheidung".

[69] Alternatively, the designation "statutory subject-matter" is used, but strictly speaking that includes subject-matter excluded by judicially-created exceptions.

[70] 35 USC § 100(a).

[71] Art. 52(2a) in conjunction with (3) EPC.

II.2. Why only "technology"?

Although the technology requirement is often considered "indispensable" and even "self-evident", in the context of this chapter we are interested in *legal* reasons only to grant patents for "technology".

II.2.1. Worldwide treaties

At the end of the nineteenth century two treaties were adopted that shape the landscape of "intellectual property" until today to a large extent. In 1883 the *Paris Convention for the Protection of Industrial Property*[72] was adopted, and in 1886 the *Berne Convention for the Protection of Literary and Artistic Works.*[73] Patents are covered by the former treaty. From the names of these treaties is seems that "industrial" is seen as the opposite of "artistic". However Art. 2(1) of the Berne Convention already creates doubts because it includes "every production in the scientific domain" in its scope. While the concepts "technology" and "art" are perhaps mutually exclusive, the concepts "technology" and "science" definitely are not.[74] On the contrary: science is indispensable for modern technology. Meanwhile the Paris Convention gives no clue about patentable subject-matter, let alone about a technology requirement.

More than a hundred years later the forthcoming member states of the World Trade Organization came to an agreement what minimum level of protection should be offered in a number of area's of "intellectual property" law, including patent law, by its – presently over a hundred and fifty[75] member states. This TRIPS Agreement[76]

---

[72] Originally dated 20 March 1883 http://www.wipo.int/treaties/en/ip/paris/pdf/trtdocs_wo020.pdf.

[73] Originally dated 9 September 1886 http://www.wipo.int/treaties/en/ip/berne/pdf/trtdocs_wo001.pdf.

[74] In some languages, the word "science" is translated by a word that includes the humanities ("Wissenschaft" in German, "wetenschap" in Dutch), while "science" doesn't.

[75] As of 10 May 2012, the WTO has 155 member states. *See* http://www.wto.org.

went into force in 1996. While the substance of this Agreement builds on earlier treaties, such as the above Berne and Paris Conventions,[77] it distinguishes itself from its predecessors by its dispute prevention and settlement procedures, enabling sanctions against member states not fulfilling the requirements of the Agreement.[78]

The European Patent Office is not a member of the World Trade Organization, so formally it is not bound by the TRIPS Agreement. However, most member states of the European Patent Organisation are members of the World Trade Organization,[79] as is the European Union. Would the EPO fail to grant patents where the Agreement requires to do so, then the member states would be individually obliged grant such patents.[80] Because the member states founded the EPO for the very reason to centralise the grant of patents, their representatives in the EPO *Administrative Council*[81] undoubtedly will urge the EPO to conform to TRIPS. The EPO Boards of Appeal also take TRIPS into account, though they are aware not to be bound directly by its provisions.[82]

---

[76] This Agreement is part of the treaties establishing the World Trade Organization. The text can be found at http://www.wto.org/english/docs_e/legal_e/27-trips.pdf. The provisions of this Agreement became binding one year after the treaties went into force, see Art. 65(1) TRIPS.

[77] Art. 2(2) TRIPS explicitly refers to these treaties.

[78] Art. 63 and 64 TRIPS. These dispute settlement procedures are created for the World Trade Organization as a whole. http://www.wto.org/english/tratop_e/dispu_e/dispu_e.htm.

[79] Exceptions are Monaco, San Marino and Serbia, although the country last mentioned has observer status at the WTO.

[80] Remember that there is still a possibility to obtain patents from national patent offices, for instance the *UK Intellectual Property Office* or the German *Deutsches Patent- und Markenamt*.

[81] Art. 26-36 EPC.

[82] *For instance* TBA 1 July 1998, no. T 1173/97, 22 *OJ* 1999, p. 609-632, at VIII (*Computer Program Product I/IBM*).

Specific provisions about patent law are found in Chapter 5 of the TRIPS Agreement.[83] What subject-matter should be eligible for patent protection is defined in the following provision:[84]

> Article 27 TRIPS - Patentable Subject-matter
>
> 1. Subject to the provisions of paragraphs 2 and 3, patents shall be available for any inventions, whether products or processes, in all fields of technology, provided that they are new, involve an inventive step and are capable of industrial application.[85] [...] patents shall be available and patent rights enjoyable without discrimination as to the place of invention, the field of technology and whether products are imported or locally produced.

The purport of this provision is that no field of technology may be excluded or discriminated. That is confirmed by the legislative history: at the time TRIPS was adopted, in particular in many jurisdictions no patents were granted on pharmaceutical products, and "TRIPS" intended to end such exceptions.[86] So the emphasis is on "*all*", but we will see in a minute that the wording of the provision is also seen as a reason *only* to grant patents for technology.

Still the provision explicitly refers to "all fields *of technology*" instead of simply "all fields". So without stretching the literal text, it could as well be interpreted in the sense that TRIPS does not oblige the WTO member states to grant patents outside the domain of technology.[87] TRIPS does not *prevent* patents to be granted in non-technical fields

---

[83] Art. 27-34 TRIPS.
[84] Emphasis added.
[85] In the original treaty text a footnote is added to this sentence: *For the purposes of this Article, the terms "inventive step" and "capable of industrial application" may be deemed by a Member to be synonymous with the terms "non-obvious" and "useful" respectively.*
[86] Straus 1996, nr. 27, p. 181.
[87] These words fell prey to a strong controversy in the framework of the negotiations for a world-wide *Substantive Patent Law Treaty*. *See* p. 24. Recently these words have also been included into European Patent Convention. *See* p. 28.

however, since the TRIPS Agreement only imposes minimum requirements upon the member states.[88]

Another observation is that this provision only requires patent protection for "inventions", without defining this concept though. While this concept in the perception of the EPO and the Germans implies a technical character requirement, the principle of autonomous interpretation of treaties[89] does not allow the TRIPS invention concept to be interpreted in the same manner, because in many jurisdictions the invention concept does not have that connotation, in particular in the United States.[90]

While the TRIPS Agreement only regulates minimum requirements, since 1986 the World Intellectual Property Organization (WIPO)[91] has been working on worldwide patent law harmonisation,[92] and since 1998 the *Standing Committee on the Law of Patents* (SCP)[93] of the WIPO has regularly meetings for that purpose. In 2000 the work of the SCP led to the *Patent Law Treaty* (PLT).[94] But this treaty makes arrangements for procedural matters only and purposely does not contain any substantive provisions.[95] From the fifth session in May 2001 the SCP negotiates about a *Substantive Patent Law Treaty* (SPLT), that strives for substantive patent law harmonisation.

Less than a year after the start of the negotiations on the SPLT, a severe controversy arose about the question whether the envisaged

---

[88] Art. 1(1) TRIPS.

[89] This principle has been codified in Art. 31(1) VCLT. The United States are not a party to this treaty, but logically they are not allowed either to give their own interpretation to treaty texts, because otherwise a treaty would hardly be meaningful at all.

[90] *See* section II.2.6, p. 48.

[91] Art. 4(i) WIPO Convention. For the history of WIPO and its predecessors see http://www.wipo.int/treaties/en/general.

[92] Schäfers 1992, nr. 6.

[93] *Standing Committee on the Law of Patents*, http://www.wipo.int/patent/law/en/scp.htm.

[94] This treaty went into force on 28 April 2005.

[95] Art. 2(2) PLT confirms this explicitly.

world wide patent law should limit itself to technology.[96] The debate centres around the following draft provision:[97]

> Article 12 Draft SPLT – Conditions of Patentability
>
> (1) Subject-matter Eligible for Protection
>
> (a) A claimed invention shall fall within the scope of subject-matter eligible for protection. Subject-matter eligible for protection shall include products and processes [, in all fields of technology,] which can be made and used in any field of activity.

The clause between square brackets is identical to a clause we just encountered in Art. 27(1) of the TRIPS Agreement. While the Americans were the driving force behind this agreement in 1995,[98] they had discovered meanwhile that this phrase was also construed in the sense that *only* technical inventions are patentable,[99] an interpretation the Americans strongly disagree with. Several delegations, in particular the delegation of the EU[100] and the EPO insisted that the square brackets were removed, in order to prevent the domain of patent law to be extended to e.g. non-technical business methods in Europe.[101] In contrast, the US delegation held the opinion that the words between the square brackets must be interpreted in the sense that inventions in *any* field should be eligible for patent protection. The Americans demanded the removal of this phrase, arguing that the harmonisation purpose would not be served by apparently ambiguous wordings.[102] The US delegation stated that it had come to the negotiations in good faith in that many provisions in the draft SPLT would require fundamental changes to the United States patent system. However, the Delegation stated that its continued participation was contingent on similar good faith from all

---

96 This happens during the seventh SCP session, held from 6-10 May 2002.

97 The square brackets have been copied from the original text. (This applies for the rather oddly placed comma's too.)

98 *See* Drahos 1995.

99 WIPO 2002a, nr. 159-160, Conclusion under nr. 173.

100 The EU was represented there by the Spanish presidency of the time.

101 WIPO 2002a, nr. 159.

102 WIPO 2002a, nr. 160.

members of the Committee". Otherwise "they might well have to reconsider their participation in those discussions".[103] Several other delegations strongly objected against the American suggestion that they would not negotiate "in good faith".[104]

At the next SCP session it was agreed that the discussion on these provisions be postponed,[105] and in later SCP sessions no progress was made on this issue either. Also an *Open Forum* was unable to resolve this stalemate.[106]

While initially SCP meetings took place every half hear, it took more than three years before in June 2008 again an official SCP meeting was held.[107] On this meeting, a list of eighteen issues was agreed,[108] and from this list, four priority issues were selected.[109] One of these issues is "exceptions from patentable subject matter".[110] A document prepared by the WIPO secretariat on this topic concentrates on subject-matter that is considered an invention, but nonetheless excluded from patentability.[111] Limitations based on a technology requirement are outside this scope, because non-technical subject-matter is not considered an invention, at least by the EPO.[112]

Meanwhile, a committee of patent scholars from all inhabited continents has made a masterly inventory of "Exclusions from Patentability and Exceptions and Limitations to Patentees' Rights" all

---

[103] WIPO 2002a, nr. 171.
[104] Pagenberg 2002, p. 737.
[105] WIPO 2002b, nr. 64. *See also* Schneider 2003, p. 353.
[106] Open Forum on the draft Substantive Patent Law Treaty (SPLT), Geneva, 1 to 3 March 2006. For a report *see* Klunker & Waldeck Pyrmont 2006.
[107] SCP/12, 23-27 June 2008.
[108] WIPO 2009b, nr. 85.
[109] WIPO 2009b, nr. 109.
[110] French: "exceptions relatives à l'objet brevetable", Spanish: "excepciones a la materia patentable".
[111] WIPO 2009a, nr. 27.
[112] *See* section II.2.2, p. 28.

over the world,[113] commissioned by WIPO.[114] With respect to the original priority issue identified by the SCP meeting, the scope is extended now to the limitation of the rights of patentees,[115] recommended by the committee as an alternative for a complete exclusions of certain subject-matter that deserves more attention.

"Exclusions", "exceptions" and "limitations" are terms that suggest a departure from a principal rule. The WIPO assignment fails to appreciate that first and foremost more clarity is needed about the principal rule, the fundamental problem to identify the limits of the domain of patent law.

At the moment, the objective of a worldwide harmonised patent law seems farther away than ever. While harmonisation has undeniable advantages – for instance for worldwide patent applications through the PCT system[116] – it should be acknowledged that sovereign states – unless (voluntarily) bound by treaties – have the fundamental right to arrange their patent law as they want: patent law is not a human right[117] (human rights only apply to patents once they have been granted).[118] Incidentally, the disadvantage of a non-harmonised patent law is limited due to the assimilation principle,[119] which implies for instance that in the United States for Europeans the same patent law applies as for Americans. Harmonisation is easily misunderstood as a reason for ever further extension of patent law, without due consideration whether that serves a purpose.[120] A writer even argues

---

[113] *See* Bently et al. 2010.
[114] WIPO 2010.
[115] Example: U.S. patent law allows medical methods to be patented, but gives medical practitioners and related health care entities a specific defence. 35 USC § 287(c). *See also* Lee 1997.
[116] http://www.wipo.int/pct.
[117] Brinkhof 2004, p. 408.
[118] ECHR 11 January 2007, no. 73049/01 (*Anheuser-Busch v. Portugal*).
[119] Art. 2 Paris Convention.
[120] In particular countries in an early stage of industrialisation can benefit from a limited patent protection: *see* Schiff 1971.

that harmonisation may prohibit countries to experiment with different regulations that may eventually enrich patent law.[121]

In sum, we can conclude that no present worldwide treaty contains an explicit provision allowing only patents for technical subject-matter. In particular, inferring a technology requirement from the wordings of the TRIPS Agreement is both questionable from a legal perspective and controversial from a political perspective.

II.2.2. European Patent Office

In "EPC 2000", the new version of the European Patent Convention agreed in 2000 that went into force late 2007[122] the words "in all fields of technology" are added to Art. 52 EPC:[123]

> Art. 52(1) EPC
>
> 1. European patents shall be granted for any inventions, in all fields of technology, provided that they are new, involve an inventive step and are susceptible of industrial application.

The emphasised words have been adopted[124] from the TRIPS Agreement,[125] according to the preparatory materials of "EPC 2000" for two reasons: on the one hand in order to align the EPC with TRIPS, and to lay down that patent protection is offered in *all* fields of technology, and on the other hand to express that patents are *only*

[121] *See* Duffy 2002.
[122] As agreed, this change went into force on 13 December 2007, two years after the fifteenth member state had ratified this change (or accepted at the time of accession, for new member states).
[123] Emphasis added.
[124] *Diplomatic Conference for the revision of the EPC* http://www.epo.org/patents/law/legal-texts/archive/EPC 2000/diplomatic-conference-nov2000.html.
[125] Art. 27(1) TRIPS. *See further* section II.2.1, p. 21.

granted for technical inventions.[126] As regards the latter aspect, the document explains:[127]

> [...] the point must be made that patent protection is reserved for creations in the technical field. This is now clearly expressed in the new wording of Article 52(1) EPC. In order to be patentable, the subject-matter claimed must therefore have a "technical character" or to be more precise - involve a "technical teaching", ie an instruction addressed to a skilled person as to how to solve a particular technical problem using particular technical means. It is on this understanding of the term "invention" that the patent granting practice of the EPO and the jurisprudence of the Boards of Appeal are based. The same considerations apply to the assessment of computer programs. [...]

Does this really mean that the technology requirement now has been codified? The rules of the law of treaties require that "[a] treaty shall be interpreted in good faith in accordance with the ordinary meaning to be given to the terms of the treaty in their context and in the light of its object and purpose".[128] The ordinary meaning of the words "in all fields of technology" is that no field of technology is excluded. And that is the meaning of these words in the pertinent TRIPS provision, because it purports to a ban on discrimination by field of technology, rather than a limitation to technology.[129] The rules of the law of treaties only allow recourse to the preparatory works as a "supplementary means of interpretation" if an interpretation based on the ordinary meaning "leaves the meaning ambiguous or obscure; or leads to a result which is manifestly absurd or unreasonable".[130] Because that is not the case here, the preparatory works can play no role for the interpretation of the new text of Art. 52(1) EPC, so that it may not be interpreted as a provision limiting patentability to technology.

---

[126] Administrative Council of the EPO, *Basic proposal for the revision of the European Patent Convention*, document MR/2/00. München, 13 October 2000, p. 43. For URL see note 124.

[127] Id., item 4.

[128] Art. 31(1) VCLT.

[129] *See* p. 23.

[130] Art. 32 VCLT.

According to the text cited above, the words "in all fields of technology" merely confirm current practice. Before "EPC 2000" went into force, the EPO considered the technology requirement as more or less "self-evident", following a German tradition, and found confirmation of this perception in *indications* in the text of the Convention, that we will discuss in a minute.

But first we turn to the question whether a technology requirement is really "self-evident". The drafters of the original European Patent Convention deliberately refrained from including a technology requirement in the Convention, as it would be difficult to reconcile the divergent views of the future member states on this issue.[131] As we will see in more detail when we discuss the case law of the pertinent jurisdictions, the Germans were actually pretty alone with their explicit technology requirement. The French requirement of a "caractère industriel"[132] was supposed to comprise both the susceptibility of industrial application and the technical character.[133] The British always rejected a separate technology requirement.[134] Also in The Netherlands "technology" was not considered a separate requirement.[135] The *Strasbourg Convention on the Unification of Certain Points of Substantive law on Patents for Invention*[136] does not contain any provision explicitly limiting patents to "technology" either.

Still the EPO maintained a technology requirement, and it motivated this requirement in several ways from the text of the EPC, long before the clause "in all fields of technology" was included in the EPC.

---

[131] Kolle 1974b, p. 145. *See* also Melullis 2002, Art. 52, Rn. 60-63.

[132] "Industrial Character".

[133] Pagenberg 1984, Art. 57, Rn. 22.

[134] *For details see* Section II.2.5, p. 45.

[135] *For details see* Section II.2.3, p. 39.

[136] While this treaty, originating from 1963 only officially went into force in 1980, much earlier it already was quite influential. *See further* Haertel 1981 and Kraßer 2009, p. 91. For The Netherlands this treaty went into force on 3 December 1987 (*Trb*. 1987, 148).

Mostly, the EPO derived the technology requirement from the text of the following EPC provision:

Article 52 EPC - Patentable inventions

(1) [...]

(2) The following in particular shall not be regarded as inventions within the meaning of paragraph 1:

(a) discoveries, scientific theories and mathematical methods;

(b) aesthetic creations;

(c) schemes, rules and methods for performing mental acts, playing games or doing business, and programs for computers;

(d) presentations of information.

(3) The provisions of paragraph 2 shall exclude patentability of the subject-matter or activities referred to in that provision only to the extent to which a European patent application or European patent relates to such subject-matter or activities as such.

In the perception of the Boards of Appeal of the EPO all subject-matter listed in subsection 2 shares an "abstract" and/or "non-technical" character,[137] and they infer from that finding that only technical subject-matter would be patentable. That leads to two questions: is the *perception* correct, and is the *conclusion* justified? As

[137] *For instance*: TBA 14 March 1989, no. T 163/85, 13 *OJ* 1990, p. 379, at 2. (*Colour television signal/BBC*); TBA 16 April 1993, no. T 833/91, at 3.1 (*Simulation of computer program external interfaces/IBM*); TBA 16 April 1993, no. T 236/91, at 4.1 (*Menu-based natural language understanding system/TEXAS INSTRUMENTS*); TBA 29 October 1993, no. T 204/93, at 3.12 (*System for generating software source code components/AT&T*); TBA 29 October 1993, no. T 790/92, at 4.6 (*Editing business charts/IBM*); TBA 31 May 1994, no. T 769/92, 18 *OJ* 1995, p. 525, at VI.1 (*General purpose management system/SOHEI*); TBA 6 July 1994, no. T 1002/92, 18 *OJ* 1995, p. 605, at 2. (*Queuing system/PETTERSSON*); TBA 8 September 2000, no. T 931/95, 24 *OJ* 2001, p. 441-457, at 2. (*Controlling pension benefits systems/PBS PARTNERSHIP*).

regards the conclusion, it should be noted that the listed subject-matter is excluded only "as such", according to subsection 3. As we will see, these words can not be interpreted in the literal sense of "as far as limited to", so they are essential to answer the question whether the old[138] Art. 52 EPC indeed implied a technology requirement. We will discuss the interpretation of subsection 2 first, and investigate the purport of subsection 3 after that.

Does the subject-matter listed in Art. 52(2) EPC indeed have something in common? Even the EPO itself once admitted that the observation that this subject-matter shares an "abstract" and/or "non-technical" character should be taken *cum grano salis*,[139] and literature is critical as well.[140] British courts persist that the list is heterogeneous.[141] In particular, in their eyes some exclusions relate to inherently unpatentable subject-matter, such as discoveries and scientific theories, while "aesthetic creations",[142] "presentations of information"[143] and also computer programs[144] appear to be listed in order to draw a line between patent law on the one hand and copyright law and design model law on the other hand. "Methods for performing mental acts" would be fundamentally excluded because of the age-old *mental steps* doctrine.[145]

The words "in particular" in the first sentence of Art. 52(2) EPC indicate that the enumeration is not limitative. That could mean different things. If the codified exclusions are similar, the list may be extended by similar exclusions. If they are dissimilar, the EPC would allow the list to be extended by arbitrary exclusions. That is unlikely,

---

[138] We refer to article 52 as it applied before "EPC 2000" went into force late 2007.
[139] TBA 15 July 1996, no. T 953/94, at 3.1 (*A method of functional analysis/GEORGES*).
[140] Pila 2010b, p. 910-11.
[141] *See* p. 46.
[142] Art. 52(2b) EPC.
[143] Art. 52(2d) EPC.
[144] Art. 52(2c) at the end EPC.
[145] *See* Elben 1960.

which makes the British conception less credible that the list is heterogeneous.

If both the text and the context of a treaty leave its meaning "ambiguous or obscure", recourse may be had to its preparatory work.[146] It shows that the drafters of the EPC primarily had the desire to follow conceptions of the contracting states.[147] The subject-matter listed in Art. 52(2) EPC always was considered unpatentable in most jurisdictions, as a matter of course.[148] For the wording of the exclusions in the EPC, the *Patent Cooperation Treaty*[149] served as an example, in particular the two provisions in the Regulations under the PCT that contain identical lists of subject-matter for which the pertinent international authorities of the contracting states are not required to conduct searches[150] and preliminary examinations.[151] The drafters of the EPC thought that it would be advisable to deviate as little as possible from the lists from the PCT,[152] that was concluded shortly before the EPC.[153] It should be noted however that the lists *added to* the PCT have a very different function than the list *within* the EPC: the PCT lists only provide what subject-matter the patent offices of the participants are not obliged to assess. Unlike Art. 52(2) EPC, they do not prevent patents from being be granted for such subject-matter.

Item (vi) of the lists in the PCT Rules in particular determines that in the case of computer programs those obligations do not exist only *to the extent* that the participating states and organisations are not

[146] Art. 32 VCLT.
[147] *See* Kolle 1974b, Pila 2005b, Pila 2010a, p. 126-164.
[148] *See for instance* PLG 1965, nr. 42, p. 13 and Banks 1970, nr. 213, p. 62 for the United Kingdom.
[149] The PCT allows "international" patent applications for multiple countries worldwide. It does *not* harmonise substantive patent law.
[150] Rule 39 Regulations under the PCT.
[151] Rule 67 Regulations under the PCT.
[152] Reversely, the working groups preparing the EPC also influenced the PCT text. Pila 2010a, p. 120.
[153] The PCT was established on 19 June 1970 in Washington, the EPC on 5 October 1973 in Munich.

equipped to assess these programs. This shows that the PCT excludes computer programs only to the extent needed for the practical reason that software patenting in 1970 was a new phenomenon not all participating patent offices were sufficiently familiar with. In contrast, the drafters of the EPC decidedly intended to limit the patentability of computer programs permanently.[154]

Two of the six types of subject-matter included in the PCT lists have been adopted in Art. 53 EPC rather than Art. 52:[155] like the PCT, the EPC excludes certain biological[156] and medical[157] methods, but still considers them inventions, unlike the subject-matter listed in Art. 52 EPC. That is another argument against the British perception. If only certain subject-matter is excluded because it is not considered an invention, it apparently has something in common, albeit that this is not a reason to assume that it is a "non-technical or abstract" nature.

A perhaps even more important deviation of the EPC from the PCT is the fact that all subject-matter listed in Art. 52(2) EPC is only excluded *as such* according to Art. 52(3) EPC, while the PCT limits just the exclusion of "presentations of information"[158] with the similar word "mere". During the EPC negotiations, it was established that discoveries, scientific theories and mathematical methods should be excluded only "as such" too, because undoubtedly practical inventions are often based on discoveries, theories etcetera. For similar reasons, it was decided to limit the other exclusions nowadays listed in Art. 52(2) EPC to the pertinent subject-matter "as such",[159] except "programs for computers".[160] Only last minute,[161] after a

---

[154] Kolle 1974b, p. 151, Pila 2005b, p. 768-770, Pila 2010a, p. 153-155.
[155] Until "EPC 2000" went into force, the pertinent medical methods were excluded via the legal fiction that they were not considered "susceptible of industrial application". But also at the time they were considered inventions. Art. 52(4) EPC 1973.
[156] Rule 39(ii) and 67(ii) PCT, Art. 53 b) EPC.
[157] Rule 39(vi) and 67(vi) PCT, Art. 53 c) EPC.
[158] PCT Rule 39(v).
[159] Pila 2005b, p. 766-67; Pila 201a, p. 151-52.
[160] Pila 2010, p. 161.

German proposal, this proviso was extended to the entire list of exclusions, in order to avoid the suggestion that the exclusion of "programs for computers" *a contrario* should be interpreted broadly.[162]

At first sight, the fact that the listed subject-matter is only excluded "as such" means that only patent applications are excluded that are *limited to* this subject-matter, and that this subject-matter is still patentable in combination with something else. Obviously, a scientific discovery is only patentable if combined with a practical application, but it is absurd to make a distinction between a "computer program as such" and a computer program combined with a computer.[163] Still the legislator apparently intended a limited exclusion of computer programs. What else could a "computer program as such" be? *Von Hellfeld* gives no less than six different interpretations from various sources,[164] and eventually he concludes that these words are so empty that they can be interpreted at will.[165] Other writers note serious confusion too.[166]

The EPO solved this problem by reversing the line of reasoning: assuming that only technology is patentable (for reasons mentioned earlier in this section), and given the fact that the EPC provides that certain subject-matter "as such" is not patentable, the EPO concluded that "as such" should be understood in the sense of "as far as non-technical". That implies that applications solely related to subject-matter listed in Art. 52(2) EPC could be patentable too. In other words, in the EPO interpretation the subject-matter listed in Art 52(2) EPC is not excluded *because* it is not technical, but only *as far as* it is non-technical. While the lists associated with the PCT enumerate

[161] That happened in March 1973. The EPC was adopted in October 1973.
[162] Nack & Moufang 2005, Rn. 42, Pila 2005b, p. 766-67, Pila 2010a, p. 151-152.
[163] *See* p. 117.
[164] *One of these sources is* Prasch 1987 p. 341 and 343.
[165] Von Hellfeld 1989, p. 476.
[166] Blind, Edler, Nack & Straus 2003, p. 116-119, nr. 26-34, quoting several other sources.

unconditional exclusions, Art. 52(2) EPC only lists subject-matter that *may* not be patentable, and requires applications involving such subject-matter to be submitted to a further test, on technical content.

So actually Art. 52(2) EPC provides little more than a list of *examples* of subject-matter that may not be patentable. That is in step with the fact that the list is not exhaustive, in view of the words "in particular" in its heading. It is unlikely that the legislator wanted an open-ended list of unconditional exclusions, because that would allow the courts to make far-reaching changes to the bounds of the legal invention concept.

The above line of thought accepts that the initial EPO presumption that all subject-matter listed in Art. 52(2) EPC lacks a technical character can not be maintained, and assumes the technical character requirement as a given. Consequently, an analysis of Art. 52(2) and (3) EPC does not answer the question why only technology would be patentable.

Perhaps conscious that the technology requirement could not entirely convincing be inferred from Art. 52 EPC,[167] the EPO also defends[168] the requirement by pointing out that the Implementing Regulations to the EPC[169] require the application to specify the *technical* field of the invention,[170] to explain the *technical* problem[171] and to define the

---

[167] Here we refer to the original Art. 52 EPC, without the words "in all fields of technology" inserted in 2007 into Subsection 1.

[168] *See e.g.* TBA 15 July 1986, no. T 208/84, 10 *OJ* 1987, p. 14 (*Computer-Related Invention/VICOM*); TBA 5 October 1988, no. T 22/85, 13 *OJ* 1990, p. 12 (*Document abstracting and retrieving/IBM*); TBA 14 March 1989, no. T 163/85, 13 *OJ* 1990, p. 379 (*Colour television signal/BBC*); TBA 29 October 1993, no. T 204/93 (*System for generating software source code components/AT&T*); TBA 31 May 1994, no. T 769/92, 18 *OJ* 1995, p. 525 (*General purpose management system/SOHEI*).

[169] In the other authentic EPC languages: "Ausführungsordnung zum Übereinkommen über die Erteilung Europäischer Patente"/"Règlement d'exécution de la Convention sur la délivrance de Brevets Européens".

[170] Rule 42(1a) EPC (Rule 27(1a) EPC old).

claims in terms of the *technical* features of the invention.[172] Specifically for the description of the invention a different form is permitted though if "owing to the nature of the invention, a different presentation would afford a better understanding or be more concise".[173] One writer argues that the "nature" may well be a non-technical one, so that this provision effectively does not imply a technical character requirement at all.[174]

More fundamentally, the whole idea seems wrong to derive such an important substantive patentability requirement from rules in the Implementing Regulations to the EPC,[175] that only prescribe the format of the patent application.[176] A British court notes that "it is something of a counsel of desperation to use what is little more than a procedural rule in place of major substantive provisions of the Convention".[177]

Literature shows that the EPO occasionally assists patent applicants in finding the right "technical" wordings.[178] That is another indication that the instructions in the EPC Rules are not supposed to have a substantive effect on patentability. It is unthinkable that the EPO helps applicants to obtain patents for substantially unpatentable subject-matter.

---

[171] Rule 42(1c) EPC (Rule 27(1c) EPC old). Whether it is ever appropriate at all to qualify a *problem* as technical will be elaborated on p. 102.
[172] Rule 43(1) EPC (Rule 29(1) EPC old).
[173] Rule 42(2) EPC (Rule 27(2) old). Prior to EPC 2000 this provision was phrased slightly differently, but the purport was the same.
[174] Jehan 2001, p. 80.
[175] In Chapter II, "Provisions Governing The Application".
[176] Pila 2005a, p. 184.
[177] Patents Court 21 July 2005, no. 2005 EWHC 1589 Pat, *RPC* 2006, 5, at 78 (*CFPH*).
[178] Beresford 2000. In chapter 3 of this book various cases are discussed where the claims were redrafted with the help of the EPO in order to "make" the invention sufficiently technical.

Finally, also the following provision in the European Patent Convention may give the impression that only technical inventions can be patented:

> Article 57 EPC – Industrial application
>
> An invention shall be considered as susceptible of industrial application if it can be made or used in any kind of industry, including agriculture.

According to the Boards of Appeal of the EPO "susceptibility of industrial application" in the sense of Art. 57 EPC *per se* is insufficient for a technical character,[179] even though such a susceptibility was mentioned occasionally to confirm the patentability of an invention with a questionable technical character.[180] The fact that susceptibility of industrial application has no independent significance for the assessment of the technical character of a patent application becomes apparent from the fact that – dependent on the meaning attached to the word "industrial" – "methods for doing business" do meet this requirement. Nevertheless such methods are not usually seen as "technical". Reversely technical inventions don't always meet the industrial applicability criterion, as it is assumed that professions don't belong to "industry" in the sense of this provision.[181] Also in literature the technical character requirement is no longer construed from the requirement of industrial applicability.[182]

In older legislation the industrial applicability requirement occasionally played a more important role, in particular if statutes –

[179] TBA 15 April 1993, no. T 110/90, at 10 (*Editable document form/IBM*); TBA 29 October 1993, no. T 204/93, at 3.13 (*System for generating software source code components/AT&T*); TBA 15 July 1996, no. T 953/94, at 3.11 (*A method of functional analysis/GEORGES*).

[180] *See* TBA 15 July 1986, no. T 208/84, 10 *OJ* 1987, p. 14 (*Computer-Related Invention/VICOM*).

[181] Jestaedt 2002, Art. 57, Rn. 5; Gramm 1984, p. 763. *Different*: Pagenberg 1984, Art. 57, Rn. 10. As far as we know there is no case law about this matter.

[182] Elben 1960, p. 21-27; Kolle 1974b, p. 146. Elben quotes sources from the time of the previous turn of the century that do assume such a relationship.

unlike the EPC – left the "invention" concept entirely open. For instance the aforementioned French requirement of a "caractère industriel" was supposed to encompass both industrial applicability and technical character.[183] No doubt there is a certain relationship between the legal invention concept and the statutory requirement of "susceptibility of industrial application",[184] even though such a susceptibility does not unambiguously imply a technical character requirement.

In Dutch language the word "industrie" has a narrower meaning than in English, referring to manufacturing industry only.[185] But the word "Gewerbe" in the authentic German EPC text refers to any kind of business, so it is not limited to manufacturing industry, like in Dutch. The word "any", and the explicit reference to agriculture further add to the impression that this provision is meant to be expansive rather than restrictive. The same applies for the identical article of the Strasbourg Convention, that served this provision as an example.[186]

In sum, the EPC does not explicitly exclude non-technical subject-matter, although it does contain various *indications*, and although a codification was *intended* in EPC 2000.

II.2.3. The Netherlands

Nowadays[187] the Dutch Patent Act too[188] provides that patents are granted "in all fields of technology".[189] According to the explanatory

---

[183] Pagenberg 1984, Art. 57, Rn. 22; Casalonga 1979, p. 413.
[184] Nack 2002, p. 153 and p. 222.
[185] The Dutch translation of the EPC is not authentic: according to Art. 177 EPC the authentic languages of this treaty are German, English and French.
[186] Council of Europe, *Convention on the Unification of Certain Points of Substantive Law on Patents for Invention Strasbourg*, Art. 3. 27 November 1963. http://conventions.coe.int/Treaty/en/Treaties/Html/047.htm.
[187] This change went into force on 13 December 2007, the same day that "EPC 2000" went into force that also was amended by this clause. *See* section II.2.2, p. 28.
[188] Art. 2(1) ROW 1995.

memorandum,[190] these words have been added in order to bring the statute in line with Art. 27(1) of the TRIPS Agreement[191] (the related change in the EPC[192] is not mentioned). The memorandum notes that this change will not lead to changes in practice since presently no area of technology is excluded. It also notes that this clause clarifies that only inventions in the realm of technology can be patented, and it mentions business methods as such as an example of non-technical subject-matter that cannot be patented.

These statements are somehow contradictory. On the one hand, the "clarification" could be seen as a substantial departure from current practice (see below), on the other hand continuity with the past is emphasised. And "business methods as such" were already excluded in The Netherlands too by Art. 2(2c) in conjunction with (3) Dutch Patent Act, even if this provision does not explicitly relate that exclusion to a lack of technical character.

Before the above legislative change went into force, never an independent Dutch court has stated the requirement of a technology requirement. There are some decisions of the (former) Board of Appeal of the Dutch Patent Office,[193] that declared several times that in Dutch patent law there is no separate technical character requirement,[194] distinguishing itself knowingly from the European Patent Office. Perhaps this can be related to the fact that the Dutch Patent Act at the time[195] did not have exclusions like the ones listed in

---

[189] *Stb.* 2007, 342.

[190] *Kamerstukken II* 2004/2005, nr. 29 874, nr. 3, p. 12.

[191] *See* p. 21.

[192] *See* p. 28.

[193] Except otherwise noted, the Dutch patent case law discussed here stems from the former Board of Appeal of the Dutch Patent Office. For details about this organisation see p. 13.

[194] Board of Appeal of the Dutch Patent Office 12 September 1985, 53 *BIE* 1985, p. 435-437 (*Schakelnetwerk*). Board of Appeal of the Dutch Patent Office 11 May 1987, 55 *BIE* 1987, p. 174-176, 4 *CR* 1987, p. 195-197, 37 *GRUR Int* 1988, p. 71-72; 11 *OJ* 1988, p. 75-78 (*Barcode*).

[195] Only in 1995 a new patent act was adopted, adapted to the EPC.

Art. 52(2) EPC. Therefore, nowadays the judgement might be different.[196] Since there are no court decisions on the patentability of software-inventions after the adoption of a new Dutch Patent Act in 1995 it is uncertain whether it makes any difference that since also in The Netherlands "programs for computers as such" are no statutory inventions.[197]

In a recent infringement case about software patents, the defendant did not even try to question the technical content.[198]

In the history of Dutch patent law, the "technical character" requirement never was considered as important as it is considered in Germany and by EPO. Still there were always somehow similar requirements. In the explanatory memorandum of the Dutch Patent Act 1910, the Dutch legislator notes that patent law relates to industrial property, and that industry produces *material* goods.[199] In the opinion of the legislator, the restriction to material production – although it is not even codified – obviates the need for various specific exclusions (as applied in other countries in past and present), such as the exclusion of "abstract science" and other limitations comparable with present-day exclusions of Art. 52(2) EPC and Art. 2(2) ROW 1995.[200] This limitation was construed at the time from the provision that requires an industrial result,[201] the equivalent of the present-day Art. 57 EPC and Art. 7 ROW 1995. As we have seen before, in the past more often a technology requirement was derived from such provisions, rather than from the exclusion of specific subject-matter *as an invention*.[202]

---

[196] Hutter 1997, p. 316.
[197] Art. 2(2c) ROW 1995.
[198] The Hague District Court 24 August 2012, no. LJN: BR5755 (*Apple v. Samsung*).
[199] Explanatory Memorandum of the Dutch Patent Act 1910: *Kamerstukken II* 1904/05, 197 nr. 3, p. 13. The same information can be found in Moorrees 1912, p. 8.
[200] "ROW" is the Dutch abbreviation for "Patent Act".
[201] "Uitkomst op the gebied of the nijverheid", to be translated as "industrial result", Art. 3 ROW 1910.
[202] *See* section II.2.2, p. 28 (at the end).

II.2.4. Germany

The German patent act was changed too by adding a reference to "all fields of technology"[203] the same day that the European Patent Convention changes agreed in 2000 went into force,[204] on 13 December 2007.[205] According to the explanatory memorandum,[206] this change intends to confirm that patents are granted in *all* fields of technology, and that *only* technology is patentable. Particularly, it is noted that this confirms that computer-supported technical inventions can be patentable in certain cases, even if computer programs "as such" are not.

In Germany, it was always considered a rule of customary law that only technical inventions are patentable. The motivation of the technology requirement in German case law was mostly apodictic. Often certain subject-matter is first designated as "obviously" unpatentable, a conclusion subsequently explained by the observation that this subject-matter lacks a technical character. To some extent, for Germans "non-technical" is *synonymous* with "unpatentable" rather than a *reason*.

For instance the Supreme Court of the German Reich (RG) decided in 1933 that a fold-out "multiplication table" in a book was not patentable, simply stating that a patentable invention ought to have a technical nature.[207] The German Federal Court of Justice (BGH) in 1958 concludes from history and purpose of patent law that an

---

[203] § 1 Abs. 1 PatG: "auf allen Gebieten der Technik".

[204] *See* section II.2.2, p. 28.

[205] Article 2 of the "Gesetz zur Umsetzung der Akte vom 29. November 2000 zur Revision des Übereinkommens über die Erteilung europäischer Patente" van 24 August 2007, *BGBl. I* Nr. 45, 5 September 2007, p. 2166 (2167).

[206] *Bundestagdrucksache* 16/4382, 2007, p. 10. http://dipbt.bundestag.de/dip21/btd/16/043/1604382.pdf.

[207] RG 12 January 1933, 38 *GRUR* 1933, p. 289-292 (290), at II.A (*Multiplikationstabelle*).

invention relates to applied knowledge in the realm of technology.[208] In this case, no further motivation is given either. The reference to history may relate to the fact that the German patent act was introduced in 1877 in order to satisfy the needs of the industrial firms of the time.[209] Just as well that could be an argument to provide patent protection for non-technical subject-matter if demanded by present-day firms.

The famous *Red Dove* decision still is considered *the* decision where the BGH laid down the technology requirement with a concrete definition.[210] That perception is incorrect. Actually the BGH decided that not just technology in the traditional sense is potentially patentable, but also subject-matter like the method to breed red doves in the present case.[211]

When the BGH made its first decision on a software-invention, it still stated that patent law must limit itself to technology:[212]

> For the concept "technical" seems also practically to be the only usefully limiting criterion with respect to different intellectual achievements of man for which patent protection is neither provided nor suitable.

This statement alludes to systematic reasons: the patent system would not just not be intended, but also unfit for the legal protection of non-technical creations. As we will elaborate later, this is a false

---

[208] BGH 21 March 1958, no. ZR 160/57, 60 *GRUR* 1958, p. 602-603 (602) (*Wettschein*): “Unter einer Erfindung ist dabei nach der Entstehungsgeschichte und dem Sinn und Zweck des Patentgesetzes nur eine angewandte Erkenntnis auf technischem Gebiet zu verstehen”.
[209] Incidentally, in the same year the Germans started the first experiments with telephony, and Morse’s telegraph is even forty years older. Information- and communication technology is older than one would believe.
[210] *See* BGH 27 March 1969, no. X ZB 15/67, 1 *IIC* 1970, p. 136-142 (*Red Dove*). *For background information about the actual case see*: Bunke 2009.
[211] For further details see section II.3.3, p. 64.
[212] BGH 22 June 1976, no. X ZB 23/74, 8 *IIC* 1977, p. 558-565 (564), at II.3 c) bb) (*Disposition Program*).

juxtaposition.[213] Even in common parlance, one refers to the "technical" skills of an artist.

The BGH recognised that the word "technical" was not mentioned in the provision that decides what subject-matter is patentable,[214] but it concluded from the frequent use of this word in other provisions of the German patent act that the legislator definitely intended to limit German patent law to "technology".[215]

After Germany acceded the European Patent Organisation as one of the founding members in 1977, and the first three subsections of Art. 52 EPC[216] were copied almost literally into § 1 of the German Patent Act,[217] the Germans persisted for a long time in their traditional perception that the technology requirement was an unwritten rule, to be applied before any statutory requirement was tested. Thus they often avoided the question whether an application relates to a "computer program as such"[218] by rejecting the application beforehand due to insufficient technical content.[219] Only since fairly recently the Germans too assess the patentability of software-inventions under Art. 52 EPC and § 1 PatG,[220] just like the EPO. The practical difference is minor though: the explicit unwritten technology requirement was replaced by an implicit written rule.

---

[213] *See in particular* Section IV.2.8, "Aesthetic creations", p. 213.

[214] Also in the German patent act of the time it was § 1.

[215] In the present German patent act the words "Technik" and "technisch" occur 47 times.

[216] Obviously, the original EPC text is meant here.

[217] Until December 2007 Art. 52 EPC had a fourth subsection. The relevant subsections were copied in § 1 Abs. 1-3 PatG. A statutory change on 28 February 2005 inserted a new subsection 2 in § 1 PatG, so that the corresponding subsections now are 1, 3 and 4.

[218] Art. 52(3) EPC, § 1 Abs. 4 PatG (was Abs. 3).

[219] *See for instance* BGH 1 June 1991, no. X ZB 24/89, 24 *IIC* 1993 p. 124-129 (*Chinese Characters*).

[220] BGH 17 October 2001, no. X ZB 16/00, 33 *IIC* 2002, p. 753-762 (756), at B.III.1 (*Search for Faulty Character Strings*). The decision cites various sources to support this change of policy.

II.2.5. United Kingdom

When "EPC 2000" went into force late 2007, the British legislator adapted its patent act too,[221] but the words "in all fields of technology" were not adopted in the act, although Section 1 of the UK Patents Act resembles the old Art. 52 EPC like two peas in a pod.

The United Kingdom has no tradition of explicitly limiting patents to technology. Following an Australian court,[222] the British believe that any attempt is bound to fail to state in general terms the ambit of "manner of new manufactures", the original concept from the centuries old *Statute of Monopolies,*[223] still a respected monument of legislation.

The "PLG"[224] committee that investigated in the early 1960s how British patent law could be modernised in view of international developments,[225] for similar reasons found that it was better not to give a statutory definition of the invention concept.[226] Consequently, there was no mention of a technology requirement.

That does not mean though that British patent law has no limits. Another committee, that reviewed the British patent system by the

[221] The following Sections were changed: 4A, 27, 58, 62, 63, 72, 75, 77, 78, 80, 81, 89B and 130. The *UK Intellectual Property Office* gives on its website detailed information about the 'Changes in UK patent law as a result of revised European Patent Convention Implementation', but it does not spend a single word on this particular change. http://www.patent.gov.uk/patent/p-decisionmaking/p-law/p-law-changes.htm.
[222] High Court of Australia 16 December 1959, *RPC* 1961, p. 134-147 (142), 102 *CLR* 252 (271) (*N.R.D.C.*). If the statutes are similar, it is not unusual in the United Kingdom to cite case law from other Commonwealth member states.
[223] Statute of Monopolies (1623), Section 6.
[224] Patents Liaison Group.
[225] The reason was the adoption of the "Strasbourg Convention on the unification of certain points of substantive law on patents for invention" in 1963.
[226] PLG 1965, p. 35. Cited in Pila 2010a, p. 181.

end of the 1960s[227] gives a list in its report of subject-matter "never" considered an invention that closely resembles the list in Art. 52(2) EPC,[228] but its entire chapter on the "Definition of Patentable Invention" does not spend a single word on the technical character of inventions.[229] A separate chapter on "The Protection of Computer Programs"[230] discusses many issues on the patenting of software, but it does not spend a word either on the technical character of computer programs, or the lack of it. Apparently an (explicit) limitation to technology was not a theme in British patent law at the time.

In the United Kingdom the wind started to blow from a different quarter when in 1977 a new patent act was adopted, adapted to the then new EPC, with a Section 1(2) very similar to Art. 52(2) and (3) EPC.[231] Since then, statute and case law provide that uniform interpretation should be strived for.[232] The British – until today – are so critical about the EPO interpretations of the above provisions though that they believe they *cannot* follow them. In their perception, the best thing they can do is to strive for similar *results* of their assessments, albeit perhaps on different grounds.

To start with, British courts disagree with the EPO[233] that all subject-matter listed in Art. 52(2) EPC[234] is similar and shares an abstract or

---

[227] This study was commissioned by the *Board of Trade* on 10 May 1967. The findings were presented to the parliament in July 1970. The rapport of this committee is usually referred to as the *Banks Report*, after the name of its chairman.

[228] Banks 1970, p. 62.

[229] Banks 1970, Chapter 7, p. 61-68.

[230] Banks 1970, Chapter 17, p. 140-144.

[231] Remarkably, the text of this provision in the British Patents Act is not a verbatim copy of the corresponding English text in the EPC. The purport is however unmistakably identical.

[232] *See* p. 16.

[233] *See* section II.2.2, p. 28.

[234] And of the virtually identical Section 1(2) UK Patents Act.

non-technical character.[235] Unlike the EPO, British judge *Peter Prescott* does not consider a technical character (or a technical contribution) a fundamental requirement:[236]

> [...] If you look at the case law on the subject, both here and in Munich, you will find many references to "technical contribution", "technical result", and so on, being touchstones by which these cases are decided. The use of the word 'technical' as a short-hand expression in order to identify patentable subject-matter is often convenient. But it should be remembered that it was not used by the framers of the Patents Act 1977 or the European Patent Convention when they wanted to tell us what is or is not an 'invention'. <u>In any case the word 'technical' is not a solution. It is merely a restatement of the problem in different and more imprecise language</u>. I am not claiming that it is wrong to decide cases with reference to the word 'technical'. It happens all the time. What I am saying is that it is not a panacea. It is a useful servant but a dangerous master.

Actually he maintains the view from aforementioned case law predating the EPO accession, that it makes no sense to try to refine the "manner of manufacture" concept in any detail in the abstract.[237]

In sum, the British do not seem convinced that the technical character is the prime criterion to assess patentability. Still in the interest of harmonisation they strive to arrive at *about* the same conclusions on the patentability of applications as the EPO, but they do not follow the EPO reasoning they reject.

---

235 Court of Appeal 27 October 2006, no. 2006 EWCA Civ 1371, at 9 (*Aerotel/Macrossan*); Patents Court 21 July 2005, no. 2005 EWHC 1589 Pat, *RPC* 2006, p. 5, at 28 (*CFPH*); Patents Court 7 November 2005, no. 2005 EWHC 2416 (pat), *RPC* 2006, p. 7, at 8 (*Shopalotto*); Patents Court 21 July 2005, no. 2005 EWHC 1623 (Pat), *RPC* 2006, p. 2, at 212 (*Halliburton*).

236 Patents Court 21 July 2005, no. 2005 EWHC 1589 Pat, *RPC* 2006, p. 5, at 14 (*CFPH*) (emphasis added). In this decision, a German decision is mentioned making similar observations: BGH 11 May 2000, no. X ZB 15/98, 33 *IIC* 2002, p. 343-348 (*Speech Analysis Apparatus*).

237 High Court of Australia 16 December 1959, *RPC* 1961, 134 (*NRDC*).

II.2.6. United States

Also in patent law, the United States seem to be the "land of unlimited opportunities", because here patents are granted for subject-matter outside the domain of technology too. Nevertheless, United States law apparently does have a statutory reason to grant only patents for "technology", because American Congress bases its competence to make patent legislation on the following constitutional mandate:[238]

> Section. 8 US Constitution.
>
> Clause 1: The Congress shall have Power …
>
> […]
>
> Clause 8: To promote the Progress of Science and <u>useful Arts</u>, by securing for limited Times to Authors and Inventors the exclusive Right to their respective Writings and Discoveries;
>
> […]

Case law pointed out several times that the present day equivalent of the term "useful arts" employed by the Founding Fathers is "technological arts".[239] Still American courts do not consider the *ab*sence of a technical character a reason not to grant a patent. At most, the *pre*sence of a technical character is occasionally seen as an argument in favour of patentability, in particular if an invention consists solely of "mental steps" instead of "physical steps", for

---

[238] *The United States Constitution,* http://www.archives.gov/exhibits/charters/constitution.html.

[239] CCPA 8 October 1970, no. 8292, 57 C.C.P.A. 1352, 1367, 431 *F.2d* 882, 893 (*In re Musgrave*); CCPA 20 April 1972, no. 9619, 59 C.C.P.A. 940, 947, 457 *F.2d* 997, 1003 (*In re Waldbaum*); CAFC 22 April 1985, no. 84-787, 760 *F.2d* 1270, 1276 (*Paulik v. Rizkalla*). "CCPA" stands for the "United States Court of Customs and Patent Appeals" that existed from 1909 to 1982 and had jurisdiction in certain patent cases. "CAFC" stands for "United States Court of Appeals for the Federal Circuit". This court was created in 1982 as – among other things – the successor of the CCPA.

instance in case of a method for seismic exploration.[240] On the other hand the presence of features related to the "liberal arts" in addition to "useful arts" features is not considered detrimental for patentability.[241] So a "technological arts" qualification would not be necessary but sufficient for patentability.

Generally speaking though, Americans decidedly reject a "technological arts" test. When the USPTO dared to reject an application for a business method with the argument that it did not belong to the *technological arts*,[242] it was immediately called to a halt.[243] While the decision was made by a relatively low level appeal board,[244] apparently it was so convincing that the USPTO did not appeal. Instead, only two months later the USPTO proposed to change the related guidelines for its *Manual of Patent Examining Procedure* (MPEP) accordingly.[245] Although these guidelines do not have force of law by themselves, they strive to reflect the current state of the law. Several reactions still considered these guidelines too restrictive.[246] While in the 2005 edition the *Computer-Related Inventions* paragraph[247] the words "technological arts" still are mentioned eight times, a year later all those words have been removed from this paragraph,[248] and they aren't mentioned anywhere anymore in the 240 page MPEP chapter on the

---

[240] *See* CCPA 8 October 1970, no. 8292, 431 *F.2d* 882 (*In re Musgrave*).

[241] CCPA 18 May 1978, no. 77-554, 575 *F.2d* 872, 877 (*In re Toma*).

[242] This business method did not even use a computer.

[243] *See* BPAI 28 September 2005, no. 2003-2088, 76 *USPQ2d* (*BNA*) 1385 (*Ex parte Lundgren*). For the idea behind Lundgrens "invention" *see* Lundgren 1996.

[244] "Board of Patent Appeals and Interferences", abbreviated as "BPAI". Its statutory basis is 35 USC § 6.

[245] USPTO 2005b, week 47, nr. 13 (22 November 2005).

[246] For an overview of these reactions see: http://www.uspto.gov/web/offices/pac/dapp/opla/comments/ab98/ab98.html.

[247] USPTO 2005a, § 2106, p. 2100-5 t/m 2100-29.

[248] USPTO 2006, § 2106, p. 5-19. This Revision 5 follows the above mentioned Revision 3 published in 2005: no Revision 4 was published of this Chapter.

patentability of inventions in general either.[249] A writer notes that the USPTO thus actually made a policy choice, while it pretended only to follow case law.[250]

The rejection of a technology test in American patent law should be seen against the backdrop of the fact that American courts over the past decades have argued again and again that the legislator intended a broad patent law, leaving little room for judicially-created non-statutory exceptions.[251] Even the statutory text alone would be a reason for that conclusion. The American patent act provides that in principle four types of inventions[252] can be patented:[253]

> 35 USC § 101 – Inventions patentable
>
> Whoever invents or discovers <u>any</u> new and useful (1) process, (2) machine, (3) manufacture, or (4) composition of matter, or <u>any</u> new and useful improvement thereof, may obtain a patent therefor, subject to the conditions and requirements of this title.

At first sight, this provision limits patentable subject-matter to four specific categories. However, case law emphasises that the expansive

---

[249] *See* USPTO 2006.

[250] Cotropia 2006, p. 55-56.

[251] The American Supreme Court emphasised this in: U.S. Supreme Court 16 June 1980, no. 79-136, 447 *U.S.* 303, 308, 100 *S.Ct.* 2204, 2207 (*Diamond v. Chakrabarty*); and: U.S. Supreme Court 3 March 1981, no. 79-1112, 450 *U.S.* 175, 182, 101 *S.Ct.* 1048, 1054 (*Diamond v. Diehr*). Also lower American courts often mention that the legislator intended a broad construction of patentable subject-matter, for instance: CCPA 29 March 1979, no. 76-712, 596 *F.2d* 952, 960 (*In re Bergy*); CAFC 12 March 1992, no. 91-1091, 958 *F.2d* 1053, 1064 (*Arrhythmia v. Corazonix*); CAFC 29 July 1994, no. 92-1381, 33 *F.3d* 1526, 1542 (*Alappat*); CAFC 23 July 1998, no. 96-1327, 149 *F.3d* 1368, 1376 (*State Street Bank & Trust v. Signature Financial Group*).

[252] Remember that the European invention concept corresponds to the American "statutory subject-matter" concept rather than the American invention concept (35 USC § 100(a)). This is merely a matter of terminology. *See* p. 20.

[253] Emphasis and numbering added.

word "any" is used twice in this provision,[254] and that the four listed categories underline the breadth of American patent law,[255] and should not be construed as limitations and conditions which the legislature has not expressed.[256]

It is often argued[257] that Congress would have desired a broad patent law because it would have stated during the discussion on a new patent act in 1952 that "everything under the sun made by man" should be patentable. But actually the Senate Committee said:[258]

> A person may have `invented' a machine or a manufacture, which may include anything under the sun that is made by man, but it is not necessarily patentable under section 101 unless the conditions of [this] title are fulfilled.

This quote unequivocally shows that Congress rather intended *not* "anything under the sun made by man" to be patentable, as a Supreme Court judge recently noted.[259]

That is still no reason however not to grant patents for business methods, the typical non-technical subject-matter. A curious systematic argument that the American legislator does not want to exclude business method patents is that the American patent act since 1999 contains a "prior use" regulation just for business methods,[260] which might be construed as an implicit statutory recognition of

---

[254] Again see the case law cited in the previous section.
[255] U.S. Supreme Court 16 June 1980, no. 79-136, 447 U.S. 303, 308, 100 *S.Ct.* 2204, 2207 (*Diamond v. Chakrabarty*).
[256] A notable exception is: CAFC 20 September 2007, no. 2006-1371, 500 *F.3d* 1346 (*In re Nuijten*). Here the decision was made that a *signal* (in the sense of communication technology) did not fall into any of the four categories.
[257] *Typically*: U.S. Supreme Court 16 June 1980, no. 79-136, 447 *U.S.* 303, 309, 100 *S.Ct.* 2204, 2208 (*Diamond v. Chakrabarty*).
[258] S. Rep. No. 82-1979 at 5 (1952); H.R. Rep. No. 82-1923 at 6 (1952).
[259] U.S. Supreme Court 28 June 2010, no. 08-964, 130 *S.Ct.* 3218, 3248-49 (*Bilski v. Kappos*).
[260] "First Inventor Defense Act", 35 USC § 273. This provision went into force late 1999, less than a year and a half after the *State Street* decision.

business method patents. However, the legislative history shows that Congress after a court decision that all but abolished all restrictions to business method patenting[261] merely recognised these patents *as a problem*. Because there was no prior use regulation in American patent law,[262] there was a risk that firms would be legally forced to stop using their own business methods. Congress chose to regulate only the prior use of business methods for the time being, in the perception that the political feasibility of a general prior use regulation would be lower.[263]

Still the U.S. Supreme Court recently considered this alleged implicit recognition of business method patents an additional argument to reject at least a categorical ban on business method patents,[264] although *Justice Stevens* gives a plethora of legal, historical and economical arguments for such a ban in a concurring opinion.[265] While Stevens acknowledges that patent law should move with the times, he explains that this is no argument to allow business method patents. On the contrary, while people have long innovated their business methods, they were never considered patentable subject-matter.[266]

Shortly before his nomination as director of the USPTO *David Kappos* again advocates a technology requirement after the European

---

[261] CAFC 23 July 1998, no. 96-1327, 149 *F.3d* 1368, 1375 (*State Street Bank & Trust v. Signature Financial Group*.

[262] This is another difference between American and European patent law. In Europe, prior use was recently regulated in art. 112a(6) EPC (in force since December 2007). And since a long time it is regulated at the national level. Examples: German Patent Act § 12, UK Patents Act Section 64, Dutch Patent Act art. 55(1).

[263] *See* Ergenzinger 2006.

[264] U.S. Supreme Court 28 June 2010, no. 08-964, 130 *S.Ct.* 3218, 3222 (*Bilski v. Kappos*).

[265] U.S. Supreme Court 28 June 2010, no. 08-964, 130 *S.Ct.* 3218, 3231-57 (*Bilski v. Kappos*).

[266] U.S. Supreme Court 28 June 2010, no. 08-964, 130 *S.Ct.* 3218, 3239 (*Bilski v. Kappos*).

example,[267] although he is warned from European side that the grass is always greener on the other side of the fence.[268]

II.2.7. Conclusion

What are the legal reasons to honour only patent applications for technology? At first sight, it seems that in Europe all uncertainty about the statutory basis of the technology requirement is over now that the words "in all fields of technology" have been added to Art. 52 EPC, a change that became effective in December 2007[269] and has been reflected in the legislation of several – but not all – EPO member states.[270] We have seen however that this clause originates from a provision[271] in the TRIPS Agreement purporting to a ban on discrimination rather than a technology requirement.[272]

Until recently, the limitation of patent law to technology was primarily seen as something self-evident, that was subsequently substantiated by various *indications* in legislation, by default of an explicit statutory rule. Remarkably the Germans, and the EPO have adopted the view that a technical character is a matter of course, while elsewhere in Europe (such as in the United Kingdom[273], and in the past also in The Netherlands[274]) there are serious doubts whether the technical content is really the appropriate and exclusive criterion characterising patentable subject-matter, although no one in Europe

[267] *See* Kappos, Thomas & Bluestone 2008.
[268] *See* Bakels 2008.
[269] *Gesetzgebungsinitiativen im europäischen Patentrecht. EPÜ 2000/Legislative Initiatives in European Patent Law. EPC 2000/Initiatives législatives en droit européen des brevets CBE 2000.* http://patlaw-reform.european-patent-office.org/EPC 2000.
[270] For instance The Netherlands (see p. 39), Germany (see p. 42) and Austria (Patentgesetz 1970, § 1(1), http://www.patentamt.at/Media/PatG.pdf).
[271] Art. 27(1) TRIPS.
[272] *See* p. 23.
[273] Section II.2.5, p. 45.
[274] Section II.2.3, p. 39.

would advocate that truly non-technical American-style business methods should be patentable here.

II.3. What is "technology" in patent law?

If patents are only granted for "technology", the next question is what should be understood by "technology" in the legal sense. By default of a statutory definition, this word ought to be understood in its ordinary meaning.[275] But this meaning is not as easy to frame as it may seem at first sight, and it is ambiguous as well. In the introduction we noted that software is definitely technical for instance for software engineers, but for other people software is not technical at all due to its intangible nature. Still for software in particular the technical content is considered decisive for patentability. Consequently, the "technology" concept must have a specific meaning in patent law. Still legislators and courts are reluctant to provide an explicit definition, since this concept is supposed to be "dynamic", for the reason that technology develops over time. This is a peculiar position however. By itself there are no objections if law is kept current by adapting the interpretation of statutes to changing circumstances, as long as the underlying principles continue to be observed. But then the underlying principles must be clear. Often tradition is presented as the underlying principle, but what is the meaning of tradition if patent law is supposed to adapt to new developments?

Consequently, it is particularly interesting to investigate *why* courts give a certain meaning to the technology concept.

II.3.1. European Patent Office

By default of a statutory definition, the term "technology" in the European Patent Convention[276] ought to be interpreted in its "ordinary" meaning according to the rules of the law of treaties,[277]

---

[275] Art. 31(1) VCLT.

[276] Art. 52(1) EPC. *See also* p. 30.

[277] Art. 31(1) VCLT.

because the EPC is an international treaty. But we just noted that the technology concept does not have a single "ordinary meaning". For the contracting states that was even a reason not to include an (explicit) technology requirement in the original EPC.[278] And although the EPO Boards of Appeal consistently assumed that only "technology" is susceptible for patent, they never gave an explicit definition of this concept.

When we discussed why EPO always only granted patents for technology, even before the technology requirement was codified,[279] we saw that one of the arguments given by EPO was that all subject-matter listed in Art. 52(2) allegedly lacks a technical character. Does that imply that all other subject-matter is technical? There is more than one reason to reject that conclusion. Firstly, it is simply substantially questionable that all that subject-matter is non-technical.[280] Furthermore, the listed subject-matter is not excluded categorically, but only "as such", and in the EPO perception that means that the listed subject matter is only excluded *as far as* the pertinent subject-matter is non-technical[281] – so it is supposed not always to lack a technical character. In sum, Art. 52 may have codified the technology requirement nowadays, but it still does not give a clue what subject-matter is sufficiently technical to be patented.[282]

As regards the technical character of computer programs, the EPO in 1998 adopted a peculiar reasoning.[283] Firstly, the EPO notes that all computer programs are technical to the extent that running a program causes "physical modifications of the hardware (for instance, electrical currents)". However, the EPO assumes that for computer programs too the words "as such" must be interpreted as

[278] Kolle 1974b, p. 145-146. *See* also p. 30 *supra*.

[279] The technology requirement is only codified in "EPC 2000", that went into force late 2007. *See* p. 28.

[280] Pila 2010b, p. 911.

[281] *See* p.35.

[282] We already discussed that this is debatable. *See* p. 29.

[283] TBA 1 July 1998, no. T 1173/97, 22 *OJ* 1999, p. 609-632, at 6.3 (*Computer Program Product I/IBM*).

the opposite of "technical",[284] so it concludes that *apparently* a program should cause a "further technical effect"[285] in order to be patentable, because otherwise the statutory exclusion of "programs for computers" would be an empty phrase.

Also a *program by itself* causing such a "further technical effect" is not considered a "*program as such*". This conclusion could be considered a "proof by contradiction" that some premise of the reasoning is incorrect – but we have seen that a more literal interpretation of the statutory exclusion of "programs for computers as such" is not as obvious as it may appear at first sight.[286] The solution to this enigma can only be given at a later stage in this study.[287]

According to case law, a *further technical effect* can be produced in various ways.[288] There is such an effect if the program is used to solve a technical problem, and also if the invention influences the internal functioning of the computer itself in a specific way,[289] for instance by enhancing the performance of the operating system leading to a reduction of the systems overhead.[290] The internal

---

284 *See* p. 35.
285 The German text of the decision as published by the EPO refers to a "weiterer technischer Effekt", the French text refers to an "effet technique supplémentaire". In Dutch, "further technical effect" is occasionally translated as "specifiek technisch effect" (Huydecoper & Van Nispen 2002, p. 118), but that is not exactly the same. In practice, the translation "verder technisch effect" could be preferred, because that is closest to the original text, even though it is not ideal from a linguistic perspective.
286 *See* p. 35.
287 *See* Chapter III, "Towards a better technology criterion", p. 133.
288 *For a summary see* EPO Examination Guidelines 2010, Section C.IV.2.3.6 op p. C IV-5.
289 TBA 1 July 1998, no. T 1173/97, 22 *OJ* 1999, p. 609-632, at 6.5 (*Computer Program Product I/IBM*). This rule reminds of the rule that was give much earlier in the following German decision: BGH 13 May 1980, no. X ZB 19/78, 82 *GRUR* 1980, p. 849-852 (*Antiblockiersystem*).
290 Computer capacity not directly devoted to applications is considered "overhead". For instance, the scheduling of tasks in a multitasking system leads to overhead.

functioning of a computer may also lead to a *further technical effect* if the invention is based on *technical considerations,* as that implies a technical problem to be solved by (implicit) technical features.[291] While the term *further technical effect* is new, the EPO notes that the requirement of such an effect is in line with previous case law.[292] In the past patents were granted already for software *by itself* – in hindsight indeed because of such an effect. Also in earlier decisions the presence of a "further technical effect" would have been sufficient[293] (in principle)[294] and the absence an objection[295] for patentability.

As far as software is not used in a conventional technical system (a system that includes hardware, and not just an ordinary computer),[296] it is apparently decisive whether the application is based on knowledge of information technology rather than knowledge of the application.

Is the EPO right to say that it is not just difficult but actually impossible to define the legal technology concept for patent law purposes? An explanation accompanying the former proposal for a European Directive for "Computer-Implemented Inventions"[297] explains why this is considered impossible:[298]

---

291 TBA 31 May 1994, no. T 769/92, 18 *OJ* 1995, p. 525, at 3.3 (*General purpose management system/SOHEI*).
292 TBA 1 July 1998, no. T 1173/97, 22 *OJ* 1999, p. 609-632, at 7.1, 7.2 and 7.3 (*Computer Program Product I/IBM*).
293 Examples given by the EPO are TBA 15 July 1986, no. T 208/84, 10 *OJ* 1987 (*Computer-Related Invention/VICOM*); TBA 31 May 1994, no. T 769/92, 18 *OJ* 1995, p. 525 (*General purpose management system/SOHEI*).
294 Of course, by itself a technical character is not a *sufficient* condition for patentability.
295 The example given by the EPO is TBA 5 October 1988, no. T 22/85, 13 *OJ* 1990, p. 12 (*Document abstracting and retrieving/IBM*).
296 Typical examples of computer controlled traditional technical systems are found in the field of control engineering in particular.
297 Proposal for a Directive of the European Parliament and of the Council on the patentability of computer-implemented inventions, Brussels, 20

> What is meant by "technical contribution"?
>
> [...] It would not be possible for a legal text such as a Directive to attempt to spell out in fine detail what is meant by "technical", because the very nature of the patent system is to protect what is novel, and therefore not previously known. In practice the courts will determine in individual cases what is or is not encompassed within the definition. [...]

This line of reasoning is unsatisfactory. If it is really impossible to give a future-proof definition of the concept of "technology", however abstract possibly, the conclusion should rather be that this concept is fundamentally unsuited to distinguish patentable subject-matter. This perception is an invitation for interested parties to extend the technology concept in creative ways.

Eventually, the question what is understood by "non-technical" by EPO should apparently be answered with: the subject-matter for which patents are considered inappropriate.[299]

II.3.2. The Netherlands

What is understood by "technology" in Dutch patent law?

Over a century ago, the Dutch legislator noted that there is no need to give a precise definition of the invention concept by excluding certain subject-matter explicitly as other legislators had done,[300] since patent law serves the purpose to define industrial property in industry, so it

---

February 2002. For the background of this Directive proposal – that was rejected meanwhile – see section II.2.2, p. 28.

[298] *Proposal for a Directive on the patentability of computer-implemented inventions - frequently asked questions.* http://europa.eu/rapid/pressReleasesAction.do?reference=MEMO/02/32.

[299] The negative wording acknowledges that a technical character is just a necessary, not a sufficient condition.

[300] Reference is made to French and Spanish acts excluding financial and credit operations, and Austrian, Hungarian Italian and Russian acts that made an exception for scientific theories.

would be limited to material production anyway.[301] That would automatically exclude "reasoning of abstract science, financial combinations, systems of education, hygienic manners of life, and surgical operations".[302] The limitation to material production (which was not codified explicitly, incidentally) leads to exclusions similar to the exclusions associated with a lack of technical content by the EPO.[303]

There is not much relevant Dutch Supreme Court case law. The most important decision in this field is about the idea to set building-lines[304] in an inventive way such that roads can be broadened without unduly reducing space for the adjacent buildings. The Supreme Court decided that this process was not patentable because it did not involve "human activity *that causes a change in nature*",[305] a requirement proposed by *Telders* some years before.[306] In present day terminology this process could be seen as a business method,[307] if not for a business,[308] but for government,[309] since a government authority determines building-lines.

---

[301] *Kamerstukken II* 1904/05, 197 nr. 3, p. 13. The same information may be found in Moorrees 1912, p. 8.
[302] In Dutch (old spelling): "Redeneeringen van abstracte wetenschap, financieele combinaties, stelsels van opvoeding, hygiënische leefwijzen, heelkundige operaties".
[303] *See* section II.3.1, p. 54.
[304] The building-line is the (imaginary) limitation of the public road. Private buildings may not extend beyond the building-line.
[305] HR 20 January 1950, 25 *NJ* 1950, 274, 18 *BIE* 1950, 36 (*Rooilijnen*). Italics added in citation.
[306] Telders 1946, nr. 42, p. 36.
[307] Art. 52(2c) EPC, Art. 2(2c) ROW 1995.
[308] Art. 3(1) ROW 1910: "Een uitvinding is slechts vatbaar voor octrooi, wanneer zij strekt tot verkrijging van enige uitkomst op welk gebied van de nijverheid ook, daaronder begrepen de landbouw". Translated: "An invention is only patentable, if it has the purpose to achieve a result in any field of industry, including agriculture."
[309] *See* De Bruijn 1944. De Reede 1944. Van Staaij 1944.

Still this interpretation seems slightly broader than the "material production" referred to in the Explanatory Memorandum we just discussed. Some years later, the Dutch Supreme Court decided that the concept of "material production" includes the application of a *permanent wave* by a hairdresser[310] – although a curl is a form rather than a substance.

The Dutch Supreme Court never made a decision about the patentability of software-inventions. There is only case law from the former Board of Appeal of the Dutch Patent Office.[311]

In 1970, in its first decision about a software-invention the Board of Appeal of the Patent Office decided that a program controlled telephone exchange could be patented neither as a product nor as a process. The application does not qualify for a product patent because its only novel aspect is its "information-content".[312] A new book, that distinguishes itself from earlier books only by its "information-content" is not patentable either, it is argued.[313] Less convincing is the argument that a computer controlled washing machine does not become a new machine either when it is loaded with a new washing program, e.g. for fine laundry, since a non-program-controlled washing machine cleaning for instance delicate fabrics in a special, inventive manner would definitely be patentable, because any inventive machine can be patented in principle.

---

[310] *See* HR 28 June 1957, 33 *NJ* 1958, 475 (*Permanent wave*).

[311] This Board was abolished on 1 September 2004. For details about this organisation see p. 13.

[312] Board of Appeal of the Dutch Patent Office 16 December 1970, 39 *BIE* 1971, p. 54-60 (*Telefooncentrale*).

[313] For explanation, the Board of Appeal only refers to its own case law. Actually, this exclusion is similar to the exclusion to (one form of) *Anweisungen an den menschlichen Geist* (directions to the human mind) in German patent law, and it is related to the *mental steps doctrine* in Anglo-Saxon patent law. These conceptions would later be codified in the exclusion of "presentations of information" in Art. 52(2d) EPC and Art. 2(2d) Dutch Patent Act 1995. We will discuss our vision on this exclusion later in this study (section IV.2.9, "Presentations of information", p. 217).

A process patent application for the program controlled telephone exchange is not accepted either, because it would not cause a "change in nature" as the Supreme Court requires,[314] and the Board of Appeal of the Patent Office holds that the patent does not relate to the realm of material production either.[315] Consequently, the applicant referred in vain to the similarity between the *voice connections* enabled by this invention and *welding connections* that are not excluded from patentability.

The Board of Appeal recognised that it would be possible – at least in theory – to implement the same inventive concept in an electronic circuit instead of a program, but it does not accept this as an argument to allow a patent for the program. The Board adds that the legislator had to draw a line somewhere, and that it is unavoidable that decisions in borderline cases occasionally are experienced as unjust.

Thirteen years later the Board of Appeal of the Patent Office resumes the thread of this decision with the observation that even at the time the possibility was acknowledged of inventions being novel only as regards the software aspect.[316] Thus it is now decided that a computer tomograph can indeed be patented,[317] although only the software is novel, and despite the fact that software by itself is still considered unpatentable. The Board of Appeal now recognises that patent protection would be an illusion if a hardware patent could be circumvented by an equivalent software implementation, if that would not be patentable.

Two years later, fifteen years after the decision on a telephone exchange discussed above, the Board of Appeal changes its opinion on the idea that merely new "information-content" can not create a

---

[314] *See* HR 20 January 1950, *NJ* 1950, 274 (*Building-lines*).

[315] Consistent with the conception of the Explanatory Memorandum we just discussed.

[316] *See* 19 January 1983, 51 *BIE* 1983, p. 104 (*Tomoscanner*).

[317] Tomography is a technology to make X-Ray images of cross-sections (τόμοι) of objects, in contrast to regular X-Ray's, that only produce some sort of shadow image.

new machine. The Board now argues that a program loaded in "directly addressable" working storage of a computer makes it a "new apparatus".[318] Like in the decision last mentioned, the Board of Appeal notes that a software implementation should be patentable as well if the equivalent hardware implementation is patentable.

In its decision, the Board refers to the guidelines issued six months before by the European Patent Office for the examination in the field of computer programs, but it indicates that it *cannot* follow these guidelines as far as they require a separate technology test, because in their view this "new apparatus" should be assessed just like any other apparatus.[319] By rejecting an explicit technology requirement this decision got international attention (together with the decision on the patentability of a method for reading barcodes to be discussed below),[320] at a time that in particular in Germany the policy still was more restrictive for software patents.

A German writer[321] concludes from this decision that a new accounting program would be patentable as well, as it changes a computer into a new accounting machine, while the EPO would reject an application for such a program since it has no technical effect. In our view, the Dutch decision is indeed consistent, because a mechanical accounting machine can definitely be an invention, despite the fact that accounting is no technical discipline. The Board of Appeal of the Dutch Patent Office once decided that even a recipe for a new kind of jam could be patentable, because manufacturing jam is an industrial process.[322]

---

[318] Board of Appeal of the Dutch Patent Office 12 September 1985, 53 *BIE* 1985, p. 435-437, 3 *CR* 1986, p. 32 with comment by Hanneman (p. 11) (*Schakelnetwerk*). *See also* Hanneman 1986.
[319] *See* Martin 1987.
[320] *Official Journal of the EPO* 1988, p. 71-74, 38 *GRUR Int* 1989 p. 705-706, `Niederländischer Octrooiraad: Computer und Programm als Patentrechtliche Einheit', 2 *Computer und Recht* 1986 p. 541-543.
[321] Betten 1988, p. 253.
[322] *See* Board of Appeal of the Dutch Patent Office 9 January 1947, 15 *BIE* 1947, 41, p. 169-170 (*Tomaten-pruimenjam*).

Not much later a software-invention drafted as a process is also decided to be patentable,[323] after in first instance the application was rejected because the invention, a method to read barcodes, would not cause a "change in nature" as required by the Supreme Court decision discussed above.[324] The Board of Appeal decided however that information can not exist without a material carrier, and such a carrier belongs to nature,[325] so that the requirement of a "change in nature" still is met. Again, the Board of Appeal states that Dutch patent law, unlike EPO law, does not require a specific test for technical character, referring to a landmark decision of an EPO Board of Appeal shortly before.[326] In an aside, the remark is added that processes involving "a human as a processor", such as accounting methods and systems, "obviously" still are not patentable.

In sum, we find that – under the old Dutch Patent Act 1910 – a separate technology test such as practiced by the EPO was explicitly rejected, but that there still was a view that patent law should limit itself to "material" products, and to processes causing "a change in nature". Whether the state of the law is still the same under the Dutch Patent Act 1995 is unknown, as there are no relevant court decisions.

---

323 *See* Board of Appeal of the Dutch Patent Office 11 May 1987, 55 *BIE* 1987, p. 174-176, 4 *CR* 1987, p. 194-197 m.nt. DWFV (*Barcode*). This "modern" decision also received international attention: 11 *Official Journal of the EPO* 1988, p. 75-78, 37 *GRUR Int* 1988 p. 71-72, `Beschwerdekammer des Niederländischen Patentamtes: Informationsverarbeitung durch Computer', 4 *Computer und Recht* 1988, p. 29-31.

324 *See* HR 20 January 1950, 25 *NJ* 1950, 274, 18 *BIE* 1950, 36 (*Rooilijnen*).

325 In the same paragraph the Board of Appeal also considers energy, for instance in the form of electromagnetic waves, as part of "nature". While no direct connection is made with "information", the consequence is that also information transmitted by radio, without carrier, causes a "change in nature".

326 *See* TBA 15 July 1986, no. T 208/84, 10 *OJ* 1987, p. 14 (*Computer-Related Invention/VICOM*).

II.3.3. Germany

German courts – unlike the EPO Boards of Appeal – have tried to give an explicit definition of "technology".

In its decision we discussed before, the Supreme Court of the German Reich[327] decided in 1933 that a fold-out multiplication table would not be patentable, with the historical words that it would not be a technical invention because it did not use *natural forces.*[328] The court, apparently inspired by *Descartes* in his distinction between mind and matter[329] relates technology to the *world of phenomena*, in contrast to the *world of ideas.*[330] The novelty of this table relates to arithmetic, qualified as brain-work, so it is decided that the table is not patentable. This decision already shows the contours of the technology concept in German patent law: a relationship with natural forces, and objections against patenting *mental steps.*[331]

Over thirty years later, the above distinction, now worded as the distinction between "the world of things"[332] and the "world of ideas"[333] appears pointless when the BGH decides that an optically readable character font is still patentable.[334]

---

327 In German: "Reichsgericht".

328 RG 21 January 1933, no. 271/1932, 38 *GRUR* 1933, p. 289-292 (290), at II.A (*Multiplication Table*).

329 Descartes distinguished "res cogitans" and "res extensa". *See* Descartes 1637.

330 In German: "Die Technik bezieht sich auf die Erscheinungswelt im Gegensatze zur Welt des Geistigen."

331 In German: *Anweisungen an den menschlichen Geist*", literally: "directions to the human mind". *See* Elben 1960.

332 In German: "Welt der Dinge"

333 In German: "Welt der Vorstellungen"

334 *See* BGH 23 March 1965, no. Ia ZB 10/64, 67 *GRUR* 1965, p. 533-536 (*Typensatz*).

In a decision about the patentability of a process for breeding red doves[335] the German Federal Court of Justice (BGH) in 1969 phrases the following famous formula:[336]

> [...] a teaching to methodically utilize controllable natural forces to achieve a causal, perceivable result could be considered patentable [...]

Since then, only this type of teaching is considered sufficiently *technical* to be patentable in German law. But actually the court notes explicitly that it is irrelevant whether the breeding process can be qualified as "technical":[337]

> It is immaterial whether, and to what extent, such utilization would fall directly under the term "technology" or whether that term can only be indirectly used in connection with biological forces and phenomena.

Rather than advocating a strict limitation to technology (in a traditional sense), this decision emphasises that patent law should be receptive to new developments, and in particular that the "invention" concept is not static:[338]

> An historical interpretation of the term invention is even more unsatisfactory [...] because invention is a basic concept in a field of law having as its most important task encompassing the patentable results of the most recent states of science and of research. Therefore, the intent of the Patent Act itself not only permits but even compels drawing upon the latest state of scientific knowledge to interpret this concept of invention, which was not construed more precisely by the legislature and which by its nature requires judicial determination.

---

335 Actually, there never was a red dove. The patent application served as a test case in a conflict about the patentability of a breeding method for red roses. *See* Bunke 2009.

336 BGH 27 March 1969, no. X ZB 15/67, 1 *IIC* 1970, p. 136-142 (138), at II.A.3 (*Red Dove*).

337 BGH 27 March 1969, no. X ZB 15/67, 1 *IIC* 1970, p. 136-142 (138), at II.A.3 (*Red Dove*).

338 BGH 27 March 1969, no. X ZB 15/67, 1 *IIC* 1970, p. 136-142 (137), at II.A.1,1 (*Red Dove*).

The actual criterion for this case becomes apparent from the second part of the official headnote,[339] which says that "[a] method for breeding animals can be patented only if the procedure is repeatable."[340] Obviously, accident is not patentable, if only because it can not be described so that it can be carried out successfully by any "person skilled in the art", as required by law.[341] And the particular process was highly unlikely to produce always a red dove.

The misunderstanding that the "Red Dove" decision provides *the* legal definition of "technology" emanates from the fact that in the traditional German perception the attribute "technical" is inherently related to the invention concept.[342] The designation "technical inventions" is not meant to distinguish such inventions from any "non-technical inventions": they do not exist in German perception. For Germans it is actually a redundant qualification.[343] If the Germans ever decide that business methods can also be considered inventions, they will probably be considered "technical" too for legal purposes.

The "force of nature" concept was introduced over a century ago in patent law by the famous German legal scholar *Josef Kohler*,[344] who defined the invention concept as "a technical expression of a product of human creativity, that by overcoming nature by using natural forces leads to a functional result, and as such is capable of satisfying human needs".[345] Kohler apparently considered inventions as human

---

339 English translation from 1 *IIC* 1970, p. 136-142 (*Red Dove*).

340 In German: "Notwendige Voraussetzung für die Patentierung eines Tierzüchtungsverfahrens ist seine Wiederholbarkeit." Of course, the word "repeatable" implies that repeatedly the intended result can be achieved.

341 In German law: § 34(4) PatG.

342 *See* e.g. Kraßer 2009, p. 119.

343 This may be related to a peculiarity of German language, that refers for instance to "food restaurants" ("Speiserestaurants") while actually no other restaurants exist.

344 1849-1919.

345 Kohler 1908, p. 13: "Erfindung ist eine zum technischen Ausdruck gebrachte Ideenschöpfung des Menschen, die unter Überwindung der

creations that teach us how to "tame" nature to satisfy our needs. "Forces of nature" are primarily presented as opportunities here. Kohler apparently did not envisage a limitation to applications of forces of nature in a narrow sense. The *Red Dove* decision we just discussed applies the "forces of nature" concept in a similar way.

In its first decision about software patenting the BGH notes that the application is limited to an "organisational and computing"-rule, that could be performed just as well by a human being. The BGH concludes that this rule is no patentable subject-matter because "human intellectual activity does not belong to the controllable natural forces", referring to the formula of the above *Red Dove* decision.[346] In an indirect way, this phrase reflects the age-old principle that *directions to the human mind* are not patentable.[347]

A commentator argues that in particular the *forces of nature* requirement of the *Red Dove* formula is decisive to prevent such mental procedures from being patented, because the requirements of a causal and perceivable result do not prevent this.[348] It is a typical German twist to consider the application of "forces of nature" a separate requirement, ignoring the essence of the *Red Dove* decision, notably the requirement of repeatability.

"Forces of nature" in German patent law are no physical but legal forces of nature: natural sciences have no relevance for the understanding of this legal concept.[349] In patent law, "forces of nature" are *matter* and *energy*,[350] and neither of those is a force in the

---

Natur durch die Benutzung der Naturkräfte zu einem funktionellen Ergebnisse führt und hierdurch tauglich ist, menschliche Ansprüche zu erfüllen.". Translation by the author of this study.

[346] In German: "Die menschliche Verstandestätigkeit aber gehört nicht zu den beherrschbaren Naturkräften". BGH 22 June 1976, no. X ZB 23/74, 8 *IIC* 1977, p. 558-565 (561), at II.3 b) bb) (*Disposition Program*).

[347] *See* note 331.

[348] Kolle 1977, p. 60.

[349] Nack 2002, p. 172.

[350] Beyer 1990, p. 400.

sense of physics.[351] A writer explains that the physical concept of force *cannot* be relevant as it has such a wide reach that a limitation to physical forces would have no effect at all.[352]

Before we discuss the German perceptions on software patenting over the years in more detail, we first devote some words to the exclusion of *mental directions* in German patent law. While it may seem far-fetched to apply this exclusion to computer programs, it is meaningful in certain cases, in particular if patents for tools are directed to the user instead of the manufacturer of those tools.

Some years after the *Red Dove* decision, the BGH decides that the intended result should be the *immediate* consequence of the application of natural forces.[353] Because of this new *immediacy principle*[354] an application for a utility model[355] for an accounting form was rejected: the form layout would be a direction to the accountant, that would only have effect on the outside world by his intervention. The BGH concludes that this form is no *technical* invention, so it cannot be patentable. Soon after, the BGH decides that the immediacy requirement not only applies for utility models, but also

---

351 In physics four fundamental natural forces are distinguished: gravity force, electromagnetic force and strong and weak nuclear force. A force in physics could be described as an effect causing (or preventing) motion. In the *Système international d'unités* a force is expressed in Newtons (1 Newton = 1 kg · m/s²).

352 Schar 1998, p. 324.

353 BGH 18 March 1975, no. X ZB 9/74, 77 *GRUR* 1975, p. 549-550 (549), at II (*Buchungsblatt*): "A technical achievement requires that the result of the newly created or improved object to have a direct effect on the external world, leading to improved usability without the use of an intermediate symbolic or corresponding mental expression." (Translation by the author of this study). Forms patent applications were already rejected before, for instance in: BGH 21 March 1958, no. ZR 160/57, 60 *GRUR* 1958, p. 602-603 (*Wettschein*).

354 German: *Unmittelbarkeitsprinzip.*

355 German: *Gebrauchsmuster,* a kind of "small" patent. While there is a separate *Gebrauchsmuster* Act, associated case law is often cited in regular patent cases.

for "genuine" patents, incidentally in a case where this requirement is fulfilled.[356]

There are in particular objections against patenting processes that require a human *judgement*,[357] as became apparent in a case about a computer program test system. The essence of this system weren't the tools but the method how a programmer might apply the tools.[358] While tools patents should not be abused to patent the use of tools instead of their production, one may wonder what actually distinguishes this process from the usual patented processes, that usually require brainwork too. That question will be discussed later in this study.[359]

Less than a month later the BGH decides that a test method that can be practiced without any human deliberation is not patentable either, because it is essentially only an "abstract logical concept".[360]

A patent application for an anti-skid braking system in first instance is rejected too because it is perceived as a non-technical abstract logical concept, a "braking philosophy".[361] The BGH decided

---

[356] *See* BGH 1 July 1976, no. ZB 10/74, 79 *GRUR* 1977, p. 152-154 (*Kennungsscheibe*).

[357] German: "abwägende Verstandestätigkeit".

[358] *See* BPatG 19 January 1978, no. 17 W (pat) 53/73, 80 *GRUR* 1978, p. 705-709 (*Programmablauf*). This is the decision of the *German Federal Patent Court* after the case has remanded by the *German Federal Court of Justice*: BGH 7 June 1977, no. X ZB 20/74, 8 *IIC* 1977, p. 363-366 (*Test Method*). The *German Federal Patent Court* roughly follows its decision in first instance: BPatG 6 August 1974, no. 17 W (pat) 53/73, *Bl. f. PMZ* 1975, 202 (only head note). *See* also Neuperth 1975, p. 250 and Kolle 1977, p. 59. "BPatG" stands for the "Bundespatentgericht", established in 1961 among other things for conflicts about the rant and the validity of patents. Before, there was no independent court for those conflicts in Germany. This court has *no* role in infringement cases.

[359] *See* p. 197.

[360] *See* BGH 14 February 1978, no. X ZB 3/76, 10 *IIC* 1979, p. 489-494 (*Error Location*).

[361] *See* BPatG 12 June 1978, no. AW (pat) 78/75, 81 *GRUR* 1979, p. 111-113 (*Antiblockiersystem*, not published in English).

however that this car part is undeniably technical. While that seems an obvious conclusion, the BGH passes over the observation made in first instance that the "braking philosophy" was insufficiently elaborated, which would have been a reason by itself to reject the application.[362]

The BGH articulates the above immediacy principle[363] in the sense that an invention must not be dependent on an *intermediate* human judgement.[364] With this requirement the formula from the Red Dove decision is further elaborated into the following rule:

> Technical is a teaching to methodically utilize controllable natural forces to achieve a causal, perceivable result, that is the immediate result of controllable natural forces without the use of human intellectual power being necessary as an intermediate step.

For many years this rule would be applied by the courts.[365] As a consequence, regularly questions arose whether systems operated by human beings would be patentable, such as an intercom system.[366] As far as we know that never lead to a rejection however. On the other hand, if a process runs fully automated, without any human intervention, that is considered an indication that the process is sufficiently technical to be patentable.[367]

Many years later the BGH decides however that a speech analysis system is a patentable invention despite the fact that it occasionally relies on a selection made by the user of this tool. The court argues

---

[362] § 34(4) PatG.

[363] Engel 1978, p. 205. Kolle 1977, p. 63.

[364] BGH 13 May 1980, no. X ZB 19/78, 82 *GRUR* 1980, p. 849-852 (851), at II.2 (*Antiblockiersystem*).

[365] *For instance* BPatG 4 October 1990, no. 117/88, 93 *GRUR* 1991, p. 195-196 (196), at II.1.1 *(Temperatursteuerung)*.

[366] *See* BPatG 7 December 1999, no. 20 W (Pat) 14/99, 102 *GRUR* 2000, p. 408-414 (*Gegensprechanlage*).

[367] *See* BPatG 14 June 1999, no. 8/99, 101 *GRUR* 1999, p. 1078-1080 (*Automatic Absatzsteuerung*).

that the *Red Dove* formula even requires human intervention.[368] Rightly this system is considered patentable, because the essence is the tool rather than its usage. Still the reference to the Red Dove formula is not entirely convincing, and fails to appreciate that tools patents may be used inappropriately to patent the *use* of tools rather than the tools themselves, as we saw a minute ago.[369] Of course, processes using tools can be patentable too, but then they should be drafted and assessed accordingly.

As announced, we now return to the German perceptions on the patentability of software. The idea that a computer is merely a technical tool to execute the non-technical programs led to the following rule:[370]

> Computer programs [...] are not patentable subject-matter, if the application of these programs merely leads to the ordinary, predetermined use of a data processing system known in its structure and design.

Case law usually refers to "the use of a standard commercially available computer for its intended purpose".[371] What use of a computer would be beyond its intended purpose? A writer suggests the use of a computer for *room heating*[372] or the use of a pocket calculator as a *paperweight*.[373] In a later article the same author explains that the essence of a common computer is its universal

---

[368] BGH 11 May 2000, no. X ZB 15/98, 33 *IIC* 2002, p. 343-348 (346), at II.1.c)bb)2.(4) (*Speech Analysis Apparatus*).

[369] *See* p. 69.

[370] BGH 22 June 1976, no. X ZB 23/74, 8 *IIC* 1977, p. 558-565 (562), at II.3. b)cc)γ) (*Disposition Program*).

[371] In German: "Bestimmungsgemäße Gebrauch eines handelsüblichen Computers". E.g. in the head notes of BGH 21 April 1977, no. X ZB 24/74, 8 *IIC* 1977 p. 459-462 (*Straken*) and BGH 16 September 1980, no. X ZB 6/80, 83 *GRUR* 1981, p. 39-42 (*Walzstabteilung*).

[372] Re-using the huge amounts of energy dissipated by large *server farms* is by all means realistic: *see for instance* http://www.channelbuzz.ca/2010/12/cold-front-can-canada-play-a-leading-role-in-the-cloud-846.

[373] Von Hellfeld 1986, p. 188.

ability to execute algorithms, so that actually every use of a computer should be deemed "conventional", unless no software is involved at all.[374]

The court decision clarifies that the above rule still allows a program to be patented[375]

> [...] if the program requires and teaches a new, inventive structure of such a system, or if it includes the instruction to use the system in a new, heretofore not customary and nonobvious way.

For brevity, in the context of this section henceforth we use the designation "special" for such programs, and "ordinary" for other programs.

For several years the German courts seemed reluctant to allow patents for any software.[376] While we saw that initially the rejection software patents was explained from the perception that software would only represent mental processes, that traditionally happen to be considered non-technical, the focus shifted to the assessment of the technical content as an independent criterion when the BGH stated that that there are both technical and non-technical programs, and added that programs and technology are not contrary concepts that exclude each other.[377] In the particular case the court decided that

---

374 Von Hellfeld 1989, p. 478 at the end.

375 BGH 22 June 1976, no. X ZB 23/74, 8 *IIC* 1977, p. 558-565 (562), at II.3 b) cc) γ) (*Disposition Program*).

376 *See* BGH 21 April 1977, no. X ZB 24/74, 8 *IIC* 1977 p. 459-462 (*Straken*); BGH 7 June 1977, no. X ZB 20/74, 8 *IIC* 1977, p. 363-366 (*Test Method*); BGH 14 February 1978, no. X ZB 3/76, 10 *IIC* 1979, p. 489-494 (*Error Location*); BGH 16 September 1980, no. X ZB 6/80, 83 *GRUR* 1981, p. 39-42 (*Walzstabteilung*).

377 BGH 13 May 1980, no. X ZB 19/78, 82 *GRUR* 1980, p. 849-852 (851), at II.4 (*Antiblockiersystem*).

the "program"[378] was technical because it was part of a conventional technical system, and therefore satisfied the Red Dove formula.[379]

More than ten years later the BGH decides that also a program that is not part of a conventional technical system can be sufficiently technical for patent, in a case about a method for a more efficient management of the "virtual memory"[380] of a computer:[381]

> Teaching related to a program is technical if it concerns the functional capabilities of the data processing unit as such and thus permits the direct interaction of the components thereof.

Incidentally, according to this decision the statutory concept of "computer programs as such"[382] is not synonymous with technical computer programs – in accordance with earlier case law,[383] but contrary to the prevailing EPO doctrine.[384]

Late last century the BGH decided[385] that a program for the verification of chip designs could be patentable because *technical*

---

[378] Actually there was no computer program involved, but just a conventional control system. The court relates this to programs.
[379] As a conventional technical system could be considered a system using equipment other than computers and related equipment. This definition is necessarily imprecise because related law is.
[380] All modern universal operating systems allow main memory to overflow – if necessary – onto disk storage, in such a way that main memory appears larger than it actually is. In analogy of virtual images that are seen but do not actually exist (such as the image in a mirror) the term "virtual memory" (or "virtual storage") is used.
[381] BGH 11 June 1991, no. X ZB 13/88, 23 *IIC* 1992, 824-828 (827) at III.5 d) (*Page Buffer*).
[382] § 1(2)3. PatG.
[383] BGH 13 May 1980, no. X ZB 19/78, 82 *GRUR* 1980, p. 849-852 (851), at II.4 (*Antiblockiersystem*): Programs as such do not always have a non-technical character. Note that this decision is based on legislation that did not refer yet to "computer programs as such".
[384] *See* section II.3.1, p. 54.
[385] *See* BGH 13 December 1999, no. X ZB 11/98, 33 *IIC* 2002, p. 231-238 (*Logic Verification*).

considerations[386] were involved in its development, although it was an "ordinary"[387] computer program in the above sense.[388] Thus the requirement was abandoned of an *immediate*[389] relationship between the use of "natural forces" and a result, that was dictated for decades by the (modified) "Red Dove" formula, but that is not seen as a problem because the BGH had emphasised in the very same "Red Dove" decision that the invention concept is not a static given, and that it is not just allowed, but even required to interpret this concept in the light of the most recent state of science and research.[390] Developments in technology would give reason for departing from earlier case law on comparable cases.[391] The prominent professor *Kraßer* wonders whether this decision went a step too far,[392] and another writer notes nothing less than a culture change in the assessment of the patentability of design methods.[393] It should be noted however that this decision does not depart from earlier decisions on the patentability of *mental steps*,[394] because the patent was for the tool, not for its use.[395]

---

[386] With the acceptance of "technical considerations" as an argument for a technical character the BGH follows a decision the EPO made five years earlier, which is cited in the decision: TBA 31 May 1994, no. T 769/92, 18 *OJ* 1995, p. 525 (*General purpose management system/SOHEI*). *See* p. 57.
[387] *See* p.71.
[388] However advanced this program perhaps was, it still was an application program running on an ordinary computer, and such programs were not considered "technical". *See* p. 75.
[389] "Immediacy principle" (German: "Unmittelbarkeitsprinzip"), *see* p. 68.
[390] BGH 27 March 1969, no. X ZB 15/67, 71 *GRUR* 1969, p. 672-676 (672) (*Rote Taube*), 1 *IIC* 1970, p. 136-142 (137) (*Red Dove*), at II.A.1.
[391] *See* BGH 21 April 1977, no. X ZB 24/74, 8 *IIC* 1977 p. 459-462 (*Straken*); BGH 16 September 1980, no. X ZB 6/80, 83 *GRUR* 1981, p. 39-42 (*Walzstabteilung*).
[392] Kraßer 2001, p. 962-63.
[393] *See* Schölch 2006.
[394] Different: Nack 2002, p. 249. But this writer does not expect that courts now will allow patents too for processes that can *only* be applied by human beings.
[395] *See* p. 69.

If the invention concept is non-static, shouldn't *information* be considered a legal force of nature too in the information age, in addition of matter and energy,[396] as has been suggested by several writers?[397] This idea has even been defended with arguments from natural science,[398] but these arguments are not even convincing as such,[399] and, again, this type of arguments can have little legal relevance. Occasionally courts have mentioned this type of considerations, but they did not adopt the idea that information is another legal "force of nature".[400] For courts the problem is not to decide whether software is technical, but in what cases software is sufficiently technical to be patented, and reference to "forces of nature" has little use for that purpose.

A writer notes that German courts basically distinguish the following types of programs:[401]

1. technical programs: programs that are part of conventional technical systems, for example in the field of control engineering,

2. non-technical programs:

    2.1. non-technical programs with technical character, such as systems software,[402] and

---

396 *See* p. 67.
397 *See* Von Hellfeld 1989, p. 484, Beyer 1990, p. 399-401, Wiebe 1994 (passim), Van Raden 1996, p. 388, Tauchert 1997, p. 149.
398 *See* Beyer 1986.
399 In physics, mass and energy, the classical legal "natural forces" are subject to "laws of conservation ", but there is no law of conservation of information.
400 Wiebe 1994 cites on p. 236 three court decisions relevant in this context: BPatG 16 March 1989, no. 31 W (pat) 50/86 (*Chinesisches Textprogramm*); BPatG 13 February 1992, no. 23 W (pat) 24/90, 94 *GRUR* 1992, p. 681-683 (*Herstellungsverfahren für ein Elektronisches Gerät*); BPatG 22 September 1988, no. 23 W (pat) 33/86, *BPatGE* 30, p. 90 (*Hochtemperatur-Kernreaktor*).
401 Winischhofer 2000, p. 60-65.
402 Systems software can be defined as software that does not directly provide functionality to an end user, as opposed to application software.

2.2. non-technical programs without technical character, such as application software.

In the first two cases, programs are sufficiently technical to be patentable, in the last case, they are not. The distinction between technical and non-technical programs in this classification could be described as the distinction made by (traditional) *engineers*, the distinction based on technical character as the distinction made by *programmers*: for them, "technical" work is work on infrastructural provisions rather than applications, but still they are no technicians in the traditional sense in that case. The design verification program we just discussed[403] actually represents a fourth category in this classification: this program is technical in the perception of an *engineer*, but not in the perspective of a *programmer*. In sum, the following combinations can be distinguished:

		technical for *engineer*	
		no	yes
technical for *programmer*	no	(non-technical)	design program
	yes	systems programming	e.g. control system

Once more, the difference in perception between traditional technicians and programmers shows that the "ordinary" meaning of the technology concept is by no means unambiguous.

In 2000 the BGH decided again that even an invention using a standard computer in a "normal" way can be patentable, this time for the simple reason that a computer is a technical device beyond doubt that does not lose its technical character by using software.[404] In the light of previous case law this is a remarkable decision. A writer is

---

Operating systems such as Linux and Windows are systems software, an accounting package is not. There is not always a sharp distinction, which is an essential problem for the legal qualification according to this classification scheme.

[403] *See* p. 73.

[404] BGH 11 May 2000, no. X ZB 15/98, 33 *IIC* 2002, p. 343-348 (345), at II.1 c) bb) (1) (*Speech Analysis Apparatus*).

concerned that every business method will be patentable if only it is implemented in a computer program.[405]

Because in the German perception at the time technical software was not the opposite of "software a such", this approach was more or less compliant with the statute,[406] and allowed the BGH to reject the idea that computer programs would only be technical in the presence of a "further technical effect", as the EPO had decided in its case law shortly before.[407] The BGH even includes this side-hit[408] in a head note.

In a case about the patentability of a spell checking method less than a year and a half later, the BGH eventually adopted the EPO perception that technical software is the opposite of "software as such".[409] In consequence, the BGH too was faced with the paradox that non-technical software actually does not exist, and – like the EPO – the BGH concluded that only more than "ordinary" technical software could be patentable, software with a certain "peculiarity",[410] a new concept in patent law. In fact, that is the German equivalent of the "further technical effect" required for software by the EPO.[411] As a matter of fact, with this decision the court has returned to the over twenty-five year old rule that programs that are not part of a conventional technical system can only be patented in special cases.

In later years, German courts emphasise that a technical problem should be solved by technical means, but then they apply

---

405 *See* Nack 2000.

406 Art. 52 EPC, § 1 PatG.

407 *See* TBA 1 July 1998, no. T 1173/97, 22 *OJ* 1999, p. 609-632 (*Computer Program Product I/IBM*); TBA 4 February 1999, no. T 935/97 (*Computer Program Product II/IBM*).

408 In German: "Seitenhieb". Hössle 2000, p. 346.

409 BGH 17 October 2001, no. X ZB 16/00, 33 *IIC* 2002, p. 753-762 (756), at B.III.1 (*Search for Faulty Character Strings*).

410 In German: "Eigenheit".

411 *See* p. 56.

"technology" concept which takes the exclusion of "programs for computer as such" rather literally:[412]

> The exclusion of computer programs as such from patentability rules out considering any teaching consisting of computer-executable instructions as patentable if such teaching goes only slightly beyond enabling the use of the program for data processing equipment. In this respect, the essential instructions of the claimed teaching must rather contribute to the solution of a concrete technical problem.

The confusing distinction between technical problems and technical solutions will be addressed when we discuss the question in what respect patent applications must be technical.[413]

Melullis, the now retired president of the tenth civil panel of the BGH, responsible for patent cases noted:[414]

> In particular, resorting to the term "technical" was unhelpful because it shifted the focus of discussion from "programs as such", a concept which was already unclear, to a further, equally ambiguous term, the meaning of which was inherently evolving and, moreover, would become further obscured as a result of the necessary distinction from subject-matter of a "not so technical" nature.[415]

It is remarkable that even this high-placed German judge is critical on the use of the technology criterion, while Germany is still the cradle of this criterion. Apparently he joins his British colleagues who questioned this criterion already before.[416]

In sum, the German courts – unlike EPO – always tried to maintain an *explicit* technology concept, although the courts – just as EPO – note that this concept is "non-static", arguing that technology is

[412] BGH 17 October 2001, no. X ZB 16/00, 33 *IIC* 2002, p. 753-763 (757), at B.III.1.b)aa) (*Search for Faulty Character Strings*).
[413] *See* p. 102.
[414] Melullis 2007, p. 186.
[415] The "not so technical nature" refers to software without "further technical effect" in EPO terminology, *see* p. 56.
[416] *See* p. 47.

subject to development.[417] The result of this view is a long series of BGH decisions, defining a slightly different technology concept all the time.

II.3.4. United Kingdom

What is understood as "technology" in British patent law? As we have seen,[418] under British patent law traditionally the technical content was not a specific criterion, but that changed when the United Kingdom joined the European Patent Organisation in 1977, and a new patent act was introduced in the United Kingdom, adapted to the EPC, but we already noted that the British definitely do not always follow EPO case law unconditionally.[419]

In 1978, still under the old Patents Act, a revocation request is rejected for a patent for – in present-day terminology – a business method,[420] arguing that the computer used in this invention to calculate the sales price of shares for instance could definitely be considered a "manner of manufacture". The fact that the computer being used is has nothing special is considered immaterial.[421] Although the British do not refer to "technology" in this decision, a German commentator concludes from this decision that the court considered the patent application sufficiently technical,[422] demonstrating again that in a German perception "patentable" is almost synonymous to "technical".

Under the new Patents Act, the opportunities to obtain a software-invention patent in the United Kingdom were greatly reduced. The

---

417 BGH 13 December 1999, no. X ZB 11/98, 33 *IIC* 2002, p. 231-238 (236), at II.4. h) (*Logic Verification*).
418 *See* Section II.2.5, p. 45.
419 *See also* Section II.1.3, "European harmonisation", p. 15.
420 *See* Patents Appeal Tribunal 16 October 1978, *FSR* 1980, p. 564 (*IBM's Application*). *About this decision see also* Hanneman 1985, p. 139.
421 In Germany however the "normal" use of a "normal" computer at the time was absolutely prohibitive for patent. *See* section II.3.3, p. 64.
422 Betten 1988, p. 253.

first time a British court made a statement about the patentability of software was in the context of a biotechnology case. The court stated that the exclusion "computer program as such"[423] implies that a computer program could never be patented, since there would be virtually no difference between a "computer program" and a "computer program as such".[424]

In the years that followed, British courts predominantly rejected applications – literally – limited to the subject-matter listed in S. 1(1) UK Patents Act *as such*.[425] Computer applications running on conventional equipment were not patentable in the United Kingdom, even if there was arguably some technical content, such as in the case of a square root algorithm "burned" into read only memory,[426] a special compiler for vector processor optimisation,[427] or a program for the automatic recognition of hostile ships.[428]

The British courts also do not allow patents for programs used to support *mental acts*. So they rejected an application for an *expert system*,[429] and an application for a program to model synthetic crystal structures.[430] For similar reasons, a computer assisted system for the design of drill bits for petroleum production was not considered

[423] Section 1(2) UK Patents Act.

[424] Court of Appeal 31 October 1988, *RPC* 1989, p. 147-287 (240) (*Genentech*).

[425] The list is almost identical to the list in Art. 52(2) EPC.

[426] *See* Court of Appeal 13 December 1990, *RPC* 1990, p. 305 (*Gale*).

[427] Patent Office 22 May 1990, *RPC* 1991, p. 415 (*Auction method/HITACHI*). A vector processor is a computer with special facilities to perform certain mathematical operations very fast. An optimising *compiler* recognises such operations in a computer program even if they have not been specified as such explicitly, so that this program is automatically performed in the most efficient way, without having been manually adapted to the facilities of the vector processor. Programs enhancing the performance of a given computer are considered "technical" for instance in Germany: BGH 11 June 1991, no. X ZB 13/88, 23 *IIC* 1992, 824-828 (*Page Buffer*).

[428] *See* Patents Court 15 March 1993, *RPC* 1993, p. 427 (*Raytheon*).

[429] *See* Patents Court 21 March 1990, *RPC* 1991, p. 463 (*Wang*).

[430] *See* Court of Appeal 6 March 1997, *RPC* 1997, p. 608 (*Fujitsu*).

patentable, although in this case there was no sufficient enabling description either.[431]

Systems to play games[432] or to wager[433] via the Internet were rejected also. An application for a wagering system was rejected because it would circumvent rather than solve a technical problem.[434] An automated securities trading system was considered an unpatentable business method, although it used a computer.[435] And a patent application for an automated method of acquiring the documents necessary to incorporate a company was rejected, because it was considered – somewhat contradictory – both a business method *as such* and a computer program *as such*.[436]

A business method for a particular setup for a *prepaid* telephone system is considered patentable however, even if it uses only conventional equipment.[437] Details about this remarkable case are discussed when we get to the question *in what respect* an invention must be "technical" in the United Kingdom in order to be patentable.[438]

While British courts nowadays are inclined to follow the EPO more closely, they are still not convinced that the exclusions in Section 1(2) UK Patents Act can solely be attributed to a lack of technical character, and consequently they still may interpret "computer

---

431 *See* Court of Appeal 15 December 2006, no. 2006 EWCA Civ 1715, 2006 (*Halliburton*).

432 *See* Patents Court 7 November 2005, no. 2005 EWHC 2416 (pat), *RPC* 2006, p. 7 (*Shopalotto*).

433 *See* Patents Court 21 July 2005, no. 2005 EWHC 1589 Pat, *RPC* 2006, p. 5 (*CFPH*).

434 There is a similarity with the following EPO case: TBA 21 April 2004, no. T 258/03, 27 *OJ* 2004, p. 575-638 (*Auction method/HITACHI*). Also in this case no patent was granted.

435 *See* Court of Appeal 21 April 1989, *RPC* 1989, p. 561 (*Merrill Lynch*).

436 *See* Court of Appeal 27 October 2006, no. 2006 EWCA Civ 1371 (*Macrossan*).

437 *See* Court of Appeal 27 October 2006, no. 2006 EWCA Civ 1371 (*Aerotel*).

438 *See* section II.4.3, p. 116.

programs as such" in a more literal sense, and reject applications limited to computer programs, irrespective of any technical content. Only lately British courts are inclined to follow the EPO more closely in this respect as well,[439] and a writer hopes that the British henceforth will be more "generous" in allowing software patents.[440] But while the present British assessment method leads to results that are more similar to the assessment by the EPO in similar cases, British courts are still reluctant to follow the EPO in the approach to assess the technical content when the inventive step is tested.[441]

In sum, since the accession to the European Patent Convention for many years the British have rejected patent applications limited to the subject-matter listed in Section 1(2) UK Patents Act 1977, the counterpart of Art. 52(2) EPC. Whether this subject-matter perhaps lacks a technical character is something the British are not really interested in.[442] In later years, the British strove to follow the EPO more closely in the interest of harmonisation, but they still disagree on the reasoning of the EPO.

II.3.5. United States

The question what Americans consider "technology" in patent law seems irrelevant, since American patent law has no technology requirement, in contrast with European patent law. Still, for over a century U.S. courts consistently exclude *abstract ideas, natural phenomena* and *laws of nature* from patentability.[443] In particular the exclusion of "abstract ideas" resembles the exclusion of non-technical

---

439 EWHC 25 January 2008, no. [2008] EWHC 85 (Pat) (*Astron*). High Court 18 March 2008, no. 2008 EWHC 518 (Pat) (*Symbian*). Confirmed in appeal: Court of Appeal 8 October 2008, no. 2008 EWCA Civ 1066 (*Symbian*).

440 *See* Teufel 2008.

441 *See* p. 100.

442 Patents Court 21 July 2005, no. 2005 EWHC 1589 Pat, *RPC* 2006, p. 5, at 14 (*CFPH*). *See* p. 47.

443 U.S. Supreme Court 16 June 1980, no. 79-136, 447 *U.S.* 303, 309, 100 *S.Ct.* 2204, 2208 (*Diamond v. Chakrabarty*), with references to older case law.

subject-matter in European patent law, actually in several respects: it is also a general criterion, undisputed in case law, and its precise meaning is equally unclear. What ideas are too "abstract" to be patented? A further parallel is that mainly software and business methods are deemed too abstract to be patentable in certain cases, just like this subject-matter is not always considered sufficiently technical to be patented in Europe.

During the past decades, American courts have developed several tests to decide whether a patent application represents an idea too abstract to be patented, but none of them lived very long. If a test is found to produce dissatisfactory results, it is usually maintained for some more time as a non-decisive "indication", a confusing situation. Remarkably, a new test usually is not presented as a correction to shortcomings, but inferred from a new analysis of legislation and precedents. While unmistakably policy considerations are involved, they are not mentioned as arguments. Perhaps that is unavoidable in the Anglo-Saxon system of binding precedents, but it makes arguments less convincing to those who are more interested in policy than legal formalism.

Patent applications that would be associated with software in Europe are related to "mathematical algorithms" in the United States, which is perhaps a more precise designation. While one may debate the mathematical nature of algorithms,[444] for now it is sufficient to note that the abstractness of these algorithms is as controversial as the lack of technical character of software in Europe. In its famous *Gottschalk v. Benson* case, the U.S. Supreme Court noted that an algorithm for a certain data conversion could not be patented, arguing that "[t]he mathematical formula involved has no substantial practical application except in connection with a digital computer [so that a] patent would wholly pre-empt the mathematical formula and in practical effect would be a patent on the algorithm itself".[445]

---

444 *See* p. 186.

445 U.S. Supreme Court 20 November 1972, no. 71-485, 409 *U.S.* 63, 72, 93 *S.Ct.* 253, 257 (*Gottschalk v. Benson*).

The decision leaves the possibility that patents are granted for algorithm-related inventions that do not monopolise the algorithm itself. From Supreme Court case law[446] the CCPA developed a criterion that became known as the "Freeman Walter Abele test"[447] (hereinafter: "FWA test") that was supposed to prevent patents on algorithms by themselves by only allowing algorithm-related patents that are restricted by *physical* "elements or process steps".

That was a mistake. It is a persistent misconception to assume that processes must operate physically upon substances in order to be patentable. Earlier the CCPA had noted[448] that this perception rests on an incorrect interpretation of a 19th century Supreme Court decision.[449] There are by all means concrete inventions that do not comply with this requirement, so soon it was concluded that FWA test compliance is perhaps sufficient, but not necessary for patentability.[450]

In the 1990s, the FWA test further crumbled away. In 1992 a court confirms the patentability of essentially an algorithm to analyse

---

446 *See* U.S. Supreme Court 20 November 1972, no. 71-485, 409 *U.S.* 63, 93 *S.Ct.* 253 (*Gottschalk v. Benson*); U.S. Supreme Court 22 June 1978, no. 77-642, 437 U.S. 584, 98 *S.Ct.* 2522 (*Parker v. Flook*); U.S. Supreme Court 3 March 1981, no. 79-1112, 450 *U.S.* 175, 101 *S.Ct.* 1048 (*Diamond v. Diehr*).

447 This test is developed in the following decisions: CCPA 30 March 1978, no. 75-531, 573 *F.2d* 1237 (*In re Freeman*); CCPA 27 March 1980, no. 79-599, 618 *F.2d* 758 (*In re Walter*); CCPA 5 August 1982, no. 81-618, 684 *F.2d* 902 (*In re Abele*).

448 CCPA 12 June 1934, no. 3314, 21 *C.C.P.A.* 1235, 1237, 71 *F.2d* 169, 170 (*In re Ernst*); CCPA 14 August 1969, no. 7987, 56 *C.C.P.A.* 1381, 1393, 415 *F.2d* 1393, 1403 (*In re Prater and Wei II*).

449 U.S. Supreme Court 19 March 1877, 94 *U.S.* 780, 788 (*Cochrane v. Deener*): "[t]ransformation and reduction of an article 'to a different state or thing' is the clue to the patentability of a process claim that does not include particular machines".

450 CAFC 3 November 1989, no. 89-1321, 888 *F.2d* 835, 839 (*In re Grams*): "Thus, though satisfaction of the Walter test necessarily depicts statutory subject matter, failure to meet that test does not necessarily doom the claim.".

electrocardiograph signals for automatic detection of dangerous arrhythmia.[451] In a concurring opinion, *Judge Rader* makes the rather dramatic observation that this application does "not disclose mere abstract ideas, but a practical and potentially life-saving process".[452] Incidentally, the court notes that case law already established that signals have a physical character[453] (here electrical signals from heart nerves are involved). Outside the legal world though, signals are not physical: they represent (analogue or digital) coded information in a communications process.

Two years later, the CAFC decides that a means for creating a smooth waveform display on the rectangular array of pixels of a digital oscilloscope is 'not a disembodied mathematical concept to be characterized as an "abstract idea," but rather a specific machine to produce a *useful, concrete, and tangible result*'.[454] In sum, algorithm-related subject-matter is not excluded *because* it is abstract, but only *if* it is too abstract.[455]

Soon after, in the ground-breaking *State Street Bank* case[456] the CAFC decides that the above criterion of a "useful, concrete, and tangible result" distinguishes patentable subject-matter from abstract

---

[451] *See* CAFC 12 March 1992, no. 91-1091, 958 *F.2d* 1053 (*Arrhythmia v. Corazonix*).
[452] CAFC 12 March 1992, no. 91-1091, 958 *F.2d* 1053, 1065-66 (*Arrhythmia v. Corazonix*).
[453] CCPA 10 June 1982, no. 81-598, 681 *F.2d* 787, 790 (*In re Taner*).
[454] CAFC 29 July 1994, no. 92-1381, 33 *F.3d* 1526, 1544 (*In re Alappat*). The associated invention resembles the invention in the well-known EPO VICOM case. In that decision signals are attributed a physical character too. TBA 15 July 1986, no. T 208/84, 10 *OJ* 1987, p. 14 (*Computer-Related Invention/VICOM*).
[455] One might say that only "mathematics as such" is no patentable subject-matter – analogous to Art. 52(a) and (c) EPC. The reader will recognise the rule of Art. 52(2c) in conjunction with (3) EPC.
[456] *See* CAFC 23 July 1998, no. 96-1327, 149 *F.3d* 1368 (*State Street Bank & Trust v. Signature Financial Group*).

ideas for business methods too.[457] In passing, the court notes that the FWA test "has little, if any, applicability to determining the presence of statutory subject matter".[458] While the court contends that actually never a specific rule prohibiting business method patents existed,[459] this decision unleashed a sudden flood[460] of business method patent applications.[461]

Only some ten years later the CAFC acknowledged that the "useful, concrete, and tangible result" criterion was too wide, and considered a limitation of business method patentability on the occasion of an appeal against the rejection of a patent application for a method of hedging risks in commodities trading. The USPTO examiner – still – based his rejection on the argument that this method was not part of the "technological arts", but the BPAI[462] notes on appeal that this argument is not supported by case law, although it rejects the application again, now basically for the reason that this method lacks a physical character.[463] After an *en banc* hearing[464] the Federal Circuit establishes that a "machine or transformation test" decides whether an application represents either patentable subject-matter or an unpatentable "abstract idea".[465] The court infers this rule from an extensive analysis of Supreme Court precedents, eventually based on a 19th century decision saying that a patentable process "is an act, or a

457 CAFC 23 July 1998, no. 96-1327, 149 *F.3d* 1368, 1373 (*State Street Bank & Trust v. Signature Financial Group*).

458 CAFC 23 July 1998, no. 96-1327, 149 *F.3d* 1368, 1374 (*State Street Bank & Trust v. Signature Financial Group*).

459 CAFC 23 July 1998, no. 96-1327, 149 *F.3d* 1368, 1375 (*State Street Bank & Trust v. Signature Financial Group*).

460 *See for instance* Meurer 2002.

461 The ensuing problems will be discussed when we consider alternative rules. *See* p. 202.

462 This *Board of Patent Appeals and Interferences* is part of the USPTO: 35 USC § 6.

463 BPAI 26 September 2006, no. 2002-2257, 2006 WL 5738364, p. 43 (*Ex parte Bilski*).

464 With all 12 CAFC judges. *See also* Vacca 2011.

465 CAFC 30 October 2008, no. 07-1130, 545 *F.3d* 943, 954 (*In re Bilski*).

series of acts, performed upon the subject-matter to be transformed and reduced to a different state or thing."[466] The business method of the present application does not pass the "machine or transformation test" because it does not involve a (particular) machine, and it does not accomplish a "transformation" either in the perception of the court.

Soon the test appears defective. To start with, it is unclear. For instance, couldn't a business transaction cause a "transformation" as well?[467] And it leads to side-effects, in particular a restriction of the patentability of software and certain diagnostic medical tools, which is criticised by the proponents[468] and applauded by the opponents[469] of this type of patents.

Also from a legal perspective the "machine or transformation test" is unsound. While the Supreme Court did use similar *words* several times,[470] in its nineteenth-century decision which is the eventual source of this test a "transformation" is actually considered *sufficient* condition rather than a *necessary* condition for patentability if no

---

[466] U.S. Supreme Court 19 March 1877, 94 *U.S.* 780, 788 (*Cochrane v. Deener*).

[467] Duffy et al. 2008, p. 25: "transactions [...] require physical communications between the parties and cannot be performed as mere mental steps."

[468] Nine *amici curiae* express their concern that the "machine or transformation test" will reduce the patentability of biomedical inventions (such as diagnostics tools), and ten *amici* fear a reduction of software patentability.

[469] Two *amici curiae* welcome a reduction of the patentability of medical methods, and four *amici* hope for a reduction of software patentability.

[470] In addition to the 19th century decision just mentioned also in: U.S. Supreme Court 20 November 1972, no. 71-485, 409 *U.S.* 63, 93 *S.Ct.* 253, 256 (*Gottschalk v. Benson*): "Transformation and reduction of an article `to a different state or thing' is the clue to the patentability of a process claim that does not include particular machines." Cited by: U.S. Supreme Court 3 March 1981, no. 79-1112, 450 *U.S.* 175, 184, 101 *S.Ct.* 1048, 1055 (*Diamond v. Diehr*).

novel machine is involved.[471] That is understandable, because from an economic perspective a "transformation" is a process creating value, and that is the eventual purpose of patented inventions.[472] An argument for a sufficient condition is no argument for a necessary condition though. So there is no ground to assume that the "machine or transformation test" should necessarily be satisfied. Proponents of more strict patentability requirements may regret this, but a test without a sound explanation is likely to erode soon.

Given these circumstances, the U.S. Supreme Court was willing to grant certiorari[473] and to review the case. That is an exceptional event, since the Supreme Court accepts only about one in hundred such petitions. It was nearly thirty years ago since the Supreme Court decided the last time about the limits of patentable subject-matter.[474] The result is disappointing though. Although the Supreme Court – as generally was expected – confirms that the actual business method of the case is too abstract to be patented, it also decides that the "machine or transformation test" is not always decisive[475] without providing a clear alternative. So this test suffers the same fate as the earlier tests we discussed above.

---

471 U.S. Supreme Court 19 March 1877, 94 U.S. 780, 788 (*Cochrane v. Deener*): "A process is [...] an act, or a series of acts, performed upon the subject-matter to be transformed and reduced to a different state or thing."
472 For instance, this becomes apparent from Art. 57 EPC and the word "useful" in 35 USC § 101.
473 "Certiorari" is the present passive infinitive of the Latin "certiorare" ("to show, prove, or ascertain"). This process is regulated in 28 USC § 1254(1).
474 *Since* U.S. Supreme Court 3 March 1981, no. 79-1112, 450 *U.S.* 175, 101 *S.Ct.* 1048 (*Diamond v. Diehr*).
475 U.S. Supreme Court 28 June 2010, no. 08-964, 130 *S.Ct.* 3218, 3221 (*Bilski v. Kappos*): 'The machine-or-transformation test is not the sole test for patent eligibility under § 101. The Court's precedents establish that although that test may be a useful and important clue or investigative tool, it is not the sole test for deciding whether an invention is a patent-eligible "process" under § 101.'

While the court gives no new interpretation rule, there had to be new guidelines for day to day use for the assessment of patent applications by the USPTO. Meanwhile the USPTO has published Interim Instructions with long lists of proposed "factors weighing toward eligibility" and "factors weighing against eligibility".[476] CAFC decisions following the *Bilski v. Kappos* decision so far don't give a clear view either. A software patent for digital image half-toning is considered "non-abstract" without much explanation.[477]

Given this unclear situation, a writer believes that *any* subject-matter test is inappropriate to prevent undesired patents, so he proposes to concentrate on the novelty and non-obviousness test,[478] but an other writer rightly points out that the former test definitely has its own, indispensable role.[479]

Despite the rejection of the "machine or transformation test" by the U.S. Supreme Court the CAFC still applies this test to a patent application for a method that allows physicians to determine the optimum dose of certain medicines (that by themselves are not part of the application), and finds a sufficient "transformation" indeed.[480] However, the Supreme Court recently decided in an unanimous decision that still the age-old rule applies that prohibits patenting of laws of nature[481] as long as the application of the law of nature brings nothing new.[482]

---

[476] *Interim Patent Subject Matter Eligibility Examination Instructions.* Latest version available via http://www.uspto.gov/patents/announce/bilski_guidance.jsp.

[477] *See* CAFC 8 December 2010, no. 2010-1037, 627 *F.3d* 859 (*Research Corp. v. Microsoft*).

[478] *See* Janis 2012.

[479] *See* Eisenberg 2012.

[480] *See* CAFC 17 December 2010, no. 2008-1403, 628 *F.3d* 1347 (*Prometheus v. Mayo*).

[481] Remember that in American patent law "abstract ideas, natural phenomena and laws of nature" are excluded in a similar manner as non-technical subject-matter in European patent law. *See* p. 82.

[482] U.S. Supreme Court 20 March 2012, no. 10-1150, 132 *S.Ct.* 1289, 1298 (*Mayo v. Prometheus*).

In sum, in this section we saw that the problems the Americans are facing to interpret the "abstract ideas" exclusion are quite similar to the problems the EPO struggles with to interpret the technology criterion: it is an undisputed principle, but it is hard to grasp in concrete interpretation rules.

II.3.6. Conclusion

In the preceding sections we saw that the "technology" concept in patent law is interpreted in various ways. Now that the technology requirement allegedly[483] has been codified in the EPC and the legislation of several EPO member states by the insertion of the words "in all fields of technology" in Art. 52(1) EPC and its corresponding provisions in national patent acts, the technology concept ought to be understood in its "ordinary" meaning. As regards the EPC, that is even required by the law of treaties.[484] However, that "ordinary" meaning appears by no means unambiguous, in particular where it is considered an essential criterion: for software.

Historically certain subject-matter always was excluded from patentability in many jurisdictions as a matter of course, and the enumeration in Art. 52(2) EPC reflects those traditional exclusions. At the time that the EPC did not provide yet that patents are granted in "all fields of technology",[485] the EPO often inferred the technology requirement from the observation that the subject-matter listed in this subsection allegedly shares an abstract or non-technical character. There is a complication however: the listed subject-matter is only excluded "as such" according to Art. 52(3) EPC. At fist sight this apparently means that only patent applications are excluded that are limited to the listed subject-matter, but in the previous sections we have seen that this interpretation is untenable, and that this subject-matter can also be patentable itself if certain conditions are met. The usual interpretation is that the listed subject-matter is not

[483] *See* p. 29.

[484] Art. 31(1) VCLT.

[485] Before 13 December 2007.

excluded *because* it is non-technical, but rather *as far as* it is non-technical.

In American patent law, we see something very similar. Courts decided that in the U.S. "mathematical algorithms" and business methods are not excluded *because* they are abstract, but only *as far as* they are.

But what is the meaning of "non-technical" if the subject-matter listed in Art. 52(2) EPC is not considered non-technical *per se*? And what means "abstract" in the US, if algorithms and business methods are not always considered abstract? Over the past decades many attempts have been made to substantiate the criteria of technical content and non-abstractness into practical interpretation rules suitable to day-to-day use by patent offices, without much success.

"Technical" may be associated with "physical", but it is a recurring misconception that only somehow physical subject-matter is patentable.[486] Still, in Germany a patent was allowed for an optically readable type font,[487] and in The Netherlands for a method for analysing barcodes,[488] codes that are not physical either by themselves. In the United States a 19th century Supreme Court decision[489] is often misunderstood as stating a physicality requirement, although that was denied a long time ago in court.[490]

If and when patent law really requires a physical result, this rule is often circumvented in order to reach an "intuitively" desired result by

---

[486] Words like "material" and "tangible" are confusing here, because they are also used in a metaphorical way *not* related to physical matter.

[487] *See* BGH 23 March 1965, no. Ia ZB 10/64, 67 *GRUR* 1965, p. 533-536 (*Typensatz*).

[488] Board of Appeal of the Dutch Patent Office 11 May 1987, 55 *BIE* 1987, p. 174-176, 4 *CR* 1987, p. 195-197, 11 *OJ* 1988, p. 75-78, 37 *GRUR Int* 1988, p. 71-72 (*Barcode*).

[489] U.S. Supreme Court 19 March 1877, 94 *U.S.* 780, 788 (*Cochrane v. Deener*).

[490] CCPA 12 June 1934, no. 3314, 21 *C.C.P.A.* 1235, 1237, 71 *F.2d* 169, 170 (*In re Ernst*).

creatively stretching the definition of "physical". For instance, in the U.S. signals[491] were considered physical,[492] and in the Dutch decision just mentioned information was attributed a physical character, with the argument that information allegedly can not exist without a physical carrier.

Still a physical result is occasionally required for the purpose to exclude certain subject-matter.[493] But the vagueness of this criterion remains a problem. For instance, one may wonder whether a form is tangible. If the essence of a certain invention is its geometry, is it relevant what material the object with the particular geometry is made from?[494] And an even more important objection is that there is no justification to discriminate the intangible: an intangible invention like a modulation technique is "susceptible of industrial application" too. Actually every invention is intangible: in essence, an invention is a *trick*.[495]

Zuse, the pioneer who built the first functioning electrical[496] computer in the early 1940s fought for decades in vain to obtain patent for his invention, and in his memoirs he complains that patent law apparently still has not escaped the preoccupation with tangible matter of Roman law.[497] For clarity: Zuse did not try to patent software, but a genuine machine.

A related idea is that "mental steps" should not be patentable, as opposed to "physical steps". In the United States, soon it became

---

491 The "signal" concept is meant here as used in communication technology.
492 CCPA 10 June 1982, no. 81-598, 681 *F.2d* 787, 790 (*In re Taner*).
493 Examples include older Dutch patent law (section II.3.2, p. 58), and the American "FWA" test (p. 84). *See also* Pila 2010b, p. 914.
494 *See* HR 28 June 1957, 33 *NJ* 1958, 475 (*Permanent wave*).
495 *See* also p. 134 in the next Chapter.
496 This computer used electromagnetic relays, so it was not an electronic computer, but the structure of this machine was basically the same as a modern electronic computer.
497 Zuse 1995, p. 148-153. *See also* Van Raden 1996, p. 384 (*German original*: Van Raden 1995, p. 452).

clear that the *mental step doctrine* was no reason not to allow software patents, despite the fact that algorithms might theoretically be executed by humans instead of machines.[498] The corresponding German doctrine that prohibits patenting "directions to the human mind"[499] has caused more confusion. The problem is that "a human as a processor"[500] obviously may not be restricted in his thoughts,[501] but that all kinds of truly technical inventions relying somehow on information processing seemingly are also within the reach of this doctrine.

Like the requirement of a physical result, due to its inherent vagueness the technology concept lends itself also more in general for "teleological" use only aiming at a particular result. For instance, "ordinary" programs running on "ordinary" computers are supposed to be non-technical, with the purpose to exclude them from patentability. That may be desirable, but this argument gives no explanation. Reversely, German writers proposed to extend the "forces of nature" concept in the German legal technology definition by "information", which would broaden software patentability.[502] They fail to appreciate that scientific arguments give no reason to change patent policy.

If the technology requirement is considered a rule of statutory or customary law, certain exclusions can be motivated by relating them to this requirement, but a drawback of this approach is that thus the desired purpose is addressed indirectly. For instance, American writers proposed a technology criterion to restrict business method patenting,[503] but probably they were unaware that technical business

---

[498] CCPA 14 August 1969, no. 7987, 56 *C.C.P.A.* 1381, 1392, 415 *F.2d* 1393, 1502 (*In re Prater and Wei II*).

[499] German: "Anweisungen an den menschlichen Geist". *See* Elben 1960.

[500] *See* Board of Appeal of the Dutch Patent office 11 May 1987, 55 *BIE* 1987, p. 174-176, 4 *CR* 1987, p. 195-197, 37 *GRUR Int* 1988, p. 71-72; 11 *OJ* 1988, p. 75-78 (*Barcode*).

[501] Nack 2002, p. 102-12 and p. 245-56.

[502] *See* p. 75.

[503] *See* Kappos, Thomas & Bluestone 2008.

methods do exist, at least in EPO perception.[504] Is the EPO right to grant a patent for a technical business method because it is still technical, or should the application be rejected because it is still a business method? Here we will not try to answer that question, but we suffice to conclude that again the technology concept proves unclear.

The ultimate step is a tautological approach: by *defining* a legal "technology" concept as patentable subject-matter it becomes absolutely certain that patents can only be granted for technology, and at the same time absolutely unclear what subject-matter constitutes "technology" in this sense. That is close to the German approach. Incidentally, this approach is acceptable from a methodological point of view: there are more legal concepts that are characterised by their consequences rather than by their properties. For instance, the consequences of "unlawfulness" are often very clear, but there is no general definition that allows a straightforward determination whether unlawfulness applies in a certain case.

In sum, there is no coherent conception as regards what subject-matter should be patentable, or: what should be considered technical subject-matter. That is even more pressing for the reason that both the European legal technology concept[505] and the American perception of patentable subject-matter[506] are supposed to be "non-static", in order to allow patent law to move with the times without repeated legislator interference.

By itself, it is acceptable if courts interpret the law in view of changing circumstances, as long as they respect the original intent of the legislator. While at least in the United States the Constitution provides the purpose of patents,[507] in practice, courts are more

---

[504] *See* TBA 12 March 1992, no. T 636/88 (*Material distribution/NAT SHIPPING BAGGING SERVICES*).

[505] *See for instance* p. 65.

[506] U.S. Supreme Court 10 December 2001, no. 99-1996, 534 *U.S.* 124, 135, 122 *S.Ct.* 593, 600 (*J.E.M. Ag Supply v. Pioneer*).

[507] U.S. Constitution, Article I, Section. 8, Clause 8.

concerned how to apply precedents, even where they are not formally bound by them. That often leads to an empty word-play, where isolated citations start to live their own life, and the purpose of the original court decisions gets out of sight. That applies just as much to the German *Red Dove* formula as the various tests ventured by the Americans to substantiate the exclusion of "abstract ideas", like the former "machine or transformation test", which eventually originates from a 19th century Supreme Court decision.[508] To some extent, a formalistic approach might be defended if it promotes legal certainty with predictable decisions – but in this chapter we have seen that this is not the case, unfortunately.

By default of a proper insight in the relationship between rules and the objectives of patent law, alleged flexibility easily leads to arbitrary decisions.

II.4. "Technical" in which respect?

The German Federal Supreme Court once noted that the patentable invention must solve a *technical* problem with *technical* means to reach a *technical* result.[509] So apparently a technical character is required in every respect. Still, there are no objections if an invention is not used in a technical field,[510] and, reversely, it is immaterial whether an otherwise non-technical invention is used in a technical field.[511]

Should specifically the novel aspect of a patent application be technical? At first sight, the answer seems affirmative: if "technology" is a requirement, it should not solely reside in the known, non-novel aspects of the application. A by itself non-technical computer

---

[508] For clarity: "originate from" is not the same as "be based on".
[509] BGH 21 March 1958, no. ZR 160/57, 60 *GRUR* 1958, p. 602-603 (602) (*Wettschein*).
[510] *See* BGH 23 November 1965, no. Ia ZB 210/63, 68 *GRUR* 1966, p. 249-251 (*Suppenrezept*); BGH 18 May 1967, no. Ia ZR 37/65, 69 *GRUR* 1967, p. 590-592 (*Garagentor*).
[511] *See* BGH 21 April 1977, no. X ZB 24/74, 9 *IIC* 1978 p. 459-462 (*Straken*).

program or business method does not become technical by using an ordinary computer, even if this is undeniably a technical machine.

Still a basic rule of patent law requires applications to be assessed *as a whole*, and that is a meaningful rule as well, for more than one reason. If considerations of novelty are involved in the assessment of the technical character, this assessment becomes dependent on the state of the art, while intuitively something that once was technical always remains technical. Furthermore, one may question whether non-technical features really exist, since only features may be specified that are needed to solve the problem set by the inventor. In particular in the case of *systems* the features are strongly interrelated, for instance in control engineering.

Mutatis mutandis exactly the same dilemma applies in the United States, if "non-technical" is replaced by "abstract". For instance, an American court was faced with the problem whether a device containing a novel algorithm should be considered a novel device like any other novel device, or whether the application should be rejected if the novelty is concentrated in the algorithm, subject-matter that was considered unpatentable at the time.

So conceivably there are two assessment methods: either the application is considered as a whole, or its (novel) essence is considered decisive. Is it possible to make a choice between the two methods, could they conceivably coexist, or are they perhaps both incorrect? Is this a dilemma or a paradox? In the following sections we will answer those questions.

For completeness we mention that we will not address Dutch law here separately, since that would not add very much.

II.4.1. European Patent Office

The European Patent Office always pretended to test applications *as a whole* for technical content. In an opposition procedure in the 1980s, the EPO explicitly rejected the so called core-theory which at the time was the rule in Germany,[512] that – as summarised by the Board of Appeal – requires to give a weighting to technical and non-technical aspects, and then to decide which aspect makes the essential contribution to the result of the invention. The Board notes that this approach has no legal basis in the EPC, and may be difficult to accomplish in practice. Furthermore, the Board believes that this approach does no justice to applications in which the technical aspect is not dominant but still novel and inventive.[513] Consequently, a computer-controlled X-ray device is deemed patentable, although the application in essence involves just the computer program, which is not considered technical in the legal sense.[514]

We mention this case first, because here the EPO itself compares its approach with the very different approach at the time in Germany. However, ten months earlier the EPO proclaimed the following rule to assess the patentability of "software":[515] "Decisive is what technical *contribution* the invention as defined in the claim when considered *as a whole* makes to the known art." In the case where this rule was stated, it led to the conclusion that a patent on an image processing system was allowed, though its essence was a mathematical algorithm. While the rule provides that the application must be considered as a whole, it still shows an early sign of later confusion because it refers to the "known art". That violates the rule that the qualification of the subject-matter of the application (under Art. 52 EPC) should not be related to the "state of the art".

The two above cases were simple insofar as these inventions consisted of systems any layman would call "technical", although these systems were computer controlled. In those early years of the EPO, the mere *presence* of conventional technical components next to

[512] For details, see section II.4.2, p. 106.
[513] TBA 21 May 1987, no. T 26/86, 11 *OJ* 1988, p. 19, at 3.4 (*X-ray Apparatus/KOCH & STERZEL*).
[514] *See* TBA 21 May 1987, no. T 26/86, 11 *OJ* 1988, p. 19 (*X-ray Apparatus/KOCH & STERZEL*).
[515] TBA 15 July 1986, no. T 208/84, 10 *OJ* 1987, p. 14, at 16 (*Computer-Related Invention/VICOM*). Emphasis added in citation.

a program was considered sufficient for many applications to be considered sufficiently technical to be patentable, even if the program might be considered the "core" of the invention.[516] But soon objections arose against applications lacking novel technical components.[517] Consequently, the EPO henceforth requires a "technical contribution in a field not excluded from patentability

516 *See* TBA 15 July 1986, no. T 208/84, 10 *OJ* 1987, p. 14 (*Computer-Related Invention/VICOM*); TBA 21 May 1987, no. T 26/86, 11 *OJ* 1988, p. 19 (*X-ray Apparatus/KOCH & STERZEL*); TBA 5 September 1988, no. T 115/85, 13 *OJ* 1990, p. 30 (*Computer-related invention/IBM*); TBA 17 November 1994, no. T 78/92 (*Terminal pour l'élaboration de programmes utilisables par un automate programmable/TÉLÉMÉCANIQUE*); TBA 6 July 1994, no. T 1002/92, 18 *OJ* 1995, p. 605 (*Queuing system/PETTERSSON*). *After*: Nack 2002, p. 189.

517 *See* TBA 5 October 1988, no. T 22/85, 13 *OJ* 1990, p. 12 (*Document abstracting and retrieving/IBM*); TBA 16 March 1989, no. T 52/85 (*Semantically-related expressions/IBM*); TBA 14 March 1989, no. T 121/85 (*Automatic spelling checking and correction process in a text processing system/IBM*); TBA 14 February 1989, no. T 38/86, 13 *OJ* 1990, p. 384 (*Text Processing/IBM*); TBA 22 June 1989, no. T 65/86 (*System for detecting and correcting contextual errors in a text processing system/IBM*); TBA 23 October 1990, no. T 95/86 (*Method for assisting an operator of an interactive text processing system/IBM*); TBA 5 December 1989, no. T 186/86 (*Method for displaying and editing spatially related data in an interactive text processing system/IBM*); TBA 12 December 1989, no. T 158/88, 14 *OJ* 1991, p. 556 (*Character form/SIEMENS*); TBA 15 April 1993, no. T 110/90 (*Editable document form/IBM*); TBA 19 March 1992, no. T 854/90 (*Kartenleser/IBM*); TBA 16 April 1993, no. T 236/91 (*Menu-based natural language understanding system/TEXAS INSTRUMENTS*); TBA 16 April 1993, no. T 833/91 (*Simulation of computer program external interfaces/IBM*); TBA 22 October 1992, no. T 167/92 (*Document composition from parts inventory/IBM*); TBA 31 May 1994, no. T 769/92, 18 *OJ* 1995 (*General purpose management system/SOHEI*); TBA 29 October 1993, no. T 790/92 (*Editing business charts/IBM*); TBA 15 July 1996, no. T 953/94 (*A method of functional analysis/GEORGES*); TBA 8 September 2000, no. T 931/95, 24 *OJ* 2001, p. 441-457 (*Controlling pension benefits systems/PBS PARTNERSHIP*); TBA 23 April 1999, no. T 619/98 (*Television set/EDICO*). *Also after* Nack 2002, p. 189.

under Art. 52(2) EPC".[518] This so-called *contribution approach* would remain in use from the late 1980s for nearly a decade.

Following this rule, a *business method* would only be patentable if it applies new technology. Nevertheless, the EPO Board of Appeal decides that a system involving a "turn-number allocating unit" is patentable,[519] because the application includes hardware, so it is not a "method for doing business *as such*".[520] Whether the hardware by itself is novel and inventive is deemed irrelevant by the TBA. The decision emphasises that the question whether the subject-matter is an "invention" within the meaning of Article 52(1) EPC is to be answered separately from the question whether the claimed subject-matter is novel and involves an inventive step. In other words: the technical aspects do not have to be new: the application *as a whole* should be assessed for technical character. Therefore this application is decided to be sufficiently technical, and subsequently it is also found sufficiently inventive to uphold the patent.

A method to interconnect various management tasks in an automated system at first sight appears a pure software-invention.[521] The EPO decided however that technical *considerations* were required to make this invention, which "lend a technical nature to the invention in that

---

518 *See* TBA 14 March 1989, no. T 121/85 (*Automatic spelling checking and correction process in a text processing system/IBM*); TBA 14 February 1989, no. T 38/86, 13 *OJ* 1990, p. 384 (*Text Processing/IBM*); TBA 23 October 1990, no. T 95/86 (*Method for assisting an operator of an interactive text processing system/IBM*); TBA 3 July 1990, no. T 603/89, 15 *OJ* 1992, p. 230 (*Marker/BEATTIE*); TBA 21 September 1993, no. T 71/91 (*Electronic document distribution network/IBM*); TBA 16 April 1993, no. T 236/91 (*Menu-based natural language understanding system/TEXAS INSTRUMENTS*); TBA 16 April 1993, no. T 833/91 (*Simulation of computer program external interfaces/IBM*); TBA 13 October 1995, no. T 77/92 (*Measuring tape/BROSELOW*).

519 *See* TBA 6 July 1994, no. T 1002/92, 18 *OJ* 1995, p. 605 (*Queuing system/PETTERSSON*).

520 Art. 52(2c) EPC.

521 *See* TBA 31 May 1994, no. T 769/92, 18 *OJ* 1995, p. 525 (*General purpose management system/SOHEI*).

they imply a technical problem to be solved by (implicit) technical features". In this case actually the "core theory" is applied too, because those considerations logically relate to the novel aspects, and they are technical, so the novel aspects are technical.

In 1998 the TBA took a new course when it acknowledged that for the technical *character* of an application (under Art. 52 EPC) its technical aspects do not have to be novel, and concluded that it is more appropriate to test the technical *contribution* (with respect to the prior art) when the novelty and the inventive step are examined (under Art. 54 and 56 EPC respectively).[522] The president of the Board or Appeal that made this decision already wrote about criticisms on the interpretation of the "contribution approach" at the time some years earlier.[523]

A little over two years later, the EPO explained its new approach in another often-cited decision even more clearly as follows:[524]

> There is no basis in the EPC for distinguishing between "new features" of an invention and features of that invention which are known from the prior art when examining whether the invention concerned may be considered to be an invention within the meaning of Article 52(1) EPC. Thus there is no basis in the EPC for applying this so-called contribution approach for this purpose. Indeed, this approach confused the requirement of "invention" with the requirements of "novelty" and "inventive step".

Apparently the application is assessed *as a whole*. Subsequently it is decided however that this invention – a pension system – is not inventive in a technical field, and therefore can not be patented. The pension scheme may be inventive, but it is designed by actuaries. According to the TBA that is no technical work: only the implementation of the system by a programmer may be technical, but

522 TBA 1 July 1998, no. T 1173/97, 22 *OJ* 1999, p. 609-632, at 8 (*Computer Program Product I/IBM*).

523 Van den Berg 1996, nr. 9-12.

524 *See* TBA 8 September 2000, no. T 931/95, 24 *OJ* 2001, p. 441-457 (*Controlling pension benefits systems/PBS PARTNERSHIP*).

the TBA considers that a routine effort, lacking an inventive step, once the pension scheme has been designed. In other words: the development of this system would not involve a relevant, *technical* "inventive step".

While the EPO rejects the "contribution approach", in fact it adopts a kind of "contribution approach 2.0", that no longer requires the technical aspects to be novel, but the novel aspects to be technical: the non-technical features are ignored for the assessment of the inventive step. That still requires a breakdown which is irreconcilable with the EPC[525] and which may be hard to accomplish as well because of interplay between technical and non-technical features. As we will see, the German courts too adopted this "contribution approach 2.0",[526] but the British reject it.[527] In this approach, the test whether the application represents an invention (under Art. 52 EPC) becomes all but redundant. A German writer even notes that time has come to say goodbye to the invention concept in patent law.[528]

The new approach would be followed in many decisions. The idea to give a mobile telephone multiple "identities" without requiring a SIM-card[529] exchange was considered not patentable: devising this idea is by itself not considered technical, and the implementation is considered insufficiently inventive by itself.[530]

In some decisions applying this "contribution approach 2.0", the non-technical elements are not ignored for the assessment of the inventive step, but they are assumed to be part of the state of the art, so they

---

525 *See for instance* Klaiber 2010 p. 566.
526 *See* section II.4.2, p. 106.
527 De British designate this approach as the "any hardware approach", because merely mentioning hardware is sufficient to pass the Art. 52 EPC test in this approach. *See* p. 119.
528 Nack 2002, p. 317: "Abschied vom Erfindungsbegriff".
529 *Subscriber Identity Module.*
530 *See* TBA 26 September 2002, no. T 641/00, 26 *OJ* 2003, p. 352-364 (*Two identities/COMVIK*).

never can be novel.[531] This approach tries to escape the objection that the application is not assessed as a whole, but in fact it still does.

A writer[532] juxtaposes the "contribution approach" (in whatever form) with the "application basis principle",[533] emanating from the statutory rule that the EPO "shall consider and decide upon the European patent application or the European patent *only in the text submitted to it*, or agreed, by the applicant for or proprietor of the patent".[534] Another writer too argues that the EPO with its new contribution approach violates the EPC.[535] Both cited writers are Germans, and in their legal culture a *contra legem* interpretation is all but unacceptable.

The fact that EPO still applies some sort of contribution approach also becomes apparent from the fact that a Board of Appeal made the observation that various day to day activities that obviously are not patentable, such as the act of writing using pen and paper actually have a technical *character* too, but that the use of technical *means* is not sufficient: a method is only patentable if it represents a technical *solution* to a technical *problem*.[536]

Should the *problem* really be technical? The nature of the problem always was a questionable criterion for the assessment of patent applications,[537] and that applies in particular to the technical content of the problem. An energy-saving combustion engine contributes to the solution of an economical problem (high fuel cost) and an

---

[531] *See* TBA 8 September 2000, no. T 931/95, 24 *OJ* 2001, p. 441-457 (*Controlling pension benefits systems/PBS PARTNERSHIP*); TBA 21 April 2004, no. T 258/03, 27 *OJ* 2004, p. 575-638 (*Auction method/HITACHI*).
[532] Klaiber 2010, p. 566.
[533] German: "Antragsgrundsatz".
[534] Art. 113(2) EPC.
[535] Von Hellfeld 2008, p. 1009.
[536] TBA 21 April 2004, no. T 258/03, 27 *OJ* 2004, p. 575-638 (585), at 4.6 (*Auction method/HITACHI*).
[537] *See* Hesse 1981; Brodeßer 1993.

environment problem (CO_2 exhaust).[538] Qualification of a problem as "technical" anticipates on the nature of the solution, so it hardly can serve as an indication for the technical content of that solution. Eventually every patent has the purpose to solve a business problem for its owner. Purchasers of patented products want to solve various problems that are not "technical" at all, like curing a headache, to name just one example.

Several decisions show that a requirement of a technical problem indeed leads to confusion. A fax machine feature would not be technical because it eventually serves the purpose of cost control.[539] Also the idea for a mobile telephone feature would not solve a technical problem because it eventually aims at cost control as well.[540]

While intuitively it stands to reason to ignore non-technical features, in practice that is hardly feasible because these features often interact with the technical features. Therefore, the EPO provides the rule:[541]

> [Non-technical features] may well form the only logical link between technical features resulting from their implementation. They must therefore be taken into consideration for the examination as to inventive step while at the same time not being permitted to contribute to it.

Even for a German commentator this is unacceptable.[542]

The cause of this confusion is that the pertinent case represents an attempt to patent the mere idea to develop a certain product (-feature). Whether "problem inventions" can be patented is controversial.[543] For instance, the BGH decidedly stated that this is

538 Von Hellfeld 2008, p. 1010.

539 *See* TBA 22 October 1999, no. T 1053/98 (*Data communication apparatus/CANON KABUSHIKI KAISHA*).

540 *See* p. 101.

541 TBA 19 September 2007, no. T 688/05, at 4.5 (*Ticket auctioning system/TICKETMASTER*).

542 *See* Von Hellfeld 2008.

543 Ochmann 1992, p. 769.

not the case,[544] and a writer explains the observation that the EPO once apparently adopted a different view[545] from the fact that in the EPO perception the legal "problem" concept includes essential elements of the solution.[546]

If the technical nature of the problem is a questionable criterion, is it a better criterion to require the *solution* to be technical? In the case of a method to hold a Dutch auction[547] in a computer network the technical character of the solution to this "technical" problem is questioned.[548] Characteristic of this type of auction is that the auctioneer begins with a high asking price, which is lowered until a bid is made. So in principle only one bid is made for each object to be sold. But if bids are made remotely via telecommunications, possibly multiple bids are made as long it is not known that anyone has made a bid, and conceivably the first bid may not arrive first, because the exchange of information in a computer network, however fast, always takes some time, which is not precisely the same for everybody, and is not predictable either.[549]

In this case, the TBA finds that the problem is not be solved in a technical manner, *but* by adapting the rules of the game, albeit preserving the essence of this type of auction as a descending-price auction. Is this really no technical solution? The designer of the system can not change laws of nature, but he can deliver a satisfactory

---

544 *See* BGH 15 November 1983, no. X ZR 27/82, 86 *GRUR* 1984, p. 194-196 (*Kreiselegge*). No English translation available.
545 *See* TBA 15 March 1984, no. T 2/83, 7 *OJ* 1984, p. 265 (*Simethicone tablet/RIDER*).
546 Melullis 2002, art. 52, Rdn. 85.
547 In Dutch such an auction is called a "Chinese veiling" ("Chinese auction").
548 *See* TBA 21 April 2004, no. T 258/03, 27 *OJ* 2004, p. 575-638 (*Auction method/HITACHI*).
549 In telecommunications (except over very short distances) usually media and equipment are shared with other users, so delays may occur. Usually a fully dedicated network is infeasible for technical and/or economical reasons.

solution by circumventing the impossible in a creative way. Engineers more often face physical limitations prohibiting a direct solution.[550]

Incidentally, this case is a fine example that a *problem* should not be qualified as "technical". The problem is here to organise a honest auction. The problem is qualified as technical because a technical solution is expected. If apparently not technical solution is available (at least in the EPO perception), that may be another reason not to qualify the problem as technical.

Finally, we mention that the – meanwhile rejected – proposal for a European Directive for "computers-implemented inventions" adopted a kind of contribution approach too. It proposed to codify the technical contribution requirement as follows:[551]

> Article 4 – Conditions for patentability
>
> 1. Member States shall ensure that a computer-implemented invention is patentable on the condition that it is susceptible of industrial application, is new, and involves an <u>inventive step</u>.
> 2. Member States shall ensure that it is a condition of involving an <u>inventive step</u> that a computer-implemented invention must make a <u>technical contribution</u>.
> 3. The <u>technical contribution</u> shall be assessed by consideration of the difference between the scope of the patent claim considered as a whole, elements of which may comprise both technical and non-technical features, and the state of the art.

While this rule nominally requires an assessment of the patent application *as a whole,* the last clause implies the presumption that technical and non-technical features can be distinguished. Apparently

---

[550] For instance, the efficiency of an electrical power plant has a theoretical limit. However, the remaining heat still can be used for heating purposes in cogeneration.

[551] Proposal for a Directive of the European Parliament and of the Council on the patentability of computer-implemented inventions, Brussels, 20 February 2002. Emphasis added. For the background of this Directive proposal see p. 17.

that is relevant, because the "technical contribution" is defined as follows:

> Article 2(b)
>
> "technical contribution" means a contribution to the state of the art in a technical field which is not obvious to a person skilled in the art.

This definition implies the presumption that conceivably also a contribution could be made in a non-technical field, so this Directive would have made the same mistake as EPOs "contribution approach 2.0".[552]

Returning to the policy of the European Patent Office, we conclude that the EPO still pretends to assess applications *as a whole*, but actually requires the novel aspects to coincide with the technical aspects.

II.4.2. Germany

The Germans too struggle with the question in which respect an application must be technical in order to be eligible for patent, and in particular with the question whether it must be technical *as a whole,* or whether specifically its inventive features must be technical (or reversely).

The first time the BGH was involved in a "software patent" case, it decided that specifically the technical features should be novel and inventive:[553]

> [...] that technical features in the claim can justify patenting only when the inventive novelty finds its expression there, but not when the invention is restricted to the nontechnical part of the teaching [...]

The court considers the "organisational and computing rule"[554] of this program a complete problem solution standing by itself.[555] It

---

552 *See* p. 101.

553 BGH 22 June 1976, no. X ZB 23/74, 8 *IIC* 1977, p. 558-565 (562), at II.3 b) cc) δ) (*Disposition Program*).

argues that this rule does not become technical because it is employed using a computer as a technical means: then the use of a pencil by a human being applying the "rule" by hand would make it technical too, since a pencil is a technical product.[556] That is what Americans call "insignificant post-solution activity".[557]

A commentator concludes from this decision that attempts to obtain patent protection for software creations have no future anymore.[558] Eventually he proved to be wrong, but this decision did mark the begin of an era of many years when software-inventions were only eligible for patent in Germany in the rare cases that a new kind of machine was used.[559]

The breakdown prescribed by the above decision may seem correct at first sight, but it also may lead to counter-intuitive results, as became apparent when a court judged that an anti-skid system[560] could not be patented because the *core* of the invention would be merely an abstract "braking philosophy" without technical character.[561] The

---

554 8 *IIC* 1977, p. 558-565 (561), at II. 3. b) bb), German: "gedanklich-logische Anweisung", (98).

555 The decision refers to a "complete problem solution", 8 *IIC* 1977, p. 558-565 (560-61), at II.3 b) bb), German: "fertige Problemlösung", 79 *GRUR* 1977, p. 96-99 (98), ibidem.

556 8 *IIC* 1977, p. 558-565 (561), at II.3 b) bb).

557 U.S. Supreme Court 22 June 1978, no. 77-642, 437 *U.S.* 584, 590, 98 *S.Ct.* 2522, 2525 (*Parker v. Flook*).

558 Kolle 1977, p. 74.

559 *See* BGH 21 April 1977, no. X ZB 24/74, 8 *IIC* 1977 p. 459-462 (*Straken*); BGH 7 June 1977, no. X ZB 20/74, 8 *IIC* 1977, p. 363-366 (*Test Method*); BGH 14 February 1978, no. X ZB 3/76, 10 *IIC* 1979, p. 489-494 (*Error Location*); BGH 16 September 1980, no. X ZB 6/80, 83 *GRUR* 1981, p. 39-42 (*Walzstabteilung*).

560 Anti-skid braking technology helps to prevent skids on slippery roads.

561 *See* BPatG 12 June 1978, no. AW (pat) 78/75, 81 *GRUR* 1979, p. 111-113 (*Antiblockiersystem*).

BGH decided however that this car part *as a whole* is definitely technical.[562]

In patent circles this decision was welcomed with relief.[563] However, one swallow does not make a summer: only a few months later the court decides that the *core* of a computer controlled system for optimised cutting of rolled bars is a "purely mental direction", rather than a patentable technical invention, even if the computer in this system is integrated with unmistakably technical equipment.[564]

Some years later, an automatic procedure for optimal regulation of fuel flow of an aircraft in order to minimise flight costs[565] was considered insufficiently technical to be patentable because "market and business factors included in the computational formula predominate over the natural forces".[566] The court repeatedly refers to the "core" of the invention, which gives the commentator a reason to introduce the term "core theory".[567] Some writers argue that the court in this case applied a more differentiated form of this core

---

[562] *See* BGH 13 May 1980, no. X ZB 19/78, 82 *GRUR* 1980, p. 849-852 (*Antiblockiersystem*).

[563] Annotator Eisenführ (a patent agent) says to be relieved that the *witch hunt* for the non-technical he feared for after the decisions of the preceding years had not materialised. BGH 13 May 1980, no. X ZB 19/78, 82 *GRUR* 1980, p. 849-852 (851), at II.4 (*Antiblockiersystem*).

[564] BGH 16 September 1980, no. X ZB 6/80, 83 *GRUR* 1981, p. 39-42 (40), at II. 3. b) (*Walzstabteilung*).

[565] Flying faster reduces flying time, saving capital cost, but it increases fuel consumption, and fuel cost therefore. At a certain velocity the costs are minimal (for a given itinerary, *ceteris paribus*).

[566] BGH 11 March 1986, no. X ZR 65/85, 19 *IIC* 1988, p. 538-545 (541-42), at II.1 (*Minimization of Flight Costs*).

[567] Comment by Jürgen Betten on: BGH 11 March 1986, no. X ZR 65/85, 88 *GRUR* 1986, p. 531-535 (534) (*Flugkostenminimierung*), 19 *IIC* 1988, p. 538-545 (543) (*Minimization of Flight Costs*), at II.1. The German word for "core" is "Kern", a word that also has the connotation of "nucleus". Because this comment was published just a few months after the Chernobyl nuclear disaster, the "core theory" would have been in a bad odour from the very beginning.

theory, that leaves room to weigh technical and non-technical elements,[568] but nevertheless the result is that this system is considered unpatentable, although it appears quite technical at first sight.

From the mid 1980's, the lower German courts gradually started to divert from the core theory more often, and to assess inventions as a whole, which made it easier to obtain a patent for a software-related invention.[569] The German courts may have been influenced by the policy of the EPO, that from its opening in 1977[570] appeared more flexible to grant patents for software-related inventions. After a guiding decision of an EPO Board of Appeal,[571] there was a certain pioneering sprit among the German proponents of such patents.[572] For this reason, at the time many Germans who wanted only a software patent for Germany went too the EPO too, instead of the DPMA,[573] accepting the risk that a German court would later revoke their patent for Germany, because in the German view at the time

---

568 Nack 2002, p. 190-191: "Abwägungslehre", which can be translated as "weighing theory".

569 *See* BPatG 12 August 1987, no. 19 W (pat) 56/85, 89 *GRUR* 1987, p. 799-800 (*Elektronisches Stellwerk*); BPatG 25 July 1988, no. 93/87, 91 *GRUR* 1989, p. 42-45 (*Rollladen-Steuerung*); BPatG 30 August 1988, no. 112/86, 91 *GRUR* 1989, p. 336-338 (*Fourier-Transformationsanordnung;* Anm. Goldrian); BPatG 8 September 1988, no. 17 W 137/86, 91 *GRUR* 1989, p. 338-340 (*Elektronisches Übersetzungsgerät*); BPatG 5 October 1989, no. 58/88, 92 *GRUR* 1990, p. 261-263 (*Seismische Aufzeichnungen*); BPatG 10 July 1990, no. W 135/89, 93 *GRUR* 1991, p. 197-198 (*Schleifverfahren*). BPatG 4 October 1990, no. 117/88, 93 *GRUR* 1991, p. 195-196 (*Temperatursteuerung*).

570 The EPO was opened on 2 November 1977 and accepts patent applications from 1 June 1978.

571 *See* TBA 15 July 1986, no. T 208/84, 10 *OJ* 1987, p. 14 (*Computer-Related Invention/VICOM*).

572 Anders 2001a tells that after this decision of the EPO Boards of Appeal there was something like a *regelrechte Aufbruchstimmung / pioneering spirit* (p. 132) *l'impression d'avènement d'une ère nouvelle* (p. 133).

573 "Deutsches Patent- und Markenamt", the German patent and trademark office. http://www.dpma.de.

European patent law did not allow all software patents granted by the EPO.[574]

The gradual change in policy of the *German Federal Patent Court* becomes apparent for instance from the decision, a little over a year after the above EPO decision, that an electronic rail traffic control system is sufficiently technical to be patentable, because all features contributing to the problem solution should be considered together, including features that might be considered non-technical by themselves.[575] This implies a clear rejection of the core theory, which is further confirmed by the order to assess the technical character of the application independent from the inventive step. This decision also notes that the features not contributing to the solution of the problem should be ignored. This may seem obvious, but it does imply that it is impossible to "make" a non-technical invention technical by adding features at will, as some opponents of a *whole contents approach* argue.[576]

Nevertheless, the highest German court four years later still applies the classical core theory to a process for entering Chinese characters into a text processing system.[577] The BGH judges that the core of this invention is an "abstract" system for arranging these characters, and decides that the equipment being used is only of minor importance and can not attribute a sufficiently technical character to the invention to allow it to be patented.

But in a case about a process for the management of the "virtual memory"[578] of a computer a mere ten days later the BGH too seems to adopt a whole contents approach: the BGH decides that the patent

---

[574] Betten 1988, p. 250.
[575] BPatG 12 August 1987, no. 19 W (pat) 56/85, 89 *GRUR* 1987, p. 799-800 (800), at II.2 (*Elektronisches Stellwerk*).
[576] *See* section II.4.5, p. 124.
[577] *See* BGH 1 June 1991, no. X ZB 24/89, 24 *IIC* 1993 p. 124-129 (*Chinese Characters*).
[578] The "virtual memory" concept has been explained in footnote 380 on p. 73.

application *as a whole* relates to a technical invention.[579] Furthermore, the BGH explicitly states that the decision whether an invention is technical does not depend on the fact whether the technical features are novel and inventive, in other words that not just its inventive *core* should be assessed for technical content.

At last, in 1992 the BGH expressly renounces the core theory in a case about a dive computer, a watch sized device that helps a scuba diver to plan a dive in order to prevent decompression sickness ("caisson disease").[580] In first instance it was decided – along the well-known scheme – that the *core* of this invention was not technical but merely consisted of a "mental scheme".[581] The BGH decided however that this application should be assessed as a whole, and thus it is found to be technical. The BGH now provides the following rule:[582]

> When inventions combining technical and non-technical features are examined for inventive step, any method of calculation must be included in an assessment of the subject-matter. It is not permissible to split the latter up and examine for inventive step - i.e. obviousness - only the part comprising the technical features.

Some years later, the BGH indeed assesses a speech analysis device as a whole.[583] While the core of this patent application is unmistakably a program, the BGH follows the literal text of the application referring to a "programmed computer" as an "apparatus". For the court, the computer as an industrially manufacturable and industrially applicable apparatus that uses[584] energy is definitely technical, and it

579 *See* BGH 11 June 1991, no. X ZB 13/88, 23 *IIC* 1992, 824-828 (*Page Buffer*).
580 *See* BGH 4 February 1992, no. X ZR 43/91, 24 *IIC* 1993, p. 645-649 (*Diving Computer*).
581 *See* BPatG 26 May 1993, no. 2 Ni 29/89, 96 *GRUR* 1994, p. 107-111 (*Diving Computer II*).
582 BGH 4 February 1992, no. X ZR 43/91, 24 *IIC* 1993, p. 645-649 (649), at 8 (*Diving Computer*).
583 *See* BGH 11 May 2000, no. X ZB 15/98, 33 *IIC* 2002, p. 343-348 (*Speech Analysis Apparatus*).
584 Between brackets and quotation marks, the court adds the word "consumes", apparently disagreeing. Thus the court respects not just

decides that the use of a program does not take away its technical character. A writer is upset and wonders whether this decision implies that now in Germany every business method using a computer is eligible for patent.[585]

Some months earlier however the BGH had established that an assessment of an application as a whole does not preclude that certain features are given more weight than others.[586] This conception still resembles the age-old "core theory", although the BGH avoids a classical mistake of this theory by saying that novelty may not be a factor in weighing features. But that raises the question whether a feature that is not novel still can carry weight, or conversely whether a novel feature may not carry weight. Furthermore, just as the classical core theory this approach requires a dissection, and that alone implies that actually the application is *not* assessed as a whole, although – obviously – the dissection starts from the application as a whole. That does not just violate a rule, but it also leads to practical dilemma's, like the question whether a small but indispensable part should be considered important or unimportant in this weighing process.

Still two years later the BGH applies this approach again for the assessment of a spell checking program.[587]

While it is a taboo henceforth to refer to the "core theory" in Germany,[588] there is still a tendency to look for the essence of patent applications, if only in order to prevent that a non-technical application is "made" technical by mentioning actually unimportant technical features, the classical objection against a whole contents approach.

---

human laws, but laws of nature too, in this case the law of conservation of energy.

585 *See* Nack 2000.

586 BGH 13 December 1999, no. X ZB 11/98, 33 *IIC* 2002, p. 231-238 (234), at II.4. f) (*Logic Verification*).

587 BGH 17 October 2001, no. X ZB 16/00, 33 *IIC* 2002, p. 753-762 (756-57), at B.III.1.b)aa) (*Search for Faulty Character Strings*).

588 Nack 2002, p. 196.

This objection ignores however that the distinction between "important" and "unimportant" is not always unambiguous. A fine example is the case of an electronic payment system. In first instance, the court focused on the organisational setup of this system, and concluded that neither the problem nor the solution is technical.[589] The BGH noted however that the solution involves secure data communication over insecure communication facilities using cryptographic techniques, and that this is technical.[590]

The irony is that both in case of an assessment as a whole, and if only the core is considered the description seems more important than the substance,[591] so that there is a risk of both manipulation and misapprehension in either approach.

While a technical *result* is required in German law, *effects* do not have to be technical.[592] Courts decided that there are no objections against patenting inventions aiming at an aesthetic result, like an iridescent surface,[593] or preventing scratches.[594] There are no objections to patents literally dealing with taste either,[595] so that a recipe for a new mushroom soup could be patented as well.[596] While in particular the two cases last mentioned are often cited in order to show that *in principle* this type of subject-matter can be patented indeed, in all these three cases eventually no patent is granted due to insufficient inventiveness. But some twenty years later the BGH upholds a patent

[589] BPatG 15 April 2003, no. 17 W (pat) 46/02, 105 *GRUR* 2003, p. 1033-1035 (1034), at II.2.3 (*Transaktion im elektronischen Zahlungsverkehr*).
[590] BGH 24 May 2004, no. X ZB 20/03, 36 *IIC* 2005 p. 242-249 (245), at II.2. b) (*Electronic Payment System*).
[591] *See* Section II.4.5, "The wording of the application", p. 124.
[592] Melullis 2002, Art. 52, Rdn. 70.
[593] *See* RG 27 November 1935, no. I 21/35, 36 *Mitt.* 1936, p. 16 (*Irisierende Oberfläche*).
[594] *See* BGH 18 May 1967, no. Ia ZR 37/65, 69 *GRUR* 1967, p. 590-592 (*Garagentor*).
[595] In common parlance tasting is no "aesthetic" experience, but the Greek word αίσθησης simply means "observation".
[596] *See* BGH 23 November 1965, no. Ia ZB 210/63, 68 *GRUR* 1966, p. 249-251 (*Suppenrezept*).

for a nicely shaped valley-gutter,[597] with the argument that the aesthetic result was reached with technical means.[598]

Is it indeed sufficient if technical means are used to achieve an aesthetic result? Again we find apparently partially technical subject-matter, and again it may seem more appropriate here to assess the *technical contribution*, rather than the *whole contents.* And again a whole contents approach appears not as counter-intuitive as it may seem at first sight because technology and aesthetics are often intertwined: there are various forms of applied art where the available technical means determine what is artistically feasible, in particular if the objective is to manufacture a commercial product. An invention that combines technology, aesthetics and commerce is the *hoarfrost candle,* a candle with a surface that suggests hoarfrost, which is perceived as beautiful by the people who like those candles.[599] The BGH decides that this candle is a technical invention as well, but it acknowledges that the objective was not simply to achieve a predetermined aesthetic result, but to find an aesthetic effect that is technically feasible as well.[600]

When late last century the BGH decided that a patent application may also be sufficiently technical if technical *considerations* are involved,[601] just like the EPO five years earlier,[602] it effectively applied some form of core theory too, because the (technical) considerations of an inventor obviously relate to the novel aspects of the invention,

---

597 A "valley gutter" is a gutter in the corner enclosed by two parts of a sloping roof.
598 *See* BGH 3 November 1987, no. ZR 27/86, 20 *IIC* 1989, p. 730-736 (*Gutter*).
599 *De gustibus non est disputandum.*
600 *See* BGH 7 October 1971, no. X ZR 57/68, 63 *Mitt.* 1972, p. 235-236 (*Rauhreifkerze*). *See also* Kolle 1974b, p. 149.
601 *See* BGH 13 December 1999, no. X ZB 11/98, 33 *IIC* 2002, p. 231-238 (*Logic Verification*). *For further information see* p. 73.
602 *See* p. 57.

that according to the core theory must coincide with its technical aspects.[603]

Around the last turn of the century the German courts followed the EPO[604] in an approach that *pretends* to assess applications as a whole, but ignores the non-technical features for the assessment of the inventive step.[605] A writer notes that this approach at least improves clarity and credibility, even if it may not substantially change the limits of patentability.[606] For instance, it would be easier to understand that only a distinction is made depending on the technical *contribution* of software, while its technical *character* is no longer questioned. Still this approach too suffers from the shortcoming that it requires a dissection that violates the German Patent Act just like it does not conform to the EPC.[607] Incidentally, the cited writer wrote several articles[608] about the complicated puzzles emanating from the perception that certain (non-technical) features in the application should be ignored.

In later years, German courts regularly involve an assessment of the technical content of the *problem* to be solved in their decision about patentability,[609] again following the EPO example. A characteristic

---

603 *See also* p. 99.

604 *See* p. 100.

605 *See* BGH 20 January 2009, no. X ZB 22/07, 111 *GRUR* 2009, p. 479-480 (*Steuerungseinrichtung für Untersuchungsmodalitäten*); BGH 22 April 2010, no. Xa ZB 20/08, 112 *GRUR* 2010, p. 613-616 (*Dynamische Dokumentengenerierung*); BGH 26 October 2010, no. X ZR 47/07, 113 *GRUR* 2011, p. 125-128 (*Wiedergabe topografischer Informationen*).

606 Anders 2001a, p. 142. He discusses the following decisions: BGH 13 December 1999, no. X ZB 11/98, 33 *IIC* 2002, p. 231-238 (*Logic Verification*); BGH 11 May 2000, no. X ZB 15/98, 33 *IIC* 2002, p. 343-348 (*Speech Analysis Device*, comment Betten), 25 *OJ* 2002, p. 454-461; BPatG 14 June 1999, no. 20 W (pat) 8/99, 101 *GRUR* 1999, p. 1078-1080 (*Automatische Absatzsteuerung*).

607 *See* p. 102.

608 *See* Anders 2001b, Anders 2004.

609 *See* BGH 17 October 2001, no. X ZB 16/00, 33 *IIC* 2002, p. 753-762 (*Search for Faulty Character Strings*);. BGH 19 October 2004, no. X ZB

statement for this view is the following citation from case law: "[...] the essential instructions of the claimed teaching must rather contribute to the solution of a concrete technical problem."[610]

We already noted that the technical content of the *problem* is a questionable criterion.[611] The BGH explains that the "objective technical problem" should be established, by investigating the actual achievement of the invention. The problem as stated by the applicant is only an aid to establish the "objective technical problem".[612] Again, actually the technical content of the solution rather than the problem seems decisive.[613]

In sum, the Germans nowadays dutifully take the application *as a whole* as a starting point, but at the same time they disregard elements considered non-technical. Thus writers note that the "core theory" is still alive and kicking,[614] and actually always has been.[615]

II.4.3. United Kingdom

While the British courts are less convinced that technical content is the decisive criterion to distinguish patentable subject-matter,[616] they also struggle with the question how to assess patent applications *partially* consisting of excluded subject-matter.[617] As we will see, the

33/03, 107 *GRUR* 2005, p. 141-143, 96 *Mitt.* 2005 p. 78-80, 8 *MMR* 2005, p. 169-170 (*Anbieten interaktiver Hilfe*); BGH 19 October 2004, no. X ZB 34/03, 107 *GRUR* 2005, p. 143-145 (*Rentabilitätsermittlung*).

[610] BGH 17 October 2001, no. X ZB 16/00, 33 *IIC* 2002, p. 753-762 (757), at B.III.1.b)aa) (*Search for Faulty Character Strings*). In German: "Die prägenden Anweisungen der beanspruchten Lehre müssen vielmehr insoweit der Lösung eines konkreten technischen Problems dienen."

[611] *See* p. 102.

[612] BGH 19 October 2004, no. X ZB 33/03, 107 *GRUR* 2005, p. 141-143 (142), at II. 4. b) (*Anbieten interaktiver Hilfe* – Offering interactive help).

[613] *See* p. 102.

[614] *See* Ganahl 2003.

[615] *See* Niedlich 2004.

[616] Section II.2.5, p. 45.

[617] Section 1(2) UK Patents Act, corresponding to Art. 52(2) and (3) EPC.

British found that there is no uniform rule to asses "mixed" applications.

In a case in the field of biotechnology the court considered that normally there are no objections against patenting applications of new scientific findings, even if only the finding is new and the application is not (as far as the distinction can be made at all).[618] So the statutory exclusion of scientific theories "as such"[619] does not imply that they are only patentable if there are *novel* non-excluded elements as well. In an *obiter* consideration, the court juxtaposed this *reductio ad absurdum* argument with another *reductio ad absurdum* argument when it noted that this rule can not apply to computer programs, because otherwise a program on a carrier would be patentable due to the carrier.[620] In a subsequent decision some months later the court noted that a computer program cannot be patented either under the guise[621] of a (conventional) computer containing the program: then it is still an excluded "computer program as such" in the perception of the court, and it noted that for patentability "something further is necessary",[622] a phrase that reminds of similar requirements developed later by the EPO[623] and the BGH.[624] In this decision, the court did not allow a patent for a computer program for the automation of securities trading, for the reason that it produces a result in an excluded field, notably business. Whatever one may think of software and business method patenting, this argumentation is questionable because usually the field of use is immaterial for patentability assessment. In literature this decision is criticised because EPO would not have been followed.[625]

---

[618] Court of Appeal 31 October 1988, RPC 1989, p. 147-287 (239-40) (*Genentech*).
[619] Art. 52(2a) EPC, Section 1(2)(a) UK Patents Act.
[620] Court of Appeal 31 October 1988, RPC 1989, p. 147-287 (240) (*Genentech*).
[621] *See* Section II.4.5, "The wording of the application", p. 124.
[622] Court of Appeal 21 April 1989, *RPC* 1989, p. 561 (569) (*Merrill Lynch*).
[623] "Further technical effect", *see* p. 56.
[624] "Eigenheit" in German. *See* p.77.
[625] *See* Hart 1989.

While the British courts thus argued that patent applications in general should be assessed as a whole, they found that for software an exception should be made in the sense that a technical contribution must be required in a field not excluded from patentability. In fact that is the (original) EPO "contribution approach".[626] Also in Germany initially a similar approach was practiced, and this approach too only allowed software patents in the exceptional case that a new kind of machine was involved.[627]

While the British courts to some extent are obliged to follow EPO case law,[628] they continued to practice this approach after late last century the EPO Boards of Appeal had abandoned the original "contribution approach" and adopted the approach to assess the technical content in conjunction with the inventive step test.[629] Incidentally, this divergence was an important reason for a proposal for a European Directive on the patentability of "computer-implemented inventions".[630]

Some years ago a British court again discussed the limits of software patentability,[631] and summarised its observations in the following four-step test:[632]

(1) properly construe the claim;

(2) identify the actual contribution;

(3) ask whether it falls solely within the excluded subject matter;

(4) check whether the actual or alleged contribution is actually technical in nature.

---

[626] *See* p. 99.
[627] *See* p. 71.
[628] *See* p. 16.
[629] *See* p. 100.
[630] *See* p. 17.
[631] Court of Appeal 27 October 2006, no. 2006 EWCA Civ 1371, at 31-35 (*Aerotel/Macrossan*).
[632] Court of Appeal 27 October 2006, no. 2006 EWCA Civ 1371, at 40 (*Aerotel/Macrossan*).

Less than a month later, in an appeal procedure the EPO notes on being asked that this approach is irreconcilable with the EPC.[633] A German writer says that the British court has not understood EPO case law.[634] That may be true – but that does not mean that EPO is right. Actually the British believe that the EPO is wrong with its "any hardware approach", as they call it.[635]

The British approach differs in particular for the assessment of applications comprising nothing else but software[636] – in British eyes excluded subject-matter. In the EPO perception this allegedly non-technical subject-matter still can be patented if it is sufficiently technical,[637] but not in the British perception. But this is gradually changing.[638] A British commentator sees a glimmer of convergence,[639] and a German commentator is inclined to forgive the British their deviant approach now that they become less restrictive in granting software patents.[640]

II.4.4. United States

Since 1952, the American patent act explicitly states that inventions should be assessed *as a whole* for meeting the non-obviousness requirement:

---

633 TBA 15 November 2006, no. T 154/04, 31 *OJ* 2008, p. 46-79 (71), at 13 (*Method of estimating product distribution/DUNS*).

634 *See* Bulling 2007.

635 Court of Appeal 27 October 2006, no. 2006 EWCA Civ 1371, at 26(3) (*Aerotel/Macrossan*).

636 *See* Patents Court 13 March 2007, no. [2007] EWHC 476 (Pat) (*Cappellini/Bloomberg*).

637 *See* p. 56.

638 *See* Patents Court 25 January 2008, no. [2008] EWHC 85 (Pat) (*Astron*); Patents Court 18 March 2008, no. 2008 EWHC 518 (Pat) (*Symbian*). After appeal by the British patent office confirmed in: Court of Appeal 8 October 2008, no. 2008 EWCA Civ 1066 (*Symbian*).

639 *See* Aplin 2008.

640 *See* Teufel 2008.

35 USC § 103 - Conditions for patentability; non-obvious subject-matter

> (a) A patent may not be obtained [...] if the differences between the subject-matter sought to be patented and the prior art are such that the subject-matter *as a whole* would have been obvious at the time the invention was made to a person having ordinary skill in the art to which said subject-matter pertains. [...]

This provision departed from the *point of novelty* approach practiced before.

Strictly speaking, this provision does not imply that the application should be assessed as a whole as well to decide whether it represents patentable subject-matter, but the U.S. Supreme Court decided that this is the case indeed.[641]

But the U.S. Supreme Court too is faced with the problem that a whole contents approach occasionally leads to counter-intuitive results. In this approach a particular warning system for the process industry might be patentable *as a whole,* although its essence is only a "mathematical algorithm" which is considered unpatentable by itself, in view of case law.[642] The Supreme Court solves this problem by considering the algorithm part of the prior art by way of fiction, so that it is not novel for patent law purposes. Because the application otherwise contains nothing novel either, the Supreme Court decides that it is not novel *as a whole.*[643]

But actually the Court did dissect the application: it distinguishes an unpatentable algorithm and a technical application that is considered "insignificant post-solution activity" outside the invention. The court notes:[644]

---

641 U.S. Supreme Court 22 June 1978, no. 77-642, 437 *U.S.* 584, 594, 98 *S.Ct.* 2522, 2527, footnote 16 (*Parker v. Flook*).
642 U.S. Supreme Court 30 January 1939, no. 127, 306 *U.S.* 86, 94, 59 *S.Ct.* 427, 431 (*Mackay Radio v. RCA*).
643 U.S. Supreme Court 22 June 1978, no. 77-642, 437 *U.S.* 584, 594, 98 *S.Ct.* 2522, 2527 (*Parker v. Flook*).
644 U.S. Supreme Court 22 June 1978, no. 77-642, 437 *U.S.* 584, 590, 98 *S.Ct.* 2522, 2525 (*Parker v. Flook*).

> The notion that post-solution activity, no matter how conventional or obvious in itself, can transform an unpatentable principle into a patentable process exalts form over substance. A competent draftsman could attach some form of post-solution activity to almost any mathematical formula.

Thus the "whole contents approach" is effectively ridiculed – although it is a basic rule of patent law. Still the Supreme Court is not alone in its approach: exactly two years before the German BGH applied the same line of reasoning.[645] Incidentally, in other jurisdictions it has been noted as well that patentability occasionally seems to be determined by the drafting skills of the patent agent rather than the substantive content of the application.[646]

While the Supreme Court presents its conclusion as a logical corollary of the statute and precedents, it does not conceal that for the time being it intended a restrictive policy as regards the patenting of "programs". While it indicates not to be opposed against patenting programs in principle, it explicitly notes that it prefers to leave the policy decisions on the patentability of programs to Congress, if only because Congress would have more information at its disposal to make a meaningful decision.[647]

A dissenting opinion[648] shows that at least some of the justices are aware that the reasoning of this decision is defective, because it "imports into its subject-matter inquiry the criteria of novelty and inventiveness". That implies that still the application is *not* assessed as a whole, but a distinction is made between novel and non-novel features.

In another famous case some years later, about a control system used

[645] BGH 22 June 1976, no. X ZB 23/74, 8 *IIC* 1977, p. 558-565 (561), at II.3 b) bb) (*Disposition Program*).

[646] *See* Section II.4.5, "The wording of the application", p. 124.

[647] U.S. Supreme Court 22 June 1978, no. 77-642, 437 *U.S.* 584, 595, 98 *S.Ct.* 2522, 2528 (*Parker v. Flook*).

[648] U.S. Supreme Court 22 June 1978, no. 77-642, 437 *U.S.* 584, 600, 98 *S.Ct.* 2522, 2530 (*Parker v. Flook*).

in a process for curing rubber, the U.S. Supreme Court clearly explains that *of course* an application must be assessed as a whole:[649]

> [...] claims must be considered as a whole. It is inappropriate to dissect the claims into old and new elements and then to ignore the presence of the old elements in the analysis. This is particularly true in a process claim because a new combination of steps in a process may be patentable even though all the constituents of the combination were well known and in common use before the combination was made. The "novelty" of any element or steps in a process, or even of the process itself, is of no relevance in determining whether the subject-matter of a claim falls within the §101 categories of possibly patentable subject-matter.

This statement acknowledges that all elements play a role in an invention so that "old" elements can not be ignored.

Gradually the CAFC applied a genuine "whole contents approach" more often, allowing patents for devices primarily distinguished by a new algorithm. So it decided that a heart monitoring device was patentable, although in essence it was based on an algorithm (for the analysis of electrocardiographic signals).[650] Similarly, a patent for a certain "mathematical" technique for a digital oscilloscope was allowed.[651] In both cases the CAFC ruled that the application *as a whole* was definitely related to a patentable device.

When the CAFC more recently made a proposal to restrict business method patentability, it indicated again that "insignificant post-solution-activity" and other insignificant "extra-solution-activity"[652]

---

[649] U.S. Supreme Court 3 March 1981, no. 79-1112, 450 *U.S.* 175, 188-89, 101 *S.Ct.* 1048, 1057-58 (*Diamond v. Diehr*).
[650] *See* CAFC 12 March 1992, no. 91-1091, 958 *F.2d* 1053 (*Arrhythmia v. Corazonix*).
[651] *See* CAFC 29 July 1994, no. 92-1381, 33 *F.3d* 1526 (*In re Alappat*).
[652] The decision mentions the following examples: CAFC 13 April 1994, no. 92-1275, 22 *F.3d* 290, 294 (*In re Schrader*) (holding a simple recordation step in the middle of the claimed process incapable of imparting patent-eligibility under § 101); CAFC 3 November 1989, no. 89-1321, 888 *F.2d* 835,

should be left out of consideration for the assessment of patentability.[653] While the U.S. Supreme Court has vacated this CAFC decision meanwhile,[654] it did not object against these ideas.

Actually the proper question is not whether "insignificant activity" should be ignored, but whether it really exists. An invention consists of a single inventive concept for which eventually all specified elements are relevant.[655]

In any case, the USPTO examiners are instructed to apply a whole contents approach. The USPTO "Manual of Patent Examining Procedure" contains a separate paragraph titled 'The claimed invention as a whole must be considered',[656] followed by a paragraph titled 'Distilling the Invention Down to a "Gist" or "Thrust" of an Invention Disregards "as a Whole" Requirement',[657] citing many court cases. Still a writer discusses the patentability of "hybrid" applications allegedly partially consisting of patentable subject-matter.[658]

In sum, we conclude that in the United States just like in Europe applications are *sometimes* assessed on the basis of their inventive core rather than as a whole, ignoring the principal rule, in order to reach an intuitively more satisfactory result. From a legal perspective it is unsatisfactory though that the result provides the rule rather than reversely.

839-40 (*In re Grams*) (holding a pre-solution step of gathering data incapable of imparting patent-eligibility under § 101).

[653] CAFC 30 October 2008, no. 07-1130, 545 *F.3d* 943, 957 (*In re Bilski*).

[654] *See* U.S. Supreme Court 28 June 2010, no. 08-964, 130 *S.Ct.* 3218 (*Bilski v. Kappos*).

[655] In the United States, a single application may include multiple inventions, but the relevant provision implicitly confirms that inventions are a unit, since the applicant may be required to split the application. 35 USC § 121.

[656] USPTO 2007, p. 123.

[657] USPTO 2007, p. 124.

[658] *See* Moy 1998.

II.4.5. The wording of the application

Obviously, for patentability the substantive *content* of the application should be decisive rather than the *wording*. But actually the wording is often more important than it should be. Again there are remarkable parallels between jurisdictions, and again, "software patents" lead to most confusion.

To start with, the German Federal Court of Justice emphasised that the wordings of a patent application could not play a role, with the following statement:[659]

> It is not the linguistic form which is decisive as to whether or not a teaching is of a technical nature, but its substantive content.

This rule has been cited in numerous decisions.[660] A German writer notes that the drafting skills of the patent agent should not be decisive for patentability.[661]

A British court also warns for this kind of deception:[662]

> [...] it cannot be permissible to patent an item excluded by section 1(2)[663] under the guise of an article which contains that item -- that is to say, in the case of a computer program, the patenting of a conventional computer containing that program.

This phrase has often been cited in later British decisions.[664]

---

659 BGH 22 June 1976, no. X ZB 23/74, 8 *IIC* 1977, p. 558-565 (560), at II.3 b) aa) (*Disposition Program*).

660 *See for instance* BGH 16 September 1980, no. X ZB 6/80, 83 *GRUR* 1981, p. 39-42 (*Walzstabteilung*); BGH 11 June 1991, no. X ZB 13/88, 94 *GRUR* 1992, p. 33-36, 23 *IIC* 1992, 824-828 (*Page buffer*).

661 Kolle 1977, p. 64.

662 Court of Appeal 21 April 1989, *RPC* 1989, p. 561 (569) (*Merrill Lynch*).

663 Section 1(2) UK Patent Act corresponds to Art. 52(2) EPC.

664 Court of Appeal 13 December 1990, *RPC* 1990, p. 305 (315) (*Gale*); Patents Court 15 March 1993, *RPC* 1993, p. 427 (433) (*Raytheon*); Patents Court 24 May 1996, *RPC* 1996, p. 511 (515) (*Fujitsu*); Court of Appeal 6 March 1997, *RPC* 1997, p. 608 (614) (*Fujitsu*); Patents Court 21 July 2005, no. 2005 EWHC 1589 Pat, *RPC* 2006, p. 5, at 76 (*CFPH*); Court of Appeal

In the United States, as early as 1966 a presidential committee was concerned that by dexterous claims drafting limitations in software patenting would be circumvented:[665]

> Direct attempts to patent programs have been rejected on the ground of nonstatutory subject-matter. Indirect attempts to obtain patents and avoid the rejection, by drafting claims as a process, or a machine or components thereof programmed in a given manner, rather than as a program itself, have confused the issue further and should not be permitted.

History has demonstrated that such a ban does not suffice to prevent confusion, as we have seen in the preceding sections.

In a decision remarkably similar to the above German decision an American court notes that:[666]

> The notion that post-solution activity, no matter how conventional or obvious in itself, can transform an unpatentable principle into a patentable process exalts form over substance. A competent draftsman could attach some form of post-solution activity to almost any mathematical formula.

This statement too was often cited.[667] Literature refers to the "the doctrine of the magic words":[668] at the time that software patentability was still more limited, patent agents knew that they could patent software more easily if they managed to give the impression that they patented a programmed machine rather than software.

---

27 October 2006, no. 2006 EWCA Civ 1371, 2006 All ER (D) 346 (Oct), at 83 (*Aerotel*).

665 President's Committee on the Patent System 1966, p. 14.

666 U.S. Supreme Court 22 June 1978, no. 77-642, 437 *U.S.* 584, 590, 98 *S.Ct.* 2522, 2525 (*Parker v. Flook*).

667 *See for instance*: U.S. Supreme Court 3 March 1981, no. 79-1112, 450 *U.S.* 175, 192, 101 *S.Ct.* 1048, 1059 (*Diamond v. Diehr*); CAFC 13 April 1994, no. 92-1275, 22 *F.3d* 290, 294 (*In re Schrader*).

668 Cohen & Lemley 2001, p. 9.

A common objection against an assessment of patent applications *as a whole* is that allegedly this approach would allow applications outside the domain of technology still to pass a technology test if arbitrarily some actually irrelevant technical features are added to the application. That would be a reason to apply the "core theory" (or one of its variants), because it concentrates on the essence of the application, and thus it would be less susceptible for word-plays. But what is the core of a patent application? That must be construed too from the text of the application, so that again its wordings are determinative. There is a substantial risk that the text of the patent application misleads the patent examiner by putting certain aspects in the foreground that actually do not deserve it. This could work out both in favour or at the detriment of the applicant: as we have seen, an unfortunate choice of words could also lead to an unjustified rejection of an application.[669]

So remarkably both in a *whole contents approach* and in an approach concentrating on the technical *core* (or *contribution*), the choice of words plays an important role. The risk of manipulations, or at least misconceptions seems inevitable.

II.4.6. Conclusion

What conclusions can be drawn from our investigations *in which respect* an invention should be technical in order to be patentable?

In all jurisdictions we discussed we found a controversy whether an application should be considered as a whole for the assessment of patentability, or whether its patentable features should coincide with its novel and non-obvious features. This applies both in the European jurisdictions that consider "patentable" synonymous with "technical" and in the United States where "patentable" is primarily associated with "non-abstract".

---

669 *See* p. 113.

The scheme below gives an overview of the differences between the "core theory" (or other approaches that actually require patentable and inventive features to coincide), and a "whole contents approach":

aspect	*core theory*, including modern variants	assessment of application *as a whole*
essence	The technical *core* of the application should be novel and inventive, vice versa.	The application is assessed as a whole.
ratio	The purpose patents is the promotion of the progress of *technology*.	Inventions are often systems and combinations.
otherwise ...	... even a reference to an ordinary computer could *make* an "abstract" invention "technical".	... the essence of an invention can be missed, in particular in case of systems (combinations).
theory	The description of inventions in patents usually consists of multiple "claims" that can be assessed individually.	According to a principal rule of patent law, applications must always be assessed as a whole.
system of patent law	The assessment of the technical *contribution* incorrectly combines Art. 52 with Art. 54 and 56 EPC, and § 101 with §§ 102 and 103 in the U.S.	Technical *character* is assessed independently from novelty and inventive step, vice versa, consistent with the system of patent law.
risk of manipulation and confusion	What appears to be in the foreground also depends on the drafting of the patent application.	By adding non-novel technical elements the technical character of inventions could allegedly be "saved".
other incongruities	What is the role of non-technical elements that still contribute to a technical result?	Various day to day activity (such as writing with a pen) *is* technical but does not make a technical *contribution*.
policy effect	Restricts the patentability of software-inventions – certainly in its original form.	Broadens the patentability of software-inventions.

Case law occasionally gives the impression that courts first determine the desired outcome intuitively, and subsequently select the theory that supports the desired outcome:[670] the "core theory" for a restrictive policy or a "whole contents approach" for wider patentability. If the "intuition" is motivated at all, it is usually by some unsubstantiated *belief* in a wide or rather a more narrow patentability. That leads to unpredictable results. A graphic representation of the extent in which German courts preferred the "core theory" in the period between 1975 and 2001 shows an undulating line that ends at about 50%: eventually just as often (a form of) the core theory is applied as a whole contents approach.[671] Don't be mistaken: that 50% does not indicate a balance, but that the situation is less clear than ever.

Is the choice between the two approaches really irrational? Don't different types of applications logically call for their own approach? For instance, a dissection of a control engineering system in its elements seems absurd, while the core theory approach is very convincing in preventing the patenting of a business method that only pretends to be technical due to a trivial computer implementation (assuming that this implementation is considered patentable, which is questionable as well in Europe).

Still there cannot be a choice for the "apparently" most appropriate approach. While a particular approach in a given case may seem more *logical,* it is by no means impossible to apply the other approach as well, typically with a very different result. A fine example is the anti-skid braking system as it is used in motor-cars. The *core* of the application would only be an unpatentable "braking philosophy", which is subsequently implemented with conventional technical means, but the German federal supreme court decided that is car part *as a whole* is definitely technical.[672] The decision of the lower court is

[670] Nack 2002, p. 188-189.

[671] Blind, Edler, Nack & Straus 2003, p. 125.

[672] *See* p. 107.

not just corrected by the supreme court, it is different in almost every respect.

In various ways lip service is paid to the principal rule that patent applications must be assessed as a whole, while actually still some sort of dissection is made. For instance, occasionally non-patentable elements are considered part of the prior art, even if they are actually novel. This fiction has the effect that apparently the application *as a whole* is not novel, let alone inventive in the case that its other elements are not inventive either. A British court has disqualified this practice at EPO[673] as “simply not intellectually honest”.[674] Still the U.S. Supreme Court occasionally has applied a similar fiction, although it was presented as a logical consequence of precedents.[675]

Several writers note that the EPO is not allowed to ignore (allegedly) nontechnical features,[676] and one writer points out that this practice is an outright violation of the EPC.[677] Is it really a problem if the statute is not followed precisely? To some extent courts can correct defective statutes. The genuine weakness of the core theory and its various variants is that it depends on a breakdown of patent applications. Apparently a breakdown is justified because patent applications typically include multiple “claims”.[678] Still one should bear in mind that a patent application may only be based on a single invention or a single “general inventive concept”.[679] Often “the whole is greater than the sum of it's parts", so that it is not just forbidden but outright impossible to make a proper dissection. For instance, it was often found in practice that allegedly non-technical features in reason

[673] *See* p. 101.
[674] Court of Appeal 27 October 2006, no. 2006 EWCA Civ 1371, 2006 All ER (D) 346 (Oct), at 27 (*Aerotel*).
[675] *See* p. 120.
[676] Haase 2003, p. 221; Tauchert 1997a, p. 153; Tauchert 1997b, Abs. 44 (same text as other article).
[677] Klaiber 2010, p. 566.
[678] Rule 43 EPC, 35 USC § 112.
[679] Art. 82 EPC. Similarly: 35 USC § 121.

can not be ignored for the assessment of patent applications.[680] Could allegedly non-technical elements that still were found to contribute to a technical effect[681] really be qualified as "non-technical"?

Conceivably, the quest for the inventive core of an application could entail a distinction between a machine and its construction, an esoteric intellectual exercise of philosophical proportions.

Alternatively, the discipline of the alleged inventor is considered a criterion for the technical content of a patent application.[682] But this criterion is ambiguous as well. Of course, for any qualification there is a grey area. However, a modern inventor is often a technician and a businessman or an artist *at the same time*. It is a creative designer who should be familiar with multiple disciplines in order to be able to develop innovative solutions.[683] The inventor that found a way to exploit the technical options to make a beautiful yet cheap candle with a good commercial potential is a technician, an artist and a businessman at the same time.[684] Technical universities increasingly educate engineers in mixed disciplines such as technical business management[685] and industrial design,[686] disciplines requiring both technical and economical or artistic skills.

For software, a tentative distinction is made between programmers who know more about applications and programmers who know more about computer science.[687] Again, it is questionable whether

---

[680] *See* p. 103.
[681] Anders 2001a, p. 142, 146. *See also* Anders 2001b, Anders 2004.
[682] *See* TBA 8 September 2000, no. T 931/95, 24 *OJ* 2001, p. 441-457 (*Controlling pension benefits systems/PBS PARTNERSHIP*).
[683] *See* Aharonian 2004, with the following reaction: Davies 2004.
[684] *See* p. 114.
[685] Anders 2001a, p. 146.
[686] For instance, the number of industrial design students at Delft Technical University in The Netherlands nowadays outnumbers the number of traditional mechanical engineering students.
[687] *See* for instance the German rule that the ordinary use of an ordinary computer is not patentable, p. 71.

this distinction really can be maintained. Perhaps the designer of an accounting program needs little knowledge about computer science, but generic software, such as word processing packages and graphic software is hard to qualify in this simple dichotomy. Linguistics are no technology, but professionals definitely will consider the problem of developing software for high speed real time dictionary retrieval in a spell checking application a *technical* challenge, although a thorough knowledge of conjugations and declensions is indispensible to arrive at an efficient solution of this problem.

In sum, there are strong arguments to assess patent applications truly as a whole, but practice shows that there is still a strong urge to identify non-patentable elements and to ignore them. While both approaches cannot coexist, courts have been unable to make a consistent choice for the lesser of two evils. If neither approach appears to be generally usable, is there perhaps another alternative? In the next chapter we will see that indeed *tertium datur*![688]

II.5. Conclusion positive law

In this chapter, we primarily discussed how in Europe the assessment is made whether an application is sufficiently technical to be patented, and how in the United States unpatentable "abstract ideas" are distinguished, a similar problem. It appears amazingly difficult to arrive at consistent, concrete rules that allow patent offices to assess efficiently and reliably whether applications relate to legally "technical" or "non-abstract" subject-matter, and that assure legal certainty to patentees and their competitors.

The legal controversy about the rules that decide whether an application is sufficiently technical in Europe, or not too abstract in the United States is by and large detached from the political controversy about patenting software and business methods, the typical non-technical or abstract subject-matter.

[688] This expression is borrowed from mathematical logic, where the assertion "tertium non datur" (there is no third alternative) was found false as well: "not true" is not necessarily the same as "false".

Legal rules are in a constant flux, not due to evolving views on innovation policy, but due to endless attempts to establish practical rules for the interpretation of the technology requirement and the exclusion of abstract ideas that conform to statutory provisions and precedents in case law, but in practice those very objectives are not met. Several writers note that the EPO interpretation outright violates the EPC,[689] and a British judge even rejects an important aspect of the EPO approach as "not intellectually honest".[690]

In Europe, the technology concept is believed to be "dynamic" because technology evolves, and likewise the subject-matter provision in the American patent act is supposed to be "a dynamic provision designed to encompass new and unforeseen inventions".[691] However, it cannot be the purpose of the patent system to fulfil all "market demand" for patents, because patents should serve the general interest rather than just the interest of patentees. Consequently, a dynamic technology concept should be buttressed by some sort of meta-rule, a fixed principle that decides the actual content of the "dynamic" rule at a certain point in time. But no such principle is known. In reality, this "flexibility" is often an excuse to adopt new rules again and again because the present rules were found to be unusable, for whatever reason.

Policy perceptions may change, but if they are not the reason to change the rules again and again, why hasn't one reached agreement about those rules, after about forty years of debate on the technical content of software, and twice that time on the technology criterion in patent law in general?

The paradoxes we found in this chapter call for a thorough investigation into the foundations of the system of patent law.

---

689 Von Hellfeld 2008, p. 1009, Klaiber 2010, p. 566.
690 Court of Appeal 27 October 2006, no. 2006 EWCA Civ 1371, 2006 All ER (D) 346 (Oct), at 27. (*Aerotel*).
691 U.S. Supreme Court 10 December 2001, no. 99-1996, 534 *U.S.* 124, 135, 122 *S.Ct.* 593, 600 (*J.E.M. Ag Supply v. Pioneer*).

III. Towards a better technology criterion

III.1. Introduction

If anything has become clear in the last chapter, it is that the precise content of the technology criterion in patent law is unclear. A basic clue however is that in those jurisdictions where patents are only granted for technology, that restriction always was presented as "obvious", as an *inherent* restriction, long before it was codified. Inherent to the word "inherent", inherent boundaries follow from the system of patent law itself, so we will start the quest for a better technology criterion in this chapter by an analysis of that system. If we know the inherent boundaries, we can use that knowledge to interpret the rules that can be associated with inherent boundaries, like the European technology requirement and the American exclusion of abstract ideas.

At first sight, this seems a rather modest approach. Aren't there many more reasons not to grant patents than a lack of technical content? Isn't "non-technical" almost synonymous to "undesired" in a German patent law tradition? Aren't all those "trivial"[692] software and business method patents highly undesired? Still we will concentrate on the inherent boundaries of patent law, since by itself that will provide strong arguments already to exclude certain controversial subject-matter, in particular business methods, even if they are completely new and definitely "non-trivial".

III.2. The inherent limits of patent law

Patent law gives a patentee certain rights for a certain type of object. An analysis of the content of that right shows that it is only suited for

[692] One usually speaks about "trivial patents", but obviously patents for trivial inventions are meant. *See for instance* Stallman 2006.

certain subject-matter. Subsequently we will show that for other subject-matter patents do not serve the purpose of patent law as it appears from the structure of patent law.

III.2.1. The contents of the rights of the patentee

Patents are granted for inventions. In common parlance, the word "invention" is used both in the meaning of a *thing* and the meaning of a *thought*: in the sentence "an inventor makes an invention", the invention is a thought, but one also says that a particular device *is* an invention.[693] Then the invention is apparently considered a thing.

The perception is widespread that patents are *things*. The highest German court once noted that inventions are related to the "world of things" rather than the "world of the mind".[694] Also in literature there is a debate whether inventions are things or thoughts. While one writer is irritated by "theoreticians" who – in his eyes – make the grave mistake to consider patents as thoughts,[695] many years later an other writer explains that inventions *always* are abstract to some extent (referring to sources from various jurisdictions in Europe and the US).[696] In legislation, this ambiguity is found too. Patent statutes usually list several acts reserved to the patentee[697] that lack a common denominator at first sight.[698] The relevant provisions often present the invention as a *thing*, for example the provision that grants the

[693] For instance in 35 USC § 101.

[694] *See* p. 64.

[695] Kumm 1963, p. 290.

[696] Blum 1977, p. 359.

[697] For completeness, we note that patent acts can only allow patent owners to act against infringement, because patent exploitation may depend on other conditions, such as the approval required to market a medicine.

[698] While the EPC almost exclusively regulates the grant of patents, the contents of a patent right are regulated (via art. 64 EPC) in the legislation of the member states, e.g. art 53 ROW 1995 for The Netherlands, § 9 PatG for Germany and Section 60 UK Patents Act for the UK. In the U.S., the contents of a patent right are regulated in 35 USC § 154(a)(1).

patent owner the exclusive right to keep his invention in stock.[699] Apparently the usual[700] distinction between product and process inventions is another sign that at least some inventions are things. Literature explains though that the object of a product patent is not the product itself, but the invention related to the product.[701] The fact that one particular invention may be claimed both as a product and a process in a single patent application[702] confirms that a product invention is not essentially different from a process invention.[703]

At last, inventions are unambiguously presented as thoughts in the provisions that require the subject-matter of a patent to be "susceptible of industrial application".[704] Furthermore, both European[705] and American[706] law require the applicant to provide a description in a manner that allows a skilled person to *carry out* the

---

699 For instance, according to the British Patents Act someone infringes a patent in the following case: "where the invention is a product, he makes, disposes of, offers to dispose of, uses or imports the product or keeps it whether for disposal or otherwise". British Patents Act Section 60(1)(a). The American patent act equates the invention to a product with the words "making, using, offering for sale, or selling the invention" in 35 USC § 154(a)(1).

700 See for instance 35 USC § 101 and Art. 27(1) TRIPS.

701 "The object of a product patent is *the invention related to the product*, not the product itself." Bacher/Melullis 2006, §1, Rn. 12 (translated, bold text in original replaced by italics). In the same sense: Gerbrandy 1946, p. 114.

702 EPO Examination Guidelines 2010, section C.III.3.1. This is related to the fact that the "process" concept is used in different meanings in patent law. In chemistry it is the process leading to a product, while for instance in the case of software the process relates to the way the product itself works.

703 In practice, the most important difference is that the protection of a process patent extends to the products directly obtained by such process. *See for instance* Art. 28(1b) TRIPS and Art. 64(2) EPC.

704 Art. 27(1) TRIPS, Art. 52(1) EPC at the end, elaborated in art. 57 EPC.

705 Art. 83 EPC.

706 35 USC § 112.

invention.[707] That shows that patent law is intended for thoughts that lend themselves to be carried out.

If an invention is a *thought*, a corollary is that it must be distinguished from its *realisation*, the result of the application of the invention. The reader who is familiar with copyright law may be surprised that this distinction is not considered obvious, because in that discipline of law it is common knowledge that the object of the right is not the physical carrier, the *corpus mechanicum* of printed paper for instance, but its information contents, the abstract *corpus mysticum*.[708] Copyright law only protects contents. Like a book *is* not a work, but only *contains* a work, a "patented product" *is* not an invention, but only *contains* an invention.

In conclusion, we note that an invention always represents a form of *knowledge, applicable knowledge* in particular.[709]

III.2.2. For what subject-matter patents are suitable?

While the awareness is still fairly common that the object of a patent in essence is applicable knowledge, one usually forgets to question whether all forms of applicable knowledge can be the object of a patent.

When more than 150 years ago *Samuel Morse* tried to claim also future applications of his well-known code system with his patent application, the U.S. Supreme Court rejected that claim.[710] While future applications might benefit from that coding system as well, Morse was not given the right to prevent others from doing things he was not (yet) able to do himself. A patent should not cover more than

[707] "Execute" might be better English, but we prefer to stick to the statutory terminology.
[708] Spoor, Verkade & Visser 2005, p. 60-61. The terms "corpus mechanicum" and "corpus mysticum" in this context are only in common use in some countries, for instance in The Netherlands and in Spain.
[709] Not all knowledge can be carried out. For instance, one can not "carry out" the knowledge that the circumference of the earth is about 40000 km.
[710] U.S. Supreme Court 30 January 1854, 56 *U.S.* 62, 112 (*O'Reilly v. Morse*).

actually has been invented:[711] it is not a "hunting license", as an American court aptly noted over a century later.[712]

An exclusive right granted for the application of knowledge not yet elaborated into concrete applications would be *disproportionate,* because it would "reward" less effort with more protection. A related objection against patenting so broad claims is that those future applications naturally are as yet unknown. In particular American patent law recognises the risk of "indefiniteness".[713]

In sum, a patent should specify exactly the applications it claims, and give a sufficiently elaborated description for those applications. Hence statutes require the description to be sufficient for any "person skilled in the [relevant] art". The EPC requires that "[t]he European patent application shall disclose the invention in a manner sufficiently clear and complete for it to be carried out by a person skilled in the art"[714] and that "[t]he claims [...] shall be [...] supported by the description."[715] The American patent act similarly provides: "[t]he specification shall contain a written description of the invention, and of the manner and process of making and using it, in such full, clear, concise, and exact terms as to enable *any* person skilled in the art to which it pertains, or with which it is most nearly connected, to make and use the same [...]".[716]

Who is this "person skilled in the art"? German literature traditionally uses the word "Durchschnittsfachmann",[717] indicating

---

[711] Case law from several jurisdictions shows, that there are various restrictions that can be explained from the principle that not more can be protected than actually has been invented. Nack 2002, p. 118-19, 133, 139, 140-41, 145, 214, 234.

[712] U.S. Supreme Court 21 March 1966, no. 58, 86 *S.Ct.* 1033, 1042, 383 *U.S.* 519, 536 (*Brenner v. Manson*).

[713] *See* Biela 2007.

[714] Art. 83 EPC.

[715] Art. 84 EPC.

[716] 35 USC § 112. Emphasis added.

[717] *See* e.g. Dreiss 1994.

explicitly that an *average* "person skilled in the art" is meant,[718] and the BGH has established that an invention is not patentable before it is elaborated sufficiently to be carried out by this person.[719] The word "any" in the provision in the American patent act emphasises that all those persons should be able to carry out the invention. Case law adds that the description should allow the person skilled in the art to carry out the invention "without undue experimentation".[720] A further indication that a person of average, not exceptional skills is meant when patent law refers to a "person skilled in the art" is that the American patent act in a related provision[721] refers to a "person having ordinary skills in the art", often abbreviated as "PHOSITA".

Still these words do not draw a bright line. Presumably the many rocket scientists working in *Kennedy Space Center* at *Cape Canaveral* locally are considered "persons skilled in the art" too, even if they literally practice "rocket science". Could a specialist having only a few colleagues all over the world still be an ordinary "person skilled in the art", in the legal sense?

This question can be answered by considering the difference between a "person skilled in the art" and an inventor. The essence of the difference is not the skill or intelligence, but the fact that a "person skilled in the art" performs duties that within reason always can be accomplished, in contrast to an inventor. For instance, every building contractor can build a house, otherwise he is no "person skilled in the art". In contrast, inventors usually conduct experiments, and experiments are not always successful by definition. One does not blame an inventor if he is unable to deliver a new medicine against a particular ailment to order. Inventing is not a planned, directed

---

[718] The translation of "Durchschnitt" is "average".
[719] BGH 10 November 1970, no. X ZR 54/67, 73 *GRUR* 1971, p. 210-214 (212), at II.B.1 (*Wildverbißverhinderung*). *See also* Dreiss 1994, p. 782-85.
[720] USPTO 2007, § 2164: 'The Enablement Requirement', section 2164.01(a) 'Undue Experimentation Factors', p. 194.
[721] 35 USC § 103, nonobviousness.

activity: inventing involves trial and error.[722] Routine inventing is a *contradictio in terminis.*

Inherent to this difference between the “person skilled in the art” and the inventor is that they use different types of knowledge. The former uses knowledge that allows *any* “person skilled in the art” to achieve a particular result. That is an invention (in European terminology).[723] In contrast, the “input” of an inventor consists of ideas, theories and bare facts that may lend themselves for *application*, but can not simply be *carried out.* Statutes confirm that mere applicability is insufficient by using the words “carry out” rather than “apply”.[724]

The reader may object that the “person skilled in the art” who executes an invention is not sure to be commercially successful either. Marketing is a separate activity however.[725] Furthermore, the likelihood of commercial success depends on *external* factors, such as market demand and the activity of competitors, thus it cannot be relevant to distinguish different types of knowledge.

The scheme below relates the two types of applicable knowledge to the roles of the scientist, the inventor and the “person skilled in the art”. While conceivably two or even all three roles may be fulfilled by the same person, the distinction between the two types of knowledge still applies, and that is eventually what matters in patent law.

---

[722] *See* Nelson 1959.

[723] *See* p. 20.

[724] For instance Art. 83 EPC, 35 USC § 112. § 34(4) PatG consistently refers to "ausführen" (execute) rather than "anwenden" (apply). Dutch patent act is different: Art. 25(1) ROW 1995 refers to "toepassen" (apply).

[725] Except for some business methods, but such methods are an exception anyway, see section IV.2.6 “Schemes, rules and methods for doing business”, p. 200.

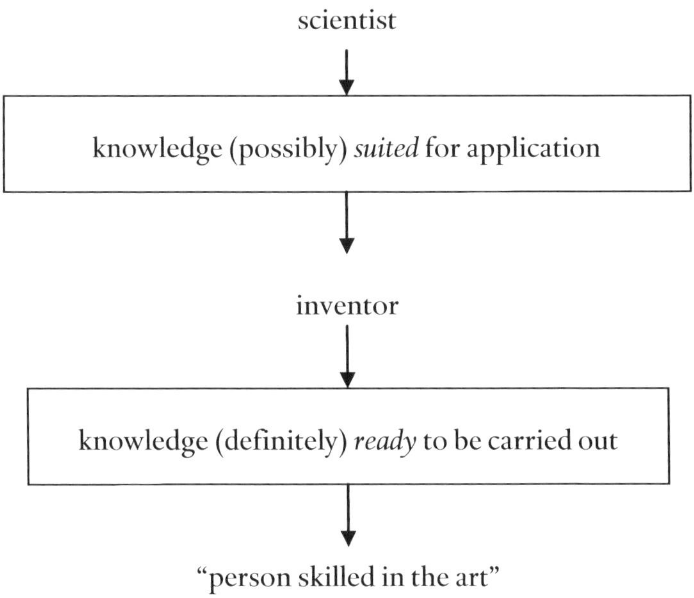

In this dichotomy of knowledge types, exclusive rights for the application of knowledge are only appropriate if that knowledge is *ready* to be *carried out,* because a right to apply mere ideas and theories would be both *indeterminate* and potentially *disproportional.* That does not mean however that such a right is not *needed.* In the next paragraph we will investigate whether that is the case.

III.2.3. For what subject-matter patents are needed?

The common justification theories of patents[726] basically give two arguments for patents, justice and utility: justice for the inventor and utility for society.

The argument of justice assumes that an inventor deserves to be rewarded for his efforts and for the service he renders to society. The idea that efforts deserve a right has been defended with the "labour theory"[727] of philosopher *John Locke.*[728] A patent as a kind of

---

[726] Machlup & Penrose 1950, p. 10-28, Machlup 1958, p. 20-25.

[727] *For an interesting account see* Ostergard 1999.

[728] Locke 1690, Chapter V, Section 27.

"property right" for knowledge is intuitively appealing because superficially the work of an inventor resembles "specification":[729] if someone makes a physical product, he becomes the owner by law,[730] so it is *apparently* logical to grant a property right for the things someone devises as well.

Still, even intuitively there is an important difference: if someone uses certain knowledge, that does not prevent other people from using the same knowledge at the same time in the same manner: knowledge is "non-rivalrous",[731] in contrast to physical objects.

Despite this fundamental difference, a little over two centuries ago the term "intellectual property" came into use. Eighteenth-century French lawyers have admitted that they purposely propagated[732] the perception of a "natural" property right for knowledge analogous to real property, in order to benefit from the fact that this right was declared an "inviolable and sacred" right in the French Revolution.[733] Until then, patents were often granted as privileges,[734] as an individual favour of a sovereign rather than to anybody fulfilling statutory requirements, but they preferred to avoid the word "privilege" because it had an unpleasant ring,[735] especially at a time when "liberté", "égalité" and "fraternité" were propagated.[736]

Soon it became apparent that the designation "intellectual property" incorrectly suggests that it would be a form of property similar to real property. In linguistic terminology, "intellectual property" is no

---

729 This is called "zaaksvorming" in Dutch law, art. 5:16(2) BW. The German term is "Verarbeitung", § 950 BGB.

730 For the precise conditions we refer to the text of the actual provisions.

731 Samuelson & Nordhaus 2010, p. 37.

732 Machlup 1958, p. 23, with further sources.

733 *Déclaration des droits de l'homme et du citoyen* of 1789 (French Civil Rights Declaration), Art. 17.

734 *See for instance* Silberstein 1961 and Bracha 2004.

735 Machlup & Penrose 1950, p. 16.

736 "Liberty, equality and fraternity", device of the French Revolution.

hyponym of property.[737] Therefore, the famous German legal scholar *Josef Kohler* proposed the term "immaterial goods" instead of "intellectual property" over a hundred years ago.[738] But the latter concept already gained too much acceptance to be stopped. Still the "immaterial goods" concept is not entirely lost, especially in the German language area.[739]

While real property nowadays[740] is considered as naturally self-evident, as a matter of justice beyond any debate about efficiency,[741] exclusive rights to "knowledge" have been instituted primarily or even exclusively because and to the extent that it is supposed to be socially useful.[742] The difference already appears from the simple fact that "intellectual property" usually has a limited term,[743] whereas real property fundamentally is not bound by a time limit. Still these insights have not become common knowledge to the extent that interested parties and their supporters can not continue to pretend that for knowledge they are entitled to similar moral, natural law-like

737 Well-known examples of a similar use of adjectives include the "fake Picasso" (which is not a Picasso at all), and the "former president" (who is no longer a president).

738 The original German term is "Immaterialgüter". For copyright: Kohler 1880, p. 1-2, for patent law: Kohler 1908, p. 13. *See also* Dölemeyer 1993.

739 For instance the German name of the *Max Planck Institute for Intellectual Property and Competition Law* is *Max-Planck-Institut für Immaterialgüter- und Wettbewerbsrecht.*

740 The Fourteenth Amendment to the United States Constitution, dating from 1868, defines private property as a civil right (Section 1). Art. 1 of the First Protocol to the ECHR codifies the protection of private property in Europe since 1954. The right of private property is not as self-obvious as it may seem, as becomes apparent for instance from the fact that China only recognises this right for a some years.

741 Still, real property *is* actually efficient, as far as it prevents the "tragedy of the commons". *See* Hardin 1968.

742 Patent law is not a human right: Brinkhof 2004, p. 408.

743 An exception are trademark rights, that can be extended forever.

"obvious" claims as to real property,[744] regardless of whether that is socially efficient or not.[745]

For completeness we note that – particular in English language – "property" may be confused with "property rights". The latter concept refers to subjective rights more in general, like they are protected for instance by the ECHR.[746] While "immaterial rights" can be the object of a property right too, there is still an essential difference with property in the more narrow sense of real property.

Here we do not discuss what existing rights deserve protection, but the preceding question what rights can be claimed legitimately. The achievement of contriving by itself is apparently no reason for a "property right", because in any case mere ideas do not qualify for such a right: "ideas are free". There is apparently *a* boundary, so the question is legitimate where it is.

The fact that patent law primarily has the purpose to serve the public interest rather than the interest of the individual patentee also becomes apparent from various regulations. It is stated particularly clearly by the *American Constitution*:[747]

> The Congress shall have power [...] To promote the progress of science and useful arts, by securing for limited times to authors and inventors the exclusive right to their respective writings and discoveries;

Case law[748] confirms that profitable exploitation by the patentee is not a purpose in itself, but only a means to the constitutional end.

---

[744] *See* e.g. Machlup & Penrose 1950, p. 11-17, Machlup 1958, p. 22-23 and Rahnasto 2003, p. 52-55.

[745] Machlup & Penrose 1950, p. 11-17; Rahnasto 2003, p. 53-59.

[746] Art. 1 of the First Protocol to the ECHR.

[747] United States Constitution, art. I, Section 8, Clause 8.

[748] U.S. Supreme Court 21 May 1945, no. 656, 325 *U.S.* 327, 330, 65 *S.Ct.* 1143, 1145, 89 *L. Ed.* 1644, 1647 (*Sinclair & Carroll v. Interchemical Corporation*); U.S. Supreme Court 11 May 1942, no. 723, 316 *U.S.* 265, 278, 62 *S.Ct.* 1070, 1078, 86 *L. Ed.* 1461, 1475 (*United States v. Masonite Corporation*); U.S. Supreme Court 9 April 1917, no. 715, 243 *U.S.* 502, 511, 37 *S.Ct.* 416, 411, 61 *L. Ed.* 871, 876 (*Motion Picture Patents v. Universal Film Manufacturing*); U.S.

The *TRIPS Agreement* contains the following statement on the purpose of patent law (and other forms of "intellectual property"):[749]

> Article 7 – Objectives
>
> The protection and enforcement of intellectual property rights should contribute to the promotion of technological innovation and to the transfer and dissemination of technology, to the mutual advantage of producers and users of technological knowledge and in a manner conducive to social and economic welfare, and to a balance of rights and obligations.

While one writer notes that this provision does not refer to the objectives of the *TRIPS Agreement* itself, but to the purpose of the protection and enforcement of "intellectual property" rights,[750] in any case the private interests of the rights owners are not put first here.

The *European Convention on Human Rights* provides the following on the protection of property:

> Article 1 First Protocol to the ECHR – Protection of property
>
> Every natural or legal person is entitled to the peaceful enjoyment of his possessions. No one shall be deprived of his possessions except in the public interest and subject to the conditions provided for by law and by the general principles of international law. [...]

Supreme Court 5 January 1942, no. 49, 314 *U.S.* 488, 492, 62 *S.Ct.* 402, 405, 86 *L. Ed.* 363, 365 (*Morton Salt v. Suppiger*). *After*: Pires de Carvalho 2010, p. 31-32.

[749] The TRIPS Agreement also covers various other forms of "intellectual property".

[750] "Contrary to the general understanding, Article 7 does not state the objectives of the TRIPS Agreement, but rather those of the protection and enforcement of intellectual property rights." Pires de Carvalho 2010, p. 197. The fact that this provision was included into the TRIPS Agreement on request of developing nations rather supports the perception that this provision states the objectives of the *Agreement* itself.

Case law notes that this provision extends to "intellectual property" as well, but that it only protects *existing* claims,[751] and does not create new claims, so it does not allow conclusions to be drawn on the purpose of "intellectual property".

Of course, the *Universal Declaration of Human Rights* ought to be mentioned too. It provides:

> Art. 27 Universal Declaration of Human Rights
>
> 1. Everyone has the right freely to participate in the cultural life of the community, to enjoy the arts and to share in scientific advancement and its benefits.
>
> 2. Everyone has the right to the protection of the moral and material interests resulting from any scientific, literary or artistic production of which he is the author.

Here the emphasis is on culture rather than technology, and participation rather than restriction. As far as subsection 2 deals with "intellectual property", it is primarily oriented towards copyright, and the moral rights of the author in particular, because they are not recognised by American copyright law to the extent that they are recognised in the European "droit d'auteur"[752] tradition. Patents were not discussed during the negotiations for the Declaration, and some delegates even argued that the right to intellectual property was not a human right at all.[753]

In sum, the American Constitution and the TRIPS Agreement indicate that patent law primarily serves a social[754] economic purpose. The ECHR at least does not derogate from this observation, and it would be misplaced to conclude anything about patents from the Universal Declaration of Human Rights.

---

751 ECHR 11 January 2007, no. 73049/01, at 64 (*Anheuser-Busch v. Portugal*).
752 "Right of the author". Due to its French origin, this concept is often worded in French.
753 Morsink 1999, p. 221.
754 The word "social" indicates that – equally economical – private interests are not meant here.

The next question is *how* patents serve their social economic purpose. Here we meet a persistent misconception. A prevailing perception is that patents serve the purpose to allow inventors to recoup their development costs. Without patent protection,[755] an inventive firm would be unable to compete with *free riders*[756] who do not incur these costs, and thus would be able to deliver similar products for a lower price. Then no one would be motivated to invest in research and development.[757] In this line of thought, patents would allow an inventor to require any competitors to contribute to the development cost via a licence fee.[758]

While this perception is widespread, it fails to explain essential aspects of the reality of patents. If indeed patents would primarily serve the purpose to allow research investments to be recovered, then the research costs would be decisive for the question when patents are appropriate. In reality neither the presence of costs is a reason to grant patents, nor is the absence of costs a reason not to grant patents. On the one hand, no patents are granted for the results of basic research that has not reached the stage of concrete applications, however costly it has been. According to the EPC, "discoveries and scientific theories as such" are not patent-eligible.[759] American patent law has a similar judicially-created exception: "natural phenomena" and "laws of nature" can not be patented in the USA.[760] On the other hand, a patent can be granted for a stroke of genius or a coincidental invention that does not require a large investment. The American patent act provides that "[p]atentability shall not be negatived by the

[755] However, secrecy may be an alternative, but it is infeasible for instance if a patented device can be reverse engineered by dismounting.
[756] *See* McMillan 1979.
[757] Whether a potential inventor is motivated so easily is disputable: Machlup & Penrose 1950, p. 21-25, Machlup 1958, p. 23-24.
[758] In the latter case, economists refer to *internalisation* of an *externality*.
[759] Art. 52 Subsection (2a) and (3) EPC.
[760] U.S. Supreme Court 16 June 1980, no. 79-136, 447 *U.S.* 303, 309, 100 *S.Ct.* 2204, 2208 (*Diamond v. Chakrabarty*), with references to older case law.

manner in which the invention was made".[761] While this remark is made in the provision on non-obviousness, it confirms that low investments are no reason to reject a patent application.

In sum, sometimes no patents are granted if it appears necessary to protect investments, and sometimes patents are granted even if there is no apparent need for such protection. If patents apparently do not serve the purpose of protecting investments, what else is their purpose?

In order to answer at question, we return to the above-mentioned problem that without patent protection nobody would be willing to invest in R&D, because without protection competitors would share the benefits of R&D without sharing the costs. Apparently, patents somehow relate to competition control. But how could that be reconciled with the common perception that competition should be promoted as much as possible?

At first sight, a maximum of competition seems desirable, because that forces suppliers to deliver the best product for the lowest price.[762] However, suppliers can make more profit if they *differentiate* themselves from their competitors. Literature[763] mentions several alternatives for differentiation: a different location, a slightly different product, a better service (or rather a "bad" service to support the suggestion of a rock bottom price image), and measures to enhance the (brand) image of a product, such as advertising and exclusive distribution via luxury shops. A consumer may be prepared to pay a little more for the same bread in one bakery than in a competing bakery because the shop is located more conveniently, because it is furnished more attractively, because it offers delicious pastry in addition to bread, or because the personnel is friendlier.

If vendors differentiate, there is no "perfect" competition in the sense that the consumer can select the cheapest vendor from multiple vendors that all offer the same product, but there is no monopoly

[761] 35 USC §103(a) at the end.

[762] "Perfect competition": Samuelson & Nordhaus 2010, p. 150.

[763] Scherer & Ross 1990, p. 571.

either, because the consumer still has a choice on this type of market. In economic terms, differentiation does not exclude "substitutes":[764] competitive products for the same market. Consumers may be prepared to pay a little more for a better product, but if they find the price difference to big they will resort to a cheaper "substitute", even if it is not entirely equivalent.

In addition to the methods mentioned above, a firm could distinguish itself as well by its exclusive *knowledge*. Knowledge as a means for differentiation can not always easily be adopted by a competitor. A snack-bar does not become a luxury restaurant overnight when an investor wants so. While every guest can see what a luxury restaurant offers, the needed knowledge can not simply be "carried out by any person skilled in the art". Thus that knowledge has a *natural* exclusivity, generally speaking. But conceivably certain knowledge indeed can be carried out by any person skilled in the art, and if that knowledge must contribute to exclusivity, its availability must be limited *artificially*, either physically (by secrecy) or by legal means. Patent law may offer that artificial exclusivity. Thus patent law makes an exception that proves the rule of freedom of competition.

After we concluded before that granting patents for knowledge that cannot be carried out by any "person skilled in the art" would lead to an *undetermined*[765] and potentially *disproportional*[766] result, now we find that patents for that type of knowledge are *unneeded* as well.

764 Samuelson & Nordhaus 2010, p. 92.

765 *See* p. 137.

766 *See* p. 137.

The scheme below gives an overview of the means for differentiation.

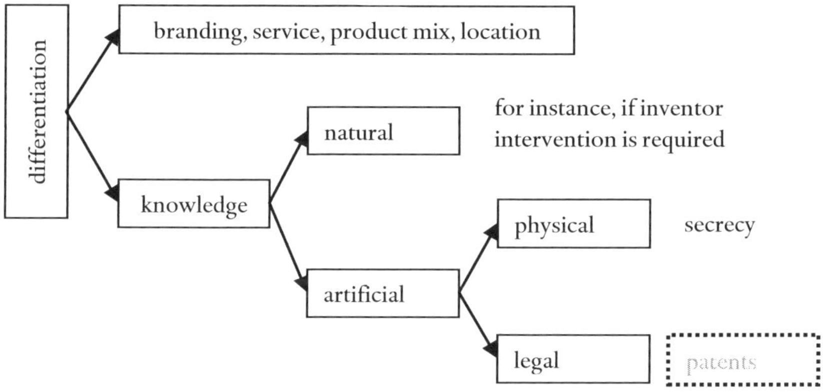

Our simple economic analysis can be refined in various ways. For instance, competition typically is a dynamic process, and a supplier who is first literally has a lead over other vendors.[767] Generally speaking, there are more ways to achieve a healthy competition without legal intervention.[768] Patents are usually associated with "protection", a word that suggests desirability. In a market economy though, protection ought to be an exception. Too much protection impedes the "creative destruction"[769] inherent to innovation.

In concrete cases where it is doubtful whether patents are really needed, it can be helpful to investigate whether a patent is needed indeed to protect against undue competition. For instance, are patents on *parts* really needed? Patents are related to inventions, while competition occurs at the level of products. If a product is covered by multiple patents,[770] patents for "knowledge ready to be carried out by a person skilled in the art" may not be needed either: then a firm still may be able to differentiate itself in a natural way by combining inventions in their products in a creative manner. In other

767 *See* e.g. Lieberman & Montgomery 1988.

768 Furthermore, conceivably there are other interventions than the grant of patents. *See* p. 156.

769 Schumpeter 1942, p. 81-86.

770 *See for instance* Somaya & Teece 2000; Rahnasto 2003, Chapter 5, "Fragmentation Problem", p. 173-181.

words, patents on parts are not always needed. Of course, parts are often traded as products in their own right. The above conclusion only pertains to parts that are not traded independently. In any case, an "interface" is not an independent product. An interface is the convention[771] enabling the connection between different products. An interface is the "cutting surface" of that connection. A cutting surface can not exist independently.

In sum, we conclude that, at most, knowledge that can be carried out by any "person skilled in the art" may need the artificial exclusivity of a patent in order to prevent undesirable "perfect competition". Legal exclusivity for the type of knowledge that is the "input" for inventors, like theories, ideas and facts is not needed to control competition, because a firm can distinguish itself in the application of this type of knowledge in a natural way.

III.2.4. Synthesis

In the preceding paragraphs first of all we found that the content of the right of a patentee in essence is a right to apply certain knowledge.[772] Thus the object of a patent obviously is applicable knowledge. However, not all forms of applicable knowledge qualify for patent, but only knowledge *any* "person skilled in the (pertinent) art" can carry out. Patents are only *suited* for this type of knowledge, because only for this type of knowledge the right is sufficiently determined, and proportional to the achievement made.[773] Subsequently, we drew the perhaps surprising conclusion, that at most for this form of knowledge there is an economic *need* for patents.[774]

---

[771] In particular in the case of information exchange, a distinction can be made between this convention, the "language", that must be compatible, and the implementation in hardware and/or software, that still can vary by product.

[772] *See* section III.2.1, "The contents of the rights of the patent", p. 134.

[773] *See* section III.2.2, "For what subject-matter patents are suitable?", p. 136.

[774] *See* section III.2.3, "For what subject-matter patents are needed?", p. 140.

Germans refer to the object of a patent as a "Lehre zum Handeln",[775] literally: a "teaching how to act". While English language literature usually refers to just "teaching",[776] the German designation rightly emphasises that a patent involves knowledge *to be carried out.*

An exclusive right to apply scientific and other "upstream" knowledge, however valuable perhaps as "input" for inventors, would be *insufficiently determined*, possibly *disproportional*, and probably *unneeded.*

III.3. Perspective

III.3.1. Exclusivity instead of reward?

Although there is a widespread perception that patents primarily serve the purpose to allow firms to recoup their development costs, still there are various indications that confirm our observation that patent law primarily serves the purpose of creating exclusivity.

For instance, never more than one inventor is granted a patent for a particular invention. At first sight, that seems reasonable, but actually it is a significant limitation, since often multiple inventors make the same invention, because certain inventions are "in the air" at some point in time, in the sense that several researchers are active in a certain field, making it more or less coincidental who is first.[777] A writer even calls this a lottery.[778] Nevertheless, the legislator has chosen only to grant a patent to the one who is first, regardless of the efforts made by the other inventors. There is no "independent

[775] Kraßer 2009, p. 125. Also in a famous German supreme court decision the invention is explicitly equated to a *Lehre*: BGH 27 March 1969, no. X ZB 15/67, 71 *GRUR* 1969, p. 672-676 (673) (*Rote Taube*), 1 *IIC* 1970, p. 136-142 (138) (Red Dove), at II.A.3.
[776] *See for instance* EPO Examination Guidelines 2010, passim. Likewise: USPTO 2007.
[777] This applies both in the traditional American "first to invent" system as in the "first to file" system used elsewhere.
[778] *See* Crouch 2008.

invention defence"[779] in case of infringement. That is a sign that the intent is to provide exclusivity, rather than to reward. This may be a remnant of times long bygone when patents where considered privileges[780] rather than a right for anyone meeting statutory requirements. In this respect patent law is essentially different from copyright law, that rewards every original author creation, even if an other author has made the same creation before.[781] That may be less likely than that the same invention is made multiple times, but that does not alter the fact that second and following inventors are not "rewarded" at all by patent law.

As a matter of fact, exclusivity is also prominent in common parlance: it is said that patent law gives the inventor a *monopoly*,[782] although strictly speaking that is incorrect, because the exclusive right of a patent does not lead to a monopoly if there are *substitutes*.[783]

In practice, patents indeed are often used for exclusivity, rather than to recoup research and development cost. For instance, firms who commercialise the results of university research often want exclusive patent licences, even if universities have less a need for patents for the results of government-funded research. This was one of the arguments for the *Bayh-Dole Act*[784] in the U.S., that facilitated patenting of the results of taxpayer paid (university) research. While this act has been criticised for various reasons,[785] it apparently fulfils a

779 Vermont 2006. The German term is "Sperrwirkung": Kraßer 2009 p. 6.
780 *See* p. 141.
781 According to the British "sweat of the brow" doctrine the effort is even a *sufficient* reason to recognise a copyright.
782 Sometimes one refers to a "legal monopoly", which is a reprehensible designation for an exclusive right because "monopoly" is an economic rather than a legal concept.
783 "Substitutes" can replace each other on a certain market. Samuelson & Nordhaus p. 92.
784 Bayh-Dole Act, in 35 USC Chapter 18 - Patent Rights in Inventions Made With Federal Assistance, § 200-212. *See* in particular 35 USC § 212, 'Policy and objective'.
785 Boettiger & Bennett 2005.

need insofar that it facilitates exclusive contracts between universities and commercial firms.[786] This exclusivity is also achieved if no licence fee is asked, that is to say, without "reward".

Also in different situations, firms apparently need exclusivity more than licence income. A fine example is the patent for a programming language element,[787] intended to prevent competitors from developing a compatible interpreter[788] for macro's[789] in text processing documents.[790]

Eventually, exclusivity is not opposite to reward, but a means to reward. For a proper understanding of patent law it is essential though to acknowledge that in a market economy patents are only a last resort to achieve exclusivity.

III.3.2. Reward instead of exclusivity?

From the persistent misconception that "intellectual property" is a form of property,[791] there is a tendency to grant patentees more rights than may be deemed to be useful.

For instance, it is assumed that a patentee has a nearly unconditional right of injunction. In Europe, a patent owner can be forced to grant a licence, but only in certain exceptional circumstances explicitly listed in the statute.[792] In the United States there is no such regulation. Still the U.S. Supreme Court recently decided that the right of injunction

---

[786] *See* Colyvas, Crow, Gelijns, Mazzoleni, Nelson, Rosenberg & Sampat 2002.

[787] A particular "operator".

[788] An "interpreter" is a program to process user programs without compilation.

[789] Macro's are (little) computer programs that may be included in text processing files to execute certain tasks during the processing of documents.

[790] *See* Bergstra & Klint 2007.

[791] *See* p. 141. Note that "property" should not be confused with "property right", see p. 143.

[792] *See e.g.* Art. 57 ROW 1995, § 24 PatG, Section 48 UK Patents Act.

of a patent owner in that case is not unconditional, but that does not give much room.[793]

In some countries, a patentee may obtain a reduction of renewal fees if he declares to be willing to grant everybody desiring so a licence for a reasonable compensation.[794] A step further is the so-called "Soft-IP",[795] a futuristic right distinguished from a patent primarily by the absence of a right of injunction, that is designed in such a way that it may be an attractive alternative for potential patentees too. An important advocate of "Soft-IP" is IBM.[796] It is particularly attractive for firms that use patents primarily to generate licence income, and fear that a tough application of the right of injunction will give patent law a bad reputation that eventually may put their income in jeopardy, but it is not attractive for firms that care more about exclusivity than licence income, and they do exist, as we noted in last section.

The idea to use patents as a "cash cow" is propagated in publications[797] that recommend managers to investigate whether their firm has knowledge that is not or no longer used, which might still be exploited by patent licensing. The suggestion is made that the income from such "Rembrandts in the Attic" goes straight to the bottom line as pure profit, because research costs of knowledge thus given a second life have been written off in the development cost of products. But actually already at the time of the initial development investment decision firms ought to take potential reuse of knowledge into account, because then an investment is more likely to be profitable. If they fail to do so, like the above publications suggest, this type of patent reuse hardly contributes to the constitutional

---

[793] *See* U.S. Supreme Court 15 May 2006, no. 05-130, 547 *U.S.* 388, 126 *S.Ct.* 1837, 164 L. Ed. 2d 641 (*eBay v. MercExchange*). *See also* Trimble 2012.

[794] In Germany and the UK the reduction is 50%. § 23 German Patent Act, Section 46 UK Patents Act ("licence of right"). If no agreement can be reached, the Patent Office may set the fee, both in Germany and the UK.

[795] European Patent Office 2007, p. 98.

[796] *See for instance* Nurton 2007.

[797] *See* Rivette & Kline 2000a, Rivette & Kline 2000b.

purpose of American patent law "[t]o promote the progress of science and useful arts".[798]

Don't all these examples show that patent law is primarily a tool for the appropriation of knowledge, to facilitate the trade of knowledge, rather than a means for market regulation via exclusivity? In order to answer that question, first of all we point out that some types of knowledge are simply unsuited for appropriation, such as purely scientific knowledge.[799] Another consideration is, that the patentee still may need exclusivity. In the last section we noted that occasionally exclusivity may even be more important than income. And otherwise it is usually in the interest of the patentee to restrict the number of licences in order to maximise his income, because in most markets the increase of volume is insufficient to compensate the decrease of price per unit beyond a certain volume.[800] A restrictive licence policy prevents the market from being flooded. Finally, we recall that the investment made by the inventor is no factor in patent law. Even a very inventive invention may be the result of a stroke of genius, or mere coincidence. Hence there is not always a reason to reward an inventor for his efforts.

Whether exclusivity or compensation is put first, in both cases a "property rule" is applied, with a more or less unconditional right-of-say of an owner.[801] In a classical article,[802] *Calabresi* en *Melamed* juxtapose "property rules" with "liability rules".[803] They note that a

[798] "The Congress shall have power [...] To promote the progress of science and useful arts, by securing for limited times to authors and inventors the exclusive right to their respective writings and discoveries". U.S Constitution, Article I, Section 8, Clause 8.

[799] *See* Section III.2.2, "For what subject-matter patents are suitable?", p. 136. *See also* Section IV.2.2, "Scientific theories", p. 182.

[800] Markets nearly always exhibit a downward-sloping demand curve, with a "negative price elasticity".

[801] To some extent, the above-mentioned "licence of right" arrangements are an exception.

[802] *See* Calabresi & Melamed 1972.

[803] They also distinguish "inalienability rules", that are not relevant for us here.

"property rule" may allow a proprietor (like a patentee) to bargain for a socially inefficient price. If a "liability rule" is applied, the price is determined using an objective standard. While it is not always easy to determine a proper "objective" price, "liability rules" still may provide a meaningful alternative for "intellectual property" as well.[804]

To put things in perspective, one should acknowledge that brainwork is rewarded in society only by way of exception by a kind of property right, that is to say a comprehensive right-of-say over the application of the results of that brainwork. Engineers, attorneys and other "knowledge workers" normally are paid by the hour,[805] not by granting them a right that – hopefully – allows them to collect an appropriate compensation for their efforts eventually. Attorneys do not claim the full value of their efforts: "no win no fee" is not allowed (in The Netherlands),[806] but "all win all fee" is unthinkable as well.[807]

In sum, a right of compensation for inventors may be a good idea, but it does not fit into the system of patent law. That needs a very different system, with more emphasis on efforts and less on exclusivity.

For completeness, we note that in certain fields, in particular in the medical realm exclusivity may be undesirable for ethical reasons, because it may have the effect that patients do not get the diagnosis or treatment they need.[808] Consequently, this type of market should preferably be controlled by more subtle means than patents. Firms invest in all sorts of industries without patent protection, so that should be possible too in the medical realm, perhaps supported by a separate statutory regulation if the free market fails to provide the ethically desired incentives.

---

[804] Van Overwalle 2009, Part IV "Liability regimes", p. 245-308.
[805] Employee patent law is an exception that confirms this rule. Rijlaarsdam 2005.
[806] *See* Faure, Hartlief & Philipsen 2006.
[807] We note that the "knowledge economy" is threatened by a kind of "claims culture" similar to liability law (see e.g. Hartlief 1997).
[808] *See for instance* Bostyn 2003 and Williams-Jones 2002.

III.3.3. Is exclusivity always effective?

Whether there is a natural exclusivity or an artificial exclusivity created by patents, a different question is whether exclusivity is effective at all. Exclusivity keeps competition healthy,[809] but by itself that is not sufficient to obtain a good return on investment. For a business justification[810] of a commercial research investment, there must be a reasonable prospect of a sufficient return on investment in the foreseeable future. For investments in truly basic science that is usually not the case: from basic research to its practical applications often many years elapse: decades or even centuries. Still such investments may be socially required. We give two examples.

For precision positioning, satellite navigation systems[811] depend on the findings of both the special and the general theory of relativity, science from about a century ago.[812] Research on nuclear fusion for energy production that started several decades ago is expected to need some more decades before it allows practical energy production application.[813] Private investors are reluctant to invest in this highly uncertain long-term project, although theorists for many years are able to calculate precisely how much energy can be produced by nuclear fusion from a given amount of fuel.[814]

---

[809] *See* p. 147.

[810] A business justification is something else than a legal justification.

[811] Such as the *Global Positioning System*, GPS, http://www.gps.gov, and the planned European "Galileo" system, http://www.esa.int/esaNA/galileo.html. The relativistic corrections amount to kilometres, so they cannot be neglected.

[812] The special theory of relativity dates from 1905, the general theory of relativity dates from 1916. The latter theory does not replace the former, but it has its own meaning.

[813] *See* http://www.iter.org for a leading new international research project in this field.

[814] Basically, this amount is given by the famous formula $E = mc^2$. A nuclear fusion process could – theoretically – produce from a single gram of fuel 90.000 kWh of energy, as much as 11 tons of coal. http://www.ipp.mpg.de/ippcms/eng/pr/fusion21/kernfusion. Note that the mass in the formula is

The "Convention Establishing the World Intellectual Property Organization"[815] defines scientific discoveries as form of "intellectual property" too.[816] By itself, that does not mean that these discoveries are protected, but only that the WIPO is given the task to promote their protection.[817] A proposed "Treaty on the International Recording of Scientific Discoveries" (1978) has never been adopted however.[818] This treaty aimed at giving scientists a certain title to unpatentable discoveries. Other proposals to grant "property rights" to basic science were not successful either,[819] which shows that this type of legal systems is actually not suited for basic knowledge.[820] The reason is that the relationship between basic research and practical application is often remote, both in time and substance, as we discussed above.

Earlier in this chapter we came to the conclusion that patents first and foremost serve the purpose to create exclusivity if there is no natural exclusivity.[821] As regards purely scientific knowledge, we now conclude that there is no market failure due to a lack of exclusivity, so that patents have no purpose here.

We already noted that an (imaginary) right to apply "upstream" knowledge would often be *indeterminate*, *disproportional* and *unneeded*,[822] and now we conclude that it may be *insufficient* as well. That such a right could be both disproportional and insufficient may sound contradictory, but actually it reflects the inherent uncertainty about the eventual applicability of such knowledge.

---

just the *decrease* in mass resulting from the nuclear reaction, which is relatively very small.

815 Hereinafter: "WIPO Treaty".

816 Art. 2 (viii) WIPO Treaty.

817 Art. 3 (i) WIPO Treaty.

818 *See also* WIPO 2004, p. 4, nr. 1.6.

819 Beier & Straus 1982, p. 14-41.

820 *See also* "property rule" on p. 155.

821 *See* p. 148.

822 *See* p. 151.

III.3.4. Reducing detrimental side-effects

Exclusivity is to the detriment of a firm that is not allowed to use an invention that is covered by someone else's patent. However, this side-effect is inevitable, otherwise patents would not be effective. Not all detrimental side-effects are unavoidable though.

Problems may arise in particular if a single product is covered by many patents that are owned by different patentees.[823] Literature refers to "complex technologies".[824] Software is a typical example.[825] A firm desiring to make such a "complex" product depends on all these patentees to be willing to grant a licence under acceptable conditions.[826] Conceivably, a single patentee may block the development of a product, in particular if it is too expensive or outright impossible to circumvent his patent. Furthermore, for this kind of products there is a substantial risk that a patent is overlooked, so that the manufacturer is forced to alter his product last minute, or still to negotiate a licence at a rather unfavourable point in time, or otherwise to withdraw his product altogether and to absorb the investments already made.

Writers note that in this situation a "tragedy of the anti-commons"[827] occurs rather than the more common "tragedy of the commons":[828] while the absence of a responsible owner may lead to overuse and neglect, in this case problems occur due to an excess of property claims.[829]

That is the reason why firms that produce this type of "complex" products take precautionary measures: by amassing as many patents as possible they arm themselves in order to be prepared to respond to

[823] *See* Cockburn & MacGarvie 2009.

[824] *See* Bessen 2003.

[825] Bakels 2011, p. 139-140.

[826] *See* Rahnasto 2003.

[827] *See* Heller 1998.

[828] *See* Hardin 1968.

[829] *See* Heller & Eisenberg 1998.

the threat of a blockade by threatening with a counter-blockade,[830] in order to arrive at cross-licensing arrangements eventually.[831] Reversely, firms may actively seek patent conflicts in the fight against competitors: "if you can't beat them, sue them". Literature distinguishes various aggressive patenting strategies, from "blocking", "blanketing" and "flooding" to "fencing" and "surrounding".[832] So-called strategic patenting[833] – both offensive and defensive[834] – is an "arms race" that – like the nuclear arms race at the time of the Cold War – leads to the prospect of *mutually assured destruction*,[835] so that no one still dares to attack, conscious that the "enemy" will strike back immediately in an equally devastating manner.

From a social perspective, strategic patenting is an undesirable phenomenon. In view of the large number of patents in a typical "strategic" patent portfolio, firms are inclined to conclude contracts for entire patent portfolios rather than for the specific patents they need.[836] Thus firms obtain, or rather regain "design freedom",[837] but patents do not contribute to efficiency by re-use of knowledge this way.[838] In the industries that practice "strategic patenting", economists observe a "patent paradox": a propensity to apply for

[830] Von Hippel 1988, p. 53.
[831] In 1990 IBM wrote that it needed patents primarily for successful licensing negotiations with other patent owners: http://www.progfree.org/Links/prep.ai.mit.edu/ibm.think.article.
[832] Granstrand 1999, p. 218-237.
[833] Blind, Cremers & Mueller 2009, p. 429: "There is no agreed definition of strategic patenting, although most experts include the use of patents to block competitors and the use of patents in negotiations with other companies."
[834] *See* Arundel & Patel 2003.
[835] Bessen & Meurer 2005, p. 14.
[836] *See* Parchomovsky & Wagner 2005.
[837] Teece 2000, Appendix A, p. 193-224.
[838] Merrill, Levin & Myers 2004, p. 37. *Specifically for software:* Blind, Edler & Friedewald 2005, p. 81-83.

large numbers of patents although individually they promise little profit.[839]

While the social benefit is questionable, participation in the strategic patenting "game" puts firms to great expenses. There is a high barrier to enter into a market in a branch of industry where strategic patenting is common.[840] That is detrimental for innovation, because young firms are more innovative by nature.

Are "strategic patenting" practices an inevitable negative side-effect of the patent system? Here patents create a detrimental exclusivity. But we established that the purpose of patents is to create artificial exclusivity if and when needed,[841] and in the light of the theory we developed there is no reason to grant the very patents that lend themselves in particular to strategic patenting practices: patents for parts.[842] Our theory that these patents are not needed is confirmed by the fact that most firms in "complex product" industries do not consider legal measures as the key means of protecting their inventions.[843]

III.3.5. In sum: the relativity of patents

Patents have the charm of simplicity: with an intuitively appealing right resembling real property, a government can support firms without any cost for the taxpayer.[844] But the simplicity is deceptive. A patent is no reward, but a means to correct the free market if and when needed, as an exception. The grant of patents is by no means the only way to compensate someone for his brainwork. The idea "I think, therefore I deserve a patent"[845] should definitely be rejected.

---

839 Hall & Ham 2001, p. 104.

840 *See e.g.* Cockburn & MacGarvie 2009.

841 *See* Section III.2.3, "For what subject-matter patents are needed?", p. 140.

842 *See* p. 149.

843 Cohen, Nelson & Walsh 2000, p. 28-29.

844 Conceivably, the grant of patents could even be profitable for the authorities, depending on tariffs.

845 After Descartes: Bostyn 2001.

In the preceding paragraphs we showed that the results of the theoretical analysis in the beginning of this chapter, while perhaps unexpected, still connect with social reality.

III.4. The "vertical" technology concept

In common parlance, knowledge an ordinary "person skilled in the art" can carry out is *technical* knowledge, as opposed to theoretical knowledge that may lend itself for application too, but only by an inventor. Thus the conclusion of the analysis earlier in this chapter could be restated as: only *technical* knowledge is inherently patentable subject-matter. In view of their respective traditions, Germans and EPO officials will not be surprised, but British will frown, and Americans will be astonished (except critics who believe that the European system is better).[846]

Although we agree with the Germans and the EPO[847] that only "technology" is susceptible for patent, we conclude that the attribute "technical" should be understood in a sense different from the way it is understood hitherto: as a designation for a certain *quality* of knowledge, rather than for a type of *products* (and *product elements*), or *disciplines*.

In the last chapter we found that the problems of the traditional assessment of the technical content of patent applications emanate (among other things) from the fact that technical and non-technical elements are often intertwined, and/or inventions have a multidisciplinary character.[848] In our perception, the only relevant criterion is whether the knowledge delivered by the inventor is sufficient to be carried out by any "person skilled in the art".

A technology concept related to knowledge quality could be designated as "vertical",[849] because it relates to a *hierarchy*: technical

---

[846] *See for instance* Kappos, Thomas & Bluestone 2008.

[847] In chronological order.

[848] *See* p. 130.

[849] *See* Bakels 2005.

knowledge encompasses theoretical knowledge, not reversely. In contrast, the traditional patent law technology concept[850] could be characterised as "horizontal", as it distinguishes disciplines at a peer level: for instance mechanical, electrical and chemical engineering are considered "technical" disciplines, while economy and linguistics are not. In this case there is no logical order.

III.4.1. Does the new technology concept cover the old?

Strictly speaking, it is impossible to answer the question whether the new technology concept covers the old one, because the traditional technology criterion in patent law is not properly defined, as we found.[851]

Still one may wonder whether the "vertical" technology criterion is as good as a barrier against "undesired" subject-matter like business methods as the traditional European technology criterion, that makes critical Americans envious.[852] Isn't there a risk that the rejection of the traditional, "horizontal" technology criterion allows American-style business method patents?

In any case, the proposed vertical technology criterion may work out more restrictively because the reasoning behind this criterion entails that *all* applications should be tested for compliance with this criterion, while traditionally only the subject matter listed in Art. 52(2) EPC is tested for technical content, like software and business methods, and the technical content in other fields is taken for granted. However, knowledge about technical *subject-matter* or knowledge in a technical *discipline* not necessarily has technical *quality*, in the "vertical" sense, as defined above. An insufficiently elaborated idea for the improvement of the diesel engine undoubtedly pertains to "horizontally" technical subject-matter, but it is not technical in the "vertical" sense.

---

[850] *See* Section II.3: 'What is "technology" in patent law?', p. 54.

[851] *See* Chapter II, "Positive law", p. 11.

[852] *See* Kappos, Thomas & Bluestone 2008.

An application not considered technical in the traditional sense is likely not to be technical in a "vertical" sense either, because knowledge in a discipline outside the realm of technology – non-technical in the "horizontal" sense – will often be hard to describe in a form sufficient to be carried out by any "person skilled in the art", i.e. in a vertically technical sense.

Literature[853] mentions several fields where "skill-based inventions" are applied by professionals that distinguish themselves from a "person skilled in the art"[854] because they need skills beyond mere craftsmanship, and because their activities are characterised by essential uncertainties just like the efforts of inventors.[855] So the related knowledge is non-technical in the "vertical" sense, in our terminology. In addition to business methods, literature mentions financial and medical[856] methods and even methods in the field of sports,[857] and gives arguments similar to the arguments we discussed not to grant patents for that type of subject-matter: these methods can not be described such that any "person having ordinary skill in the art" can carry them out unconditionally. While in all these cases there is no "vertical" technical character, these methods may pass a classical technology test, for instance because of the use of technical means. Again, the vertical technology criterion proves more restrictive.

Incidentally, there is no reason for concern that the vertical technology criterion will be so restrictive that it excludes socially desired applications, because this criterion is based on the analysis of desirabilities we gave in the beginning of this chapter, unlike the present technology criterion, which has an unclear, ambivalent basis, as we have seen in last chapter.

---

853 Arora 2005, p. 22.

854 Or: "person having ordinary skill in the art" according to American patent law.

855 *See* p. 138.

856 In the United States also medical methods can be patented.

857 *See* Section IV.2.5, "Schemes, rules and methods for playing games", p. 198.

III.4.2. Is the vertical technology concept really different?

As we have seen in last chapter,[858] since late last century the EPO no longer primarily assesses whether patent applications involve technical subject-matter,[859] but whether their technical aspects are novel and inventive.[860] This approach would reflect that various day to day activities have a technical *character*, but are not *inventive* in a technical sense, such as writing with pencil on paper.[861]

One may wonder whether this policy change relates to the replacement of a "horizontal" technology test by a "vertical" technology test we propose. At first sight, a similarity is that both in the new EPO approach and our approach the application is assessed by looking at *actors* rather than *products*. But the new EPO approach does not solve the problem either of "mixed" subject matter that requires both technical and non-technical skills in the same person.[862]

In our perception it is immaterial whether the subject-matter of a patent application is delivered by a (technical) scientist, an artist, a businessman or person combining some of these qualities, as long has he delivers knowledge ready to be carried out by any "person skilled in the art" without further experimentation or creativity.

III.4.3. Vertical technical content and the inventive step

We designated knowledge as "vertically" technical that is superior to mere ideas and theories because the latter still must be elaborated. Inventiveness also has the connotation of superiority: inventive

---

[858] *See* p. 100.
[859] Art. 52 EPC.
[860] Art. 54 and 56 EPC.
[861] TBA 21 April 2004, no. T 258/03, 27 *OJ* 2004, p. 575-638 (585), at 4.6 (*Auction method/HITACHI*).
[862] *See* p. 130.

knowledge is "non-obvious".[863] Still both qualifications are independent. The scheme below illustrates that one qualification does not imply the other.

		"vertical" technical content: extent of elaboration for application	
		low	high
inventive step: extent of (non-) obviousness	high	theory of relativity	patentable invention
	low	(irrelevant)	"detailed blueprint"

While the theory of relativity is by all means "non-obvious", by itself it can not be carried out, so it is not vertically technical, and thus it is not patent-eligible. Present-day technology applies relativistic findings, for instance in satellite navigation systems,[864] but that does not alter the fact that the theory by itself is not patentable. On the other hand, a fully elaborated blueprint for a complicated device is vertically technical if it describes knowledge sufficiently to be carried out by any person skilled in the pertinent art, but it cannot be patented unless it is inventive as well. Knowledge "not obvious to a person skilled in the art" is certainly not always ready to be carried out by that "person skilled in the art", and the opposite is not always true either.

Patents can only be granted for subject-matter that is both vertically technical and makes a sufficient inventive step.

---

[863] Art. 56 EPC, 35 USC § 103.

[864] *See* note 811.

III.4.4. Interpretation of the present rules in the light of the findings

Now that we know the inherent limits of the patent law domain, in principle we know how to interpret the rules associated with these inherent limits.

That evokes the question what rules relate to inherent limitations. For Europe, the structure of the European Patent Convention points the way: it makes a distinction between subject-matter that is excluded because it is not considered an invention (like "discoveries as such"),[865] and subject-matter that is considered an invention, but still is excluded.[866] This distinction shows that the former exclusions are inherent, while the latter are policy-based.[867] For instance, the EPC prohibits patenting of certain medical methods, although they still are designated as inventions.[868] During the EPC negotiations, they were initially included in the list of non-inventions, but following a proposal from the German delegation they were removed from this list.[869] The fact that American law does not prohibit patenting medical methods[870] confirms that the European exclusion is policy-based rather than inherent. *A contrario* this example too shows that the Art. 52 EPC exclusions have an inherent nature.

Art. 52 EPC draws the boundary between the subject-matter listed in subsection 2 "as such" and the same subject-matter *not* "as such". That is apparently the inherent boundary of the patent law domain, so the words "as such" *must* be interpreted in the sense of: "as far as not

---

[865] Art. 52(2) and (3) EPC.

[866] Art. 53 EPC.

[867] *See* p. 34 for background information.

[868] Kolle 1974b, p. 153-54, Moufang 1993, p. 29-30, Pila 2005b, p. 767-68, Nack & Moufang 2005, nr. 44 and 347-48, Pila 2010a, p. 152-53.

[869] Originally these methods were supposed not to be "susceptible of industrial application" (Art. 52(4) EPC old), nowadays they are explicitly excluded (Art. 53(c) EPC). For the moment it is only relevant that they are *not* included in the list of Art. 52(2) EPC.

[870] However, medical practitioners can't be sued for infringement due to the "Physician's Immunity Statute", 35 USC § 287(c).

vertically technical". This interpretation seemingly violates the rule that treaties should be interpreted as literally as possible,[871] but in the last chapter we found that the words "as such" cannot be interpreted in a more literal sense,[872] and then the law of treaties allows the context and the "object and purpose" of the treaty to be considered[873] – and that is exactly what we did in this chapter.

This conclusion implies that we share the EPO perception that an invention[874] in the legal sense is synonymous with technical subject-matter, and that "as such" in Art. 52(3) EPC is the opposite of "technical" so to say, but our analysis shows that "technical" should be understood *in a vertical sense.* Since this is an "ordinary" meaning of the word "technical" as well,[875] this interpretation complies with the technology requirement as prescribed nowadays in Art. 52(1).[876]

Although there are major differences between American and European patent law, in essence it is a patent system like any other patent system: it grants exclusive rights[877] to carry out certain knowledge. Consequently the inherent boundaries we established will apply to American patent law as well. Because American courts consistently and decidedly reject patents for "abstract ideas",[878] in a climate that generally opposes restrictions on patentable subject-matter, this restriction is most probably an inherent restriction. Since

---

871 Art. 31(1) VCLT.
872 *See* p. 35.
873 Art. 31(1) VCLT again.
874 We remind the reader that the invention concept has a very different meaning in American patent law, where it is defined in 35 USC § 100(a). *For further information see* Section II.1.4, "Terminology" on p. 20.
875 *See* Section III.4, 'The "vertical" technology concept', p. 162.
876 Here we ignore the fact that the clause "in all fields of technology" in Art. 52(1) taken literally does not codify a technology requirement. *For details, refer to* p. 28.
877 More precisely: patent systems actually only provide the right to exclude others from applying an invention.
878 *See* e.g U.S. Supreme Court 1874, 87 *U.S.* (20 Wall.) 498 (*Rubber-Tip Pencil Company v. Howard*).

we know from our analysis what the inherent limits of patent law are, we know now that "abstract ideas" in American patent law must correspond to knowledge that is not technical in a vertical sense.

Our earlier conclusion[879] that American patent law too *logically* excludes non-technical subject-matter – in a "vertical sense" – apparently was irreconcilable with the fact that American courts categorically reject a technology test (albeit in the traditional meaning),[880] but now we find that this conclusion actually fits very well in the system of American patent law, even if Americans are not used to associate "abstract" with "non-technical". Still Americans are aware that the lack of a proper description may indicate that the pertinent subject-matter should not be considered patentable,[881] which is an important indication for insufficient "vertical" technical content in our perception.[882] Of course, the inadequacy of a description may also result from simple negligence. What matters here is that certain subject matter that is excluded by the vertical technology criterion (like ideas and theories) *cannot* be described as required by patent law.

In sum: in this section we saw how the "vertical" technology provides the key for the interpretation of the European technology criterion and the American exclusion of abstract ideas, since both are related to the inherent boundaries of the domain of patent law.

III.4.5. Conformity to the TRIPS Agreement

Even if the interpretation we found is compatible with today's legislation, for the sake of completeness we must also verify whether it conforms to the TRIPS Agreement, that binds all presently 155 members[883] of the World Trade Organization.[884] Does "TRIPS"

[879] *See* Section III.4, 'The "vertical" technology concept', p. 162.

[880] *See* p. 49.

[881] Moy & Erstling 2008, p. 12-14. *See also* Bruzga 1987.

[882] *See* p. 137.

[883] On 10 May 2012, *Samoa* became the 155th WTO member.

[884] For more information on the framework of international treaties related to patents please refer to Section II.2.1, "Worldwide treaties", p. 21.

allow the "vertical" technology test? As we have seen in the last section, this test is an implementation of *an* invention concept, the European invention concept. The TRIPS Agreement introduces the "invention" concept in the following provision:[885]

Article 27 TRIPS. Patentable Subject Matter

1. Subject to the provisions of paragraphs 2 and 3, patents shall be available for any inventions, whether products or processes, in all fields of technology, provided that they are new, involve an inventive step and are capable of industrial application. Subject to paragraph 4 of Article 65, paragraph 8 of Article 70 and paragraph 3 of this Article, patents shall be available and patent rights enjoyable without discrimination as to the place of invention, the field of technology and whether products are imported or locally produced.

2. Members may exclude from patentability inventions, the prevention within their territory of the commercial exploitation of which is necessary to protect ordre public or morality, including to protect human, animal or plant life or health or to avoid serious prejudice to the environment, provided that such exclusion is not made merely because the exploitation is prohibited by their law.

3. Members may also exclude from patentability:

    (a) diagnostic, therapeutic and surgical methods for the treatment of humans or animals;

    (b) plants and animals other than micro-organisms, and essentially biological processes for the production of plants or animals other than non-biological and microbiological processes. However, Members shall provide for the protection of plant varieties either by patents or by an effective sui generis system or by any combination thereof. The provisions of this subparagraph shall be reviewed four years after the date of entry into force of the WTO Agreement.

---

[885] Emphasis added. A footnote attached to this provision has been omitted.

The first subsection indicates that the "invention" concept includes both products and a processes, but the treaty does not give an explicit definition of the concept. Consequently, the invention concept too should be interpreted "in good faith in accordance with the ordinary meaning to be given to the terms of the treaty in their context and in the light of its object and purpose".[886] But there is no unambiguous "ordinary meaning" of the invention concept: for instance its meaning in Europe is very different from its meaning in the United States.[887] In that case the law of treaties allows recourse to the "preparatory work".[888] During the negotiations about the TRIPS Agreement, various proposals have been made for lists of exclusions like the lists contained in the Patent Cooperation Treaty,[889] the EPC[890] and various national statutes,[891] but eventually the only reflection of those discussions is that TRIPS merely requires patent protection for *inventions,* not for "something" that can not be called an invention. That shows that the invention concept is used here in a European, or at least non-American manner, since it is not a criterion in the United States.[892]

A further source for the interpretation of the invention concept in the TRIPS Agreement is its context.[893] The above TRIPS provision – similar to the EPC – distinguishes the *absolute* criterion of "being an invention" from the *relative* criteria of novelty and non-obviousness[894] and from *policy-based* criteria covered in the second

---

[886] Art. 31(1) VCLT.

[887] 35 USC § 100(a). *See* p. 20.

[888] Art. 32 VCLT.

[889] *See* p. 33.

[890] Art. 52(2) EPC.

[891] Straus 1996, nr. 36 and note 115, p. 187, with further references; Schiuma 2000, p. 39.

[892] In American patent law, no patent application is ever rejected for not relating to an invention. *See* p. 20.

[893] Again art. 31(1) WVV.

[894] The requirement of "capability of industrial application" (according to a footnote in the *Agreement* to be equated to "usefulness") in practice plays a negligible role and requires no further discussion here therefore.

and third subsection. Thus by elimination we find that the "invention" concept should be interpreted here like in European patent law: as subject-matter that inherently fits in the patent system. According to our analysis that is knowledge with a "vertical" technical character.

As we have seen, nowadays in Europe the technology requirement is inferred from the words "in all fields of technology" in the first subsection of the above TRIPS provision, a conclusion just as incredible as controversial.[895] However, as the above reasoning shows, these words have no relevance to decide whether the "vertical" technology criterion conforms to the TRIPS Agreement.

A different issue is that the present "horizontal" technology test actually does not comply with the ban on discrimination by field of technology as laid down in Subsection 1,[896] since in the current EPC interpretation only the subject-matter listed in Art. 52(2) EPC is submitted to this test.[897] While the EPO never was blamed for violating the TRIPS Agreement in this respect, one may wonder for instance whether TRIPS allows a test for "technical contribution" specifically for software-inventions. The meanwhile rejected proposal for a "European Directive on the patentability of computer-implemented inventions"[898] was also at odds with the above discrimination prohibition as it gave specific rules for certain subject-matter. A specific regulation for biotechnological inventions[899] is

[895] *See* p. 24.
[896] The legislative history shows that the purpose of the provision was to end discrimination of certain "fields of technology" that was common at the time, notably medicines. Straus 1996, nr. 27, p. 181.
[897] *See* p. 35.
[898] Proposal for a Directive of the European Parliament and of the Council on the patentability of computer-implemented inventions, Brussels, 20 February 2002. *See also* p. 17.
[899] Directive 98/44/EC of 6. July 1998 on the legal protection of biotechnological inventions.

justified insofar as this subject-matter requires specific organisational measures for practical reasons.[900]

In contrast, the "vertical" technology criterion does not discriminate, because it applies to all patent applications.

In sum, there is apparently no objection to interpret the "invention" in the TRIPS Agreement as "subject-matter with vertical technical character". On the contrary, this approach observes the TRIPS ban on discrimination by field of technology, while the present EPO interpretation might be considered a violation.

III.5. Conclusion

In this chapter we found that the limitation of patent law to the domain of technology follows from the structure of the system of patent law. The finding that "technology" is an inherent delimitation of the domain of patent law apparently confirms an age-old German perception. But we found that "technical" should be understood quite differently from its present legal interpretations, as a designation for a certain *quality* of knowledge, instead of type of *product* or a kind of *discipline*.

Technical knowledge is knowledge that any "person skilled in the (pertinent) art" can carry out *unconditionally*, in contrast to knowledge that *may be* usable, only for an inventor, like purely scientific knowledge. The true invention is not just susceptible of industrial application, but any "person having ordinary skill in the (pertinent) art" should be able to carry out the invention, as is confirmed by the provisions that require a corresponding description. This meaning of the word "technical" is compliant too with common parlance: technical knowledge is distinguished from theoretical knowledge. Consequently, the law of treaties allows this

[900] For instance, the applicant of a patent on certain micro-organisms must deposit a culture of the micro-organism with a recognised depositary institution because otherwise the invention can not be reproduced by a "person skilled in the art". Rule 28 EPC.

interpretation for the application of the technology requirement as intended by "EPC 2000".

Whoever believes that the proposed delimitation is too narrow is reminded that there is a reason not to consider patent law as a general means for appropriation of knowledge, and that there are alternatives for the protection of knowledge. Whoever believes that the proposed delimitation is too wide is reminded that applications with sufficient technical content still may not pass the inventive step test. However, applications with insufficient technical content can not be honoured, however inventive they may be.

In any case, the delimitation we advocate has clear reasons, unlike the traditional technology criterion. That contributes to legal certainty, because those reasons provide a better base for the motivation of decisions than the word games that traditionally dominate the application of the technology criterion. The same applies to the exclusion of "abstract ideas" in American patent law. While American courts decidedly reject a traditional "technological arts" test, American patent law too is inherently limited to technical subject-matter in the "vertical" sense.

Unlike present interpretations,[901] the proposed approach follows legislation faithfully, and at last it resolves the paradox how allegedly partially technical subject-matter should be assessed. Like all paradoxes, this paradox is not resolved by an answer, but by the finding that the question was wrong: partially technical subject-matter does not require a special treatment, because it simply does not exist from the perspective of the theory of the vertical technology concept, and this theory does not need a "further technical effect" either to distinguish more and less technical software, because it acknowledges that knowledge about a technical object is not necessarily technical: a mere idea or theory is not technical, even if it relates to (technical) software.

---

[901] *See* last chapter.

In view of the history of Art. 52 EPC,[902] it is perhaps more lucky than wise that this provision *also* lends itself for an interpretation fully in concert with the purpose of patent law, that follows the statutory system precisely. As *Van Raden* says: *the law is probably wiser than its makers and its interpreters.*[903]

[902] *See* Kolle 1974b, Pila 2005b; Pila 2010a, p. 126-164.
[903] Van Raden 1996, p. 389.

IV. The application of the "vertical" technology criterion

IV.1. Purpose of this chapter

In this chapter we will investigate whether the "vertical" technology criterion could serve as the *general* criterion to delimit patentable subject-matter.

Traditionally both European and American patent law exclude various categories of subject-matter, from discoveries to algorithms, but on both sides of the Atlantic it was also established that such matter is not excluded *because*, but only *to the extent that* it is insufficiently technical or too abstract.

That means that the assessment of a patent application first requires the question to be answered whether it relates to one of these categories of subject-matter, for instance "software". If the answer is affirmative, subsequently an assessment should be made whether the application is sufficiently technical, or not too abstract. Not all jurisdictions share the EPO perception that the technical content of this subject-matter is decisive for patentability. British courts always emphasised that the technical content is not the sole criterion,[904] and American courts decidedly reject a "technological arts test". In this chapter we will show, that the technical content in the "vertical" sense makes a meaningful distinction for all those categories of subject-matter, obviating the need for additional rules. This observation, combined with the fact that according to the theory of the vertical technology concept all patent applications should be tested for vertical technical content,[905] implies that the first question no longer has to be answered. So the enumeration in Art. 52 (2) EPC should be understood as a list of examples of matter that is not always technical, rather than a list of subject-matter requiring different treatment.

---

[904] *See* p. 46.

[905] In the last chapter we showed that knowledge that is not technical in a vertical sense does not fit in the system of patent law.

In the second part of this chapter[906] we will again pay attention to American patent law in an overview of developments in American patent law since mid-nineteenth century, that shows that the Americans at the time already applied some sort of vertical technology test *avant la lettre*. That only changed when from about 1970 confusion arose about the patentability of "mathematical algorithms" and business methods.

For clarity, we remind the reader that meeting the vertical technology criterion is no more or less than a *necessary* condition for patentability. A "trivial" invention may meet this criterion, but it will be rejected for obviousness. On the other hand, subject-matter that does not meet this criterion is not patentable, however brilliant piece of science it may be.

Case law about the exclusions is not discussed extensively here but only to the extent needed in view of the purpose of this chapter. More about this case law can be found in the chapter "Positive law"[907] and an abundance of literature.[908]

IV.2. Application of the vertical technology concept to the exclusions of Art. 52 EPC

The European Patent Convention lists four categories of subject-matter that "a such" is considered no invention:[909]

a. discoveries, scientific theories and mathematical methods;
b. aesthetic creations;
c. schemes, rules and methods for performing mental acts, playing games or doing business, and programs for computers;

---

[906] *See* Section IV.3, "The vertical technology concept in American patent law", p. 221.
[907] Chapter II, p. 11.
[908] *See for instance* EPO Case Law 2010 or Melullis 2002, Art. 52. For a comparative overview of several jurisdictions (including the U.S.) *see* Nack 2002, and for a more historical overview *see* Pila 2010a.
[909] Art. 52(2) EPC.

d. presentations of information.

In the subsequent sections, for each of these categories we will first investigate what they really mean. Subsequently we will assess whether the vertical technology criterion is sufficient to make the distinction between patentable and non-patentable subject-matter of that category.

In this context we will also pay attention to American law. The above subject-matter is often considered not patentable in the United States too, which could actually be expected because we deal with restrictions inherent to the system of patent law.

IV.2.1. Discoveries

According to the EPC discoveries "as such" are no inventions,[910] so they can not be patented. In contrast, the American patent act equates discoveries to inventions: 'The term "invention" means invention or discovery.'[911] Apparently there are no statutory objections to patent discoveries in the US. But age-old case law excludes "physical phenomena",[912] and such phenomena pre-eminently are discoveries. Not every discovery is a "physical phenomenon" though.

But what is a "discovery" really? The word "dis-covery" suggests that something pre-existent is found, that only had to be "uncovered". In contrast, the word "invention" would denote a more active process (or its result) that teaches us something about something that did not exist before.[913] Nonetheless the words invention and discovery are used interchangeably in common parlance, as if they were synonyms.

---

[910] Art. 52(2)a in conjunction with (3) EPC.

[911] 35 USC § 100(a).

[912] U.S. Supreme Court 16 June 1980, no. 79-136, 447 *U.S.* 303, 309, 100 *S.Ct.* 2204, 2208 (*Diamond v. Chakrabarty*). American patent law excludes "laws of nature" as well. They will be covered in the next Section ("Scientific theories").

[913] The word "invention" in common parlance refers to both the act of inventing and its result.

Alexander Fleming *discovered* in 1928 penicillin,[914] when in the process of experiments with a very different purpose he noticed by coincidence that the fungus *Penicillium Notatum* produced a bacteria-killing substance, an *invention* that took medical science an important step forward. The fact that Fleming did not conduct his research in a directed manner (or at least did not look for a bacteria-killing substance) actually confirms that he made a genuine invention, because a patentable invention is "non-obvious",[915] so often it is *not* the result of a directed, deductive development endeavour. Literature gives various other examples where the words "invention" and "discovery" are used as synonyms.[916]

Whether the inventor has made an active contribution to science, or whether he has only observed and described a phenomenon is irrelevant for more than one reason. Firstly the presumption of the existence of knowledge that only has not yet been found evokes philosophical questions. In a platonistic conception everything is already there, so mankind must only discover it.[917] Furthermore, the amount of effort made by the inventor commonly is considered immaterial in patent law: there is no "sweat of the brow"[918] requirement. The Americans even codified that: "Patentability shall not be negatived by the manner in which the invention was made".[919] When we analysed the system of patent law in the last chapter we already noted that for legal purposes the amount of effort made by the inventor is immaterial.[920]

---

914 Alexander Fleming (1881-1955) was awarded in 1945 the Nobel Prize for medicine for the *discovery* of penicillin.
915 Art. 54 EPC.
916 Nack 2002, p. 225-235.
917 "Theory of forms" (ideas), see e.g. http://www.philosophicalsociety.com/Archives/Plato%20And%20The%20Theory%20Of%20Forms.htm.
918 This is a biblical expression, Genesis 3:19. It is related to a British copyright doctrine.
919 35 USC § 103 (a) (at the end).
920 *See* section III.2.3, "For what subject-matter patents are needed?", p. 140.

Efforts should not be confused with achievements: the value of a patent only depends on the applicability of the associated invention. Fleming may not have worked very hard, but his discovery was very valuable: he saw what others did not see. Not everybody has such a power of perception. The talent to find something useful without specifically looking for it is referred to as *serendipity*.[921]

The fact that many discoveries still cannot be patented follows directly from the vertical technical character requirement: a description of a natural phenomenon may lend itself for application, but it is not an *activity* that can be carried out by a "person skilled in the art". There are exceptions however: sometimes even an average person skilled in the art knows how to apply a discovery without further directions, such as in the example of penicillin. Here the discovery (even "as such") is vertically technical, and therefore it still could be patented.[922] That conclusion should be accepted, because the theory of the vertical technology criterion gives *rational* arguments to distinguish patentable subject-matter.

In sum, what really matters is not a possible philosophical difference between the process of "discovering" and the process of "inventing", but the result. The vertical technical character test only allows "knowledge ready to be carried out by any relevant person skilled in the art" to be patented and prevents other subject-matter from being patented like mere descriptions of observations. Consequently, there is no need for a separate exception for "discoveries" (as such) if all patent applications are assessed for "vertical" technical content, as we propose.

---

[921] The concept *serendipity* was introduced by the English writer and politician Horace Walpole (1717-1797) in one of his letters.

[922] Actually, Fleming never applied for patent, believing that his invention would be more useful to society this way.

IV.2.2. Scientific theories

According to the EPC, scientific theories "as such" are no inventions, so they can not be patented. This exclusion resembles the exclusion of "laws of nature" in American patent law.[923]

Similar to the word "discovery", the word "theory" has multiple, rather different connotations. Because an invention must be distinguished from its realisation,[924] it is always theoretical to some extent. The adjective "scientific" suggests a limitation no *natural* sciences, but the word "wissenschaftlich" in the equally authentic[925] German EPC text has a wider meaning. It seems odd that the EPC does not explicitly restrict the patenting of other theories.[926]

In philosophy of science theories are *preliminary* in the first place. Here a theory is a *hypothesis*, that can be "verified" or "falsified":[927] a theory (in this meaning) does not have to be *correct*, but it should only allow verification, and the result of the verification may be negative. Natural scientists cannot prove however that a theory is "correct" or "incorrect". They can only establish how accurate a theory describes and predicts observations, and even if a theory appears 100% accurate, correctness still has not been *proven* because observations inevitably suffer from measurement errors,[928] and because observations always relate to specific cases so that one must be

---

923 U.S. Supreme Court 16 June 1980, no. 79-136, 447 *U.S.* 303, 309, 100 *S.Ct.* 2204, 2208 (*Diamond v. Chakrabarty*).

924 *See* p. 136.

925 Art. 177 EPC.

926 Perhaps a non-scientific theory may be seen as a "method for performing mental acts", excluded "as such" by Art. 52(2c) EPC. *See also* Section IV.2.4, "Schemes, rules and methods for performing mental acts", p. 194.

927 Popper 1963, p. 36.

928 "Measurement errors" are no mistakes, but inevitable accuracies. If the dimensions of an object are measured in millimeters, the "measurement error" can be estimated at ± 0.5 mm. If a microscope is used, the error may perhaps be reduced to ± 0.5 μm, but not to zero.

careful not to make undue generalisations. Proving correctness is only reserved for mathematicians and perhaps for lawyers.

Let us take mechanics as an example. Newton's classical mechanics[929] describes various everyday phenomena very accurately, but still not precisely, since there are always deviations due to relativistic effects, as we know meanwhile. For daily use they are negligible, and practically immeasurable. However, phenomena on a cosmic scale significantly differ from what Newton's theories predict, such as the orbit of the planet Mercury.[930] Einsteins theory of relativity[931] is able to explain this orbit, and various other phenomena,[932] but it fails too to describe phenomena on a subatomary scale where quantum phenomena appear. Still quantum mechanics has it limitations if it comes to really elementary particles.

In common parlance, "theory" is often contrasted with "practice", but actually theories can be very useful in practice. Engineers use the – for them by no means preliminary – theories of mechanics to make designs at the drawing board that are ready to be built. An engineer designing a bridge does not experiment: he applies the theory of mechanics of materials to determine how thick the concrete should be. Engineers are not interested in the theory that provides the most accurate results: they use the theory that provides a balance between accuracy and simplicity, considering that the facts are never precisely known, like the total weight of the vehicles that will ever be on the bridge in the example.

Still there are reasons not to allow patents for all theories that are somehow useful in practice. It is useful to know that the amount of

---

[929] *See* Newton 1687.

[930] Mercury is an exception due to its proximity to the sun with its strong gravity field.

[931] Strictly speaking, there are two such theories, the special and the general theory of relativity. The two theories they complement each other.

[932] Think of the famous experiment by *Michelson* and *Morley* in 1887, or the observation by astrophysicist *Arthur Eddington* in 1919 at the occasion of a solar eclipse that starlight is deflected by the solar gravity field, a phenomenon predicted very accurately by the general theory of relativity.

energy produced by a nuclear reaction can be calculated with the formula $E = mc^2$, but this knowledge is insufficient to build a nuclear bomb or a nuclear power plant. In the last chapter we noted that a distinction must be made between knowledge that can be *applied* (perhaps only by an inventor) and knowledge that can be *carried out* (by any relevant "person skilled in the art"),[933] and we established that patents are only appropriate for the latter type knowledge, so-called *vertically technical* knowledge.

The European Patent Convention acknowledges that there is no reason to exclude scientific theories categorically by excluding them only "as such". At first sight that gives the impression that no patents should be granted for applications that include nothing but a scientific theory, but that perception fails to appreciate the above observation that a theory by itself may well be "vertically technical". Moreover, considering an application a "mix" of a theory and its application raises the inappropriate question whether either the theory or its application is novel, and this misconception leads to severe complications in case law.[934]

For those reasons, the words "as such" are better interpreted in the sense of "as far as not vertically technical". That is a clear, meaningful limitation.

American patent law avoids the ambiguous word "theory" and excludes "laws of nature",[935] which more clearly indicates knowledge that may lend itself for *application*, but usually cannot be *carried out,* and which is not vertically technical therefore in our terminology.

Recently U.S. Supreme Court involvement was needed to reconfirm that mere scientific knowledge is not patentable.[936] In the particular

---

933 *See* p. 139 for a categorisation of knowledge.

934 *See* Section II.4, '"Technical" in which respect?', p. 95.

935 U.S. Supreme Court 16 June 1980, no. 79-136, 447 *U.S.* 303, 309, 100 *S.Ct.* 2204, 2208 (*Diamond v. Chakrabarty*).

936 *See* U.S. Supreme Court 20 March 2012, no. 10-1150, 132 *S.Ct.* 1289 (*Mayo v. Prometheus*).

case the patent application relates to the problem that it is difficult to determine the optimum dose of medicines that are metabolised differently by different patients, while the blood levels of the metabolites[937] (rather than the medicine itself) should stay within certain limits in order that the medicine is effective without causing harmful side-effects. An obvious and well-known solution is to measure those blood levels and to use that information to determine the dose for the individual. The patent was only for the scientific fact of the blood level limits of the metabolites for a particular medicine, not for the medicine itself, nor for the measurement method, let alone for the idea to measure the blood levels of metabolites to determine the optimum dose.

Knowledge of these limits by itself can not be *carried out*, so it is not patentable, in a classical perception too.[938] The applicant does mention certain actions that must be carried out, like administering the medicine and determining the blood level (without indicating how these actions should be performed), but the Court rightly notes that they cannot justify patentability.[939]

In sum, the EPC exclusion of "scientific theories as such" is redundant if a vertical technical character test is applied,[940] and the exclusion of *laws of nature* in American patent law is covered by this test too.

---

937 A metabolite is a substance produced by the human body by transformation of (in this case) a medicine.

938 *See* p. 151.

939 U.S. Supreme Court 20 March 2012, no. 10-1150, 132 *S.Ct.* 1289, 1297 (*Mayo v. Prometheus*).

940 Similarly: Nack 2002, p. 320.

IV.2.3. Mathematical methods

According to Art. 52(2a) EPC "mathematical methods" are considered no inventions, but according to subsection 3 again that applies only to those methods "as such". Remarkably the EPC excludes mathematical *methods* rather than mathematical *theories*, and this is no coincidence: during the EPC negotiations, the Swiss argued that even the practical application of mathematics is an "intellectual activity", so that it would be more appropriate to exclude "mathematics" completely instead of merely "as such".[941]

There is no similar exclusion in the American patent act. But in this very country the patentability of "mathematical algorithms" was often contested in court,[942] because patent applications that would be associated with software in Europe typically are related to these algorithms in the U.S. That is correct insofar that "software patents" protect the underlying ideas rather than the program code itself,[943] but it is questionable whether a computer "algorithm" like "gross = net + VAT" should be qualified as "mathematical".

Hence we will discuss "mathematical methods" here separately, also because they are mentioned separately in the EPC.

While the designation "mathematical algorithm" suggests the existence of non-mathematical algorithms, in particular the opponents of software patents argue that all algorithms are mathematical,[944] and that they should not be patentable consequently.[945] However, an American court noted that every step-by-step process constitutes an algorithm in the broader sense of the term,[946] and that processes constitute statutory subject-matter,[947] so

---

[941] Pila 2005b, p. 766. Pila 2010a, p. 149-150.

[942] Nack 2002, p. 120-133. *See also* Fellas 1999.

[943] *See* Section IV.2.7, "Computer programs", p. 205.

[944] *See for instance* Gerwinski 2010.

[945] *See also* Klemens 2005.

[946] CAFC 7 November 1989, no. 89-1019, 888 *F.2d* 1370, 1374 (*In re Iwahashi*).

that there could be no objection against patenting algorithms in general. The court was bound however by the Supreme Court decision that associated *mathematical* algorithms with unpatentable laws of nature.[948] So the lower court felt obliged to make a *legal* distinction between "mathematical" and other algorithms – which was heavily criticised by a prominent computer scientist.[949]

What is "mathematics" really? For mathematicians this question is no less complex than the question what "law" really is for lawyers. At first sight, mathematics is associated with formulas. Still, mathematics is not merely a "language". An EPO Board of Appeal once noted[950] that a "mathematical" description in patent applications is not just allowed but even preferred if that serves clarity and conciseness as required by the EPC.[951] A modern inventor with a university degree may be more inclined to use mathematical notation than the archetypical hobbyist-inventors of the past,[952] if such people ever really existed. Reversely, any "mathematical" formula could conceivably also be phrased in ordinary language, although it is cumbersome and potentially detrimental to unambiguity. But obviously neither the ban on patenting "mathematical methods as such" in European patent law nor similar restrictions in American patent law can be avoided by replacing formulas in applications by words that mean essentially the same.[953] It has been said so many times: the wordings of the application can't be decisive for patentability.[954] In sum, neither the presence nor the absence of formulas in a patent application is relevant to decide whether it is "too mathematical" to be honoured.

---

947 35 USC § 101 in conjunction with 35 USC § 100(b).

948 U.S. Supreme Court 20 November 1972, no. 71-485, 409 *U.S.* 63, 67, 93 *S.Ct.* 253, 255 (*Gottschalk v. Benson*).

949 *See* Knuth 1994.

950 TBA 15 July 1986, no. T 208/84, 10 *OJ* 1987, p. 14, at 8. (*Computer-Related Invention/VICOM*).

951 Art. 84 EPC.

952 Horns 2000, Abs. 12.

953 CCPA 6 October 1977, no. 77-519, 563 *F.2d* 1026, 1030 (*In re Richman*).

954 *See* section II.4.5, "The wording of the application", p. 124.

For further illustration: mathematical notation may even be used for legal purposes. Lawyers are familiar with rules that depend on cumulative conditions, i.e. that the specific consequence only applies if all required conditions are fulfilled. If one of the conditions is not satisfied, then the consequence does not apply, obviating the need to test the other conditions. In Boolean algebra,[955] an algebra of variables that can only be "true" or "false", this rule can be written as the following identity[956] for the case that there are two conditions *a* and *b*:

$$\text{NOT}\ (a\ \text{AND}\ \text{b}) = (\text{NOT}\ a)\ \text{OR}\ (\text{NOT}\ b)$$

or in a "more mathematical" form as:

$$\neg(a \wedge b) = \neg a \vee \neg b$$

Above we concluded that the form of notation is immaterial to distinguish mathematics. Should we conclude that the rules governing the combination of cumulative and alternative conditions in law are "mathematical", even if not written in mathematical notation? The question could be answered with the counter-question whether it really matters. Likewise, for patent law the True Nature of "mathematics" is not relevant either. It is only relevant for patent law whether mathematical knowledge could be technical in a vertical sense, i.e. whether such knowledge could be elaborated to the level that it can be carried out by any "person skilled in the art" who is master of his discipline. Hence we focus now on the practical application of mathematics.

A "mathematical" formula can be both a problem[957] and a solution. Various geometrical, physical, technical, economical and other

---

955 Named after George Boole (1815-1864).

956 An *identity* is a relationship that holds for all values of its variables, in contrast to an *equation*, that only holds for specific values, the solution. So an identity has no solution.

957 The word "problem" is used here in its original meaning of "task to be accomplished" rather than in the sense of "difficulty". In mathematics, the word "problem" is often used in that sense.

practical problems can be described in "mathematical" form, in particular in mathematical equations.[958] Then that equation is a *solution*: it describes a relationship between quantities, as the outcome of theory building, usually based on observations.[959] Subsequently, the equation is a *problem* for someone who wants to use a theory thus described in "mathematical" terms to make a prediction for a concrete case. Then there is a need for an *algorithm*: a recipe showing what arithmetical operations must be performed to find that prediction.

As a *solution*, a particular equation can describe various phenomena, and as a *problem* it usually can be solved in various ways. The figure below gives a schematic overview:

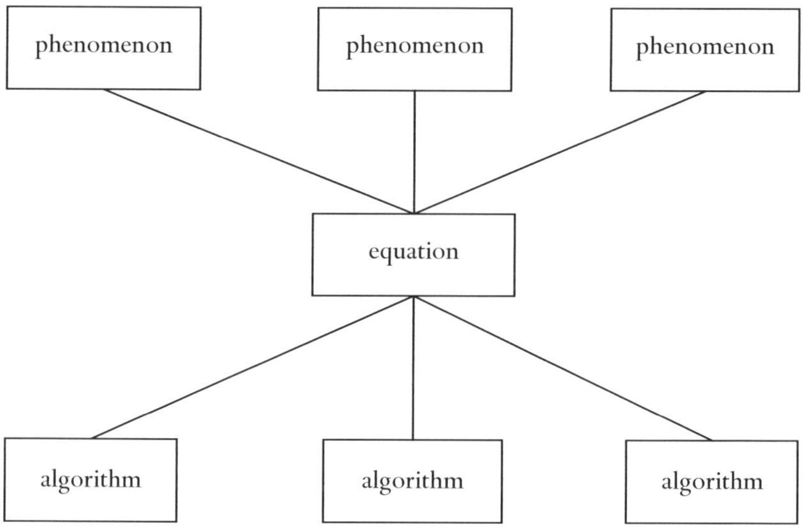

A simple example may illustrate this analysis. Assume that a cyclist has a map and a clock, but no speedometer, and wants to know how fast he cycles. The first thing he needs is to know the relationship between the quantities distance, time and velocity. If the velocity is

958 In mathematics, an equation is so to say a formula including an equal sign (=), describing the relationship between certain values.
959 Observations may or may not result from experiments. Astronomers and economists usually do not experiment.

constant, the relationship is *proportional*,[960] which can be expressed by the following "mathematical" equation:

$$s = v\,t$$

in which *s* is the distance covered, *v* is the velocity and *t* the elapsed time.[961] This equation answers the question just raised about the relationship between those quantities, and as such it is therefore a *solution*.

But in order to find the velocity in a concrete case, we are not just interested in the relationship, we also want to know how the velocity can be calculated from a given distance and time. Mathematics learns that the solution of this *problem* is the following expression:[962]

$$v = s\,/\,t\;(t \neq 0)$$

If we have found that in two hours 30 kilometres have been covered, then after substitution[963] of these data into this formula the velocity is found to be:

$$v = s\,/\,t = 30\,/\,2 = 15\ \text{km/h}$$

In this example the solution can be calculated in one's head. But not always it is so simple: if the journey took only one hour and 59 minutes, the calculation is much more complicated. Then the velocity can be calculated by means of a long division, but in practice one will

---

960 For simplicity sake, here we have chosen a relationship that follows from a definition: the definition of the velocity concept. An example of a proportional relationship in a law of nature is the relationship between force and acceleration in Newton's Second Law of Motion: F = m a.
961 As usual in mathematics no multiplication sign is used.
962 Mathematics is very simple here: if one of the factors of a given product of two numbers is unknown, it is found by division.
963 Mathematicians talk about *substitution* where lawyers talk about *subsumption*.

use a calculator.[964] A long division is an *algorithm*, and a calculator performs an algorithm as well: a process of simpler operations producing the quotient.

In order to solve the problem of the example we have to know two things: firstly the fact that there is a proportional relationship between the distance and the velocity, and secondly a method to calculate the velocity with a given distance and time (with an algorithm that produces the numerical result of the division). Those are two separate things. In both cases, there is vertically technical knowledge: any "person skilled in the art" who knows the relationship between the observed quantities and the unknown quantity can calculate the unknown quantity. And any "person skilled in the art" who knows the algorithm to perform that calculation can write a program for that purpose, "burn" a chip, or perhaps perform the calculation manually with a long division.

A ("mathematical") equation by itself does not describe an *act* at all, so it can never be an invention. An equation is useless unless it is either related to a phenomenon, or solution directions are given. Whoever knows mathematical notation conventions can devise as many equations as he likes.

The inventor of the relationship between the quantities is a practitioner of an empirical science like physics or economics.[965] He uses "mathematical" concepts, but he is no mathematician.

The algorithm is a separate invention. The development of algorithms is a specialism by itself, and a task with the typical characteristics of inventing: even a specialist is often unable to deliver an algorithm "to order", in particular if there are performance

---

964 Then one will find that the velocity is *about* 15,126050420168066678 km/h (if the observations are sufficiently accurate to justify this level of precision).

965 Again: for simplicity the relationship in the example is not really a law of nature.

constraints,[966] and for some problems it even appears impossible to find a usable algorithm.[967] Those characteristics are more relevant for patent law than the fact that the specialists who develop advanced algorithms usually are called "mathematicians".

Incidentally, algorithms in an average computer program are unlikely to be associated with mathematics. In order to find the total of a list of expenses, the individual expenses are simply added. However simple this algorithm is, it is still vertically technical, but obviously it is neither novel nor inventive. Still it is impossible to draw a bright line between advanced, "mathematical" algorithms and the basic algorithms used by programmers every day. For instance, every experienced programmer knows the basic *bubble sort* algorithm by heart, but the development of more efficient algorithms to sort large amounts of data is a science by itself.[968]

If an algorithm is the solution for a practical problem that can be implemented by any competent programmer in an operational computer program, it is vertically technical knowledge. Is there then still a reason to restrict algorithm patenting?

American courts used to have objections against patents for algorithms *themselves*, covering all their applications.[969] Still an exclusive right for an algorithm does not necessarily lead to a monopoly: as the example shows, other algorithms may offer

[966] For instance, supercomputers compete on the level of the number of arithmetic operations they can perform by second – which is not only dependent on the speed of the electronics, but also on the quality of the algorithms that are applied.
[967] An example is the factorisation of very large numbers. Cryptographic systems exploit this impossibility. Of course, a number can always be factorised using a "brute force attack", i.e. simply by trying, but for larger numbers the required amount of computing time soon becomes prohibitive, even if a supercomputer is used.
[968] Here "sort" means: put in a specific, for instance alphabetic order.
[969] U.S. Supreme Court 20 November 1972, no. 71-485, 409 *U.S.* 63, 72, 93 *S.Ct.* 253, 257 (*Gottschalk v. Benson*).

substitutes,[970] even in the apparently simple case of division arithmetic.[971] Generally speaking there is no reason why the monopoly risk would be higher in case of an algorithm patent than for patents in other fields.

A very different objection against algorithm patents is that in theory they may be executed by human beings as well, at least if there are no time constraints like in the case of real time applications.[972] Here we face confusion who applies the knowledge of a mathematical method. Normally patented knowledge is applied by a manufacturer to make a product, in this case a program that executes an algorithm rather than a human being executing the algorithm "by hand" *instead of* a program. This confusion is promoted if algorithms are patented as processes. At first sight, algorithms are indeed a kind of process, but these processes are executed by *products* (programs in particular) rather than their *manufacturers*. Processes in the legal sense normally are carried out by manufacturers, originally mainly in chemistry. That is the reason why the "product obtained directly by that process" is covered too by the protection of a process patent.[973] A process patent for an algorithm executed by a program has the odd effect that the output of the computer program is covered by the patent too according to the statute. Thus it is more appropriate to patent products executing algorithms as products.[974] In this light it is

[970] This is an economical concept. "Substitutes" may replace each other on a certain market. Samuelson & Nordhaus p. 92.
[971] Alternative algorithms obviously do not distinguish themselves by their results, but by their efficiency. A better algorithm delivers faster the solution of a given problem with given computing facilities with a certain number of decimals.
[972] For instance, an algorithm in a control engineering application should produce a result before the state of the controlled system has changed significantly. Another example are noise-cancelling headphones that reduce unwanted ambient sounds using algorithms that calculate "anti-sound" (almost) instantaneously.
[973] Art. 28(1b) TRIPS Art. 64(2) EPC Art. 53(1b) ROW 1995, § 9(3) PatG, Section 60(1)(c) UK Patents Act, 35 USC § 271 (g), etc.
[974] *See* Bakels 2003.

remarkable that initially patenting software as a product was not allowed.[975] Confusion can be avoided by acknowledging that an invention always represents knowledge that is carried out by a "person skilled in the art", both in the case of process and product patents.[976] Programmers as "manufacturers" do not execute algorithms, they only code them for machine use.

Eventually we agree with the American court that noted that there is no ground for a separate "mathematical algorithm exception", and that undesired patents are prevented by a proper application of the *general* criteria,[977] but in our perception the vertically technical character is one of these general criteria too. Mathematical methods an ordinary "person skilled in the art" can not carry out thus are insufficiently technical for a European patent, and too abstract for an American patent. They are excluded due to the general criteria of a technology requirement in Europe, and the American ban on "abstract ideas" patents.

IV.2.4. Schemes, rules and methods for performing mental acts

According to the EPC "schemes, rules and methods for performing mental acts as such" are no inventions. This exclusion is rooted in a long tradition. Long before the above rule was codified in the EPC, German patent law excluded *directions to the human mind*.[978] In American patent law one refers to the *mental steps doctrine*.[979]

---

975 *See* TBA 1 July 1998, no. T 1173/97, 22 *OJ* 1999, p. 609-632 (*Computer Program Product I/IBM*); CAFC 12 May 1995, no. 95-1054, 53 F.3d 1583 (*In re Beauregard*).

976 *See* p. 136.

977 CAFC 23 July 1998, no. 96-1327, 149 F.3d 1368, 1373 (*State Street Bank & Trust v. Signature Financial Group*).

978 In German: "*Anweisungen an den menschlichen Geist*". *See* Elben 1960. Melullis 2002, Art. 52, Rn. 175-179. Incidentally this concept is also used in a different meaning, notably for products essentially carrying a certain information-content, even if that can not be qualified as a "direction".

By itself it seems obvious that people should not be limited in their thoughts by patent law – if that could be enforced at all.[980] The Dutch Patent Office once stated that inventions involving "man as a processor" could not be patented.[981] On the other hand, conceivably no invention ever could be realised or used if one would not use his brains at any moment.[982] So logically not all "mental work" is outside the domain of patent law.

In the German perception, *directions to the human mind* in the legal sense only relate to mental steps that do not extend into the physical world.[983] They do not use "natural forces",[984] which characterises them in a German perception as non-technical almost by definition, although reversely not all non-technical subject-matter is such a *direction*.[985]

Americans used to contrast "mental steps" with "physical steps".[986] But the Americans question already for a long time whether there is a place for a separate "mental steps doctrine".[987] In one of the first conflicts about the patentability of algorithms, a court decided that this doctrine merely prohibits patenting activities that *only* the "human mind" can perform successfully, and that it is no obstacle to patent processes that are executed by machines, even if they could

---

Elben 1960, p. 59-60. Kolle 1974a, p. 14-15. The latter aspect of this concept is discussed in section IV.2.9, "Presentations of information", p. 217.
979 *See for instance* Sutton 1970.
980 This would also conflict with human rights. Nack 2002, p. 249-250.
981 Quoted from: Board of Appeal of the Dutch Patent Office 11 May 1987, 55 *BIE* 1987, p. 174-176, 4 *CR* 1987, p. 195-197, 37 *GRUR Int* 1988, p. 71-72; 11 *OJ* 1988, p. 75-78 (*Barcode*).
982 Nack 2002, p. 173 and p. 248-249.
983 Elben 1960, p. 17.
984 *See* p. 66.
985 Elben 1960, p. 17.
986 *See* CCPA 6 March 1951, no. 5723, 38 *C.C.P.A.* 945, 188 *F.2d* 165 (*In re Abrams*).
987 *See* Ambrose 1981.

theoretically be executed by human beings as well.[988] As we noted in the last section, a "process" in patent law is a process executed by a manufacturer rather than its product,[989] so this distinction is inappropriate here.

In contrast, business methods are applied by manufacturers, or businesses at least. As we will see, there are reasons to restrict business method patentability.[990] Therefore it is remarkable that the mental steps doctrine plays no role in the debate about business method patents. In a proposal for a revision of the guidelines for examination of patent applications the USPTO some years ago simply stated that a (separate) "mental step test" or "human step test" is inappropriate.[991]

If we follow the German perception that a method just for performing "mental acts" is more or less synonymous with a non-technical method in general, then it should not come as a surprise that the exclusion overlaps with the other exclusions. That might be the reason that only since 2006 the case law guide published periodically by the EPO pays attention specifically to this exclusion.[992] Incidentally, nearly half of the cases mentioned under this heading

---

[988] CCPA 14 August 1969, no. 7987, 56 *C.C.P.A.* 1381, 1392, 415 *F.2d* 1393, 1502 *(In re Prater and Wei II)*.

[989] *See* p. 193.

[990] *See* Section IV.2.6, "Schemes, rules and methods for doing business", p. 200.

[991] USPTO 2005b, p. 46-47.

[992] EPO Case Law 2009, Section I.A.2.5.2, p. 28-30. This topic is covered in *EPO Examination Guidelines* only in a short section (C.IV.2.3.5) without any reference to case law. Compare EPO Case Law 2006. *See also* EPO Examination Guidelines 2010.

relates more to "presentations of information",[993] a separate exclusion in the EPC[994] we will discuss later.[995]

Interestingly, the EPO regularly rejects patent applications for design methods, arguing that these methods constitute "mental acts". But "mental acts" too are only excluded "as such" by the EPC. While the EPO usually interprets these words in the sense of "as far as non-technical", it rejects technical design methods too, arguing that they only deliver a design and no physical product as yet,[996] although an exception is made if the design method is sufficiently close to the product,[997] a rather vague distinction. Patenting design methods is also controversial under German law.[998]

Where the traditional, horizontal technology concept leads to confusion here, the vertical technology concept provides clarity: decisive is whether a design method is sufficiently elaborated to be carried out by any relevant "person skilled in the art" for the realisation of the eventual product. The vertical technology criterion does not exclude mental labour *per se*, but it only allows unambiguous procedures to be patented that require no further experiments or creativity, nothing more than an "ordinary skill in the art". On the other hand, the mere idea to solve a problem – however technical perhaps – is not technical in a vertical sense, and actually according to the present state of the law those "problem inventions" usually are not patentable either, but there is some confusion.[999] Here the vertical technology criterion provides clarity too.

---

993 *See* TBA 19 March 1986, no. T 51/84, 9 *OJ* 1986, p. 226 (*Coded Distinctive Mark/STOCKBURGER*); TBA 10 May 2005, no. T 125/04 (*Assessment system/COMPARATIVE VISUAL ASSESSMENTS*); TBA 18 October 2005, no. T 49/04 (*Text processor/WALKER*).

994 Art. 52(2d) EPC.

995 Section IV.2.9, "Presentations of information", p. 217.

996 *See* TBA 31 May 1994, no. T 453/91 (*Method for physical VLSI-chip design/IBM*); TBA 12 July 2005, no. T 914/02 (*Loading determination method/GENERAL ELECTRIC CO*).

997 *See* TBA 10 May 2001, no. T 474/98 (*Kabushiki Kaisha/TOPCON*).

998 *See* p. 73.

999 *See* p. 103.

In sum, we find that "schemes, rules and methods for performing mental acts" can be patentable if and only if they really have vertical technical character. So again there is no need for an explicit exclusion if all patent applications are tested for vertical technical content.

IV.2.5. Schemes, rules and methods for playing games

Although in practice the exclusion of "schemes, rules and methods for playing games as such" is not as important as exclusions that follow,[1000] we keep to the sequence of the EPC here.

Does this exclusion apply to playing games or to the games themselves? In other words: does this exclusion apply to methods applied by players or to methods applied by manufacturers of games? The English EPC text refers to "playing games", which unambiguously indicates that the former interpretation is meant, but the equally authentic[1001] German and French texts are not as clear here: the words "für Spiele" and "en matière de jeu" could also apply to the games themselves instead of just playing games. Still apparently *playing* games is meant, since this exclusion is combined in the same list item with mental activities.[1002]

Nonetheless the EPO primarily applies this exclusion to limit the patentability of games *as products*. As usual, the EPO considers the technical content decisive for patentability, and rejects patent applications for technically non-inventive implementations of inventive game ideas,[1003] thus making the usual mistake again to dissect applications into a technical and a non-technical part. While

[1000] Art. 52(2c) in conjunction with Subsection 3 EPC.
[1001] Art. 177 EPC.
[1002] German: "gedankliche Tätigkeiten", French: "activités intellectuelles".
[1003] *See* TBA 11 October 2007, no. T 336/07 (*Electronic multi-play poker/IGT*); TBA 6 February 2009, no. T 12/08 (*Game machine and storage medium/NINTENDO*); TBA 29 June 2007, no. T 1543/06 (*Game machine/GAMEACCOUNT*); TBA 7 September 2006, no. T 717/05 (*Auxiliary game/LABRONIX*).

that may seem appropriate at first sight, games too must be assessed as a whole according to the principal rule, and that is definitely a meaningful rule here, since in the very case of games there is a strong interplay between (creative) design and (technical) possibilities. A professional computer game designer is an artist and an engineer at the same time, who knows how to exploit the technical capabilities to the extreme in order to achieve a spectacular result.[1004]

The vertical technology criterion prevents patents to be granted for an insufficiently elaborated game idea, that still requires (and allows) creative choices. That is what really matters, because that prevents patent law from being abused to obtain exclusive rights for game *concepts* that are left free by copyright due to the "idea-expression dichotomy".[1005] A writer points out that this principle should not be thwarted by patent law.[1006]

Returning to the original purport of this exclusion as explained above, we note that patents for methods that are applied by players of games do exist: in the United States indeed *sports patents* have been granted.[1007] American writers argue that professional sports are big business, and they understand that there is a desire to secure the enormous financial interests in this "industry" sector with patents.[1008] In fact, professional sports are more a form of entertainment than sports in the original meaning of the word. On the other hand, patents reduce the entertainment value of games if the players have unequal chances due to unequal patent rights.[1009] That affects business adversely too.

1004 In the UK, games patents are usually treated as software patents: Patents Court 21 July 2005, no. 2005 EWHC 1589 Pat, RPC 2006, p. 5 (*CFPH*); Patents Court 7 November 2005, no. 2005 EWHC 2416 (pat), RPC 2006, p. 7 RPD&TC 293-298 (*Shopalotto*).

1005 *See for instance* art. 9(2) TRIPS and 17 USC § 102(b), a codification of the classical decision: U.S. Supreme Court October 1879, 101 *U.S.* 99, 25 *L. Ed.* 841 (*Baker v. Selden*). *Different*: Schricker 2008, p. 203-04.

1006 *See* Ghosh 2009.

1007 *See* e.g. Kukkonen III 1998; Bambauer 2005.

1008 *See* Kieff, Kramer & Kunstadt 2009.

1009 Bambauer 2005, p. 402, Smith 1999, p. 1083.

The traditional "horizontal" technology criterion would not prevent such sports patents, because – apart from mind games – methods for playing games are even technical according to the strict German "forces of nature"[1010] criterion, since eventually these methods are based on mechanics.

In contrast, the "vertical" technology criterion gives a reason not to grant patents for such methods. The sportsman or sportswoman is not a "person skilled in the art", but rather a person with unique skills that allow him or her to win – and who can never be sure to win. That puts him on a par with an inventor. Sports methods are *skills based inventions*[1011] that give sportsmen ample opportunities to distinguish themselves from "competition" by their skills.[1012]

In sum, irrespective whether the exception is conceived as an exception for methods to play games or to make games, only the vertical technology criterion leads to an understandable and desirable result. Again, a separate statutory exclusion is redundant if all patent applications are tested for vertical technical character.

IV.2.6. Schemes, rules and methods for doing business

According to the EPC, "schemes, rules and methods for doing business as such" are no inventions.[1013]

It is difficult to give a precise definition of "business methods". The placement of these methods together with "mental acts" in Art. 52(3c) EPC shows that business methods are associated with this subject-matter, which is non-technical almost by definition in an age-old German tradition.[1014] Still the EPC does not exclude business methods categorically, but only "as such". As always, EPO interprets

---

[1010] *See* p. 65.
[1011] Arora 2005, p. 18.
[1012] *See* section III.4.1, "Does the new technology concept cover the old?", p. 163.
[1013] Art. 52(2c) EPC (at the end).
[1014] *See* p. 195.

these words in the sense of "as far as non-technical", and it accepts the logical consequence that technical business methods may exist as well, of which there are even examples.[1015] The inference that technical business methods *must* exist if "as such" is interpreted in the usual EPO manner could equally be considered a "proof by contradiction" that these words mean something else here.

If a lack of technical content is not considered distinctive to identify business methods, what else? Application in an economic field is no conclusive criterion either, because eventually every patented invention is destined for an economic purpose, if only because of the statutory requirement of being susceptible of industrial application.[1016] When a commission in 1965 advised the British government to exclude "commercial, financial and propaganda schemes", it expressed already its *hope* that a "comprehensive formula" would be found to prevent attempts to obtain patents for such subject-matter on the grounds that they are of use in industry.[1017] Incidentally, as a basic patent law rule the eventual product does not have to serve a technical purpose: basically there are no objections against patenting business machines.

The USPTO found in the 1990s that its personnel had difficulty in properly treating claims directed to methods of doing business, so it decided that "claims should not be categorized as methods of doing business. Instead such claims should be treated like any other process claims."[1018] In 1998 the CAFC stated that the supposed "business method" exception was a misconception, and it endorsed explicitly the USPTO approach.[1019] It argued that business method patent applications often were rejected for not meeting *general* patentability

[1015] *See* TBA 12 March 1992, no. T 636/88 (*Material distribution/NAT SHIPPING BAGGING SERVICES*).
[1016] E.g. Art. 57 EPC. In U.S. law, patentable inventions must be useful (35 USC § 101, equivalent according to a footnote attached to Art. 27(1) TRIPS).
[1017] PLG 1965, nr 42(iii), p. 13.
[1018] Examination Guidelines, 61 *Fed.Reg.* 7478, 7479 (1996).
[1019] CAFC 23 July 1998, no. 96-1327, 149 *F.3d* 1368, 1377 (*State Street Bank & Trust v. Signature Financial Group*). *See also* p. 85.

criteria, like novelty,[1020] but never explicitly for the reason that they related to business methods.

While the court suggested that nothing really changed, this decision still caused a landslide. It was a total surprise for the USPTO, which was not prepared to handle the flood of often bizarre[1021] business method patent applications that followed, and severe patent quality problems[1022] ensued. The USPTO initiated extensive quality programs[1023] that would have solved the quality problems by now.[1024] Incidentally, some authors argue that never such problems really existed.[1025]

Many applications related to "trivial" business methods, for instance the mere computer automation of a well-known business method. But triviality denotes insufficient inventiveness, and there is no reason to assume that all business methods are trivial. Are there also objections against "non-trivial" high quality business method patents? Doesn't a solid business method that required a multimillion investment deserve patent protection just as much as an invention in a traditional technical field? These questions need a rational answer. Tradition is no convincing objection against business method patents: modern times require modern patents. Courts on both sides of the Atlantic have stated repeatedly that the limits of patentable subject-matter are not static, even in Germany.[1026]

[1020] *Example*: Circuit Court of Appeals, Second Circuit 10 March 1908, 160 *F.* 467, 1908 *U.S. App.* LEXIS 4220 (*Hotel Security Checking v. Lorraine*).
[1021] Thomas 2000, p. 47-48.
[1022] The "patent quality" concept is used in different meanings. Here we deal with *legal* patent quality, which relates to the extent patents meet the statutory requirements. A good legal quality is not sufficient, and occasionally not even necessary for a good *economic* patent quality, a concept related to the commercial, or the social value of patents.
[1023] In March 2000 the USPTO established a "second pair of eyes" review for business method patent applications. Dickinson 2000, p. 399.
[1024] *See* Hunter 2004.
[1025] *See* Allison & Tiller 2003.
[1026] *See* p. 94.

When we developed the theory of the vertical technology concept in the last chapter, we noted that most business methods can not be carried out by any "person skilled in the (pertinent) art". A businessman has the characteristics of an inventor,[1027] because business methods are similar to the ideas and theories that typically are the "input" of an inventor, rather than inventions, that are the "output" of an inventor.[1028] The amount of investment is immaterial for the patentability of business methods no more than for the patentability of scientific theories etcetera.[1029]

The reader may object that certain business methods actually are business procedures that can be carried out very well by any "person skilled in the art", so they still are technical in a "vertical" sense. If such a business method is sufficiently inventive, there is no reason to refuse a patent. That is in line with the fact that business methods are not categorically excluded, on both sides of the Atlantic. This is a consequence of the vagueness of the "business method" concept. Decisive is the vertically technical content rather than the qualification as a "business method".

If the application of the vertical technology criterion to a particular application does not immediately lead to a clear result, then there is the possibility to investigate whether the reasons of this criterion indeed apply to the specific case. For instance, one might consider whether a firm without patent protection for its business method inevitably would fall prey to devastating price competition, or whether there are still sufficient possibilities for *differentiation*.[1030]

Genuine business methods are a fine example of subject-matter that does not need patent protection, even if it occasionally requires huge investments.[1031] Our analysis[1032] shows that patents serve the purpose

---

[1027] *See* p. 138.
[1028] *For a schematic overview see* p. 139.
[1029] *See* p. 146.
[1030] *See* p. 147.
[1031] *See* section III.2.3, "For what subject-matter patents are needed?", p. 140.
[1032] *See* p. 147.

to prevent excessive, detrimental competition in the case that firms are unable to *differentiate* themselves from their competitors,[1033] as an exception to the freedom of competition that is the rule in our western society. A true businessman competes by distinguishing himself on the market, rather than by prohibiting competition by means of patents. A strong firm has no fear for the competition of a "free rider"[1034] who tries to copy his method, because business success requires a special skill beyond mere knowledge.

In sum, we find again that the vertical technical content is the decisive criterion. Because all patent applications should be tested for vertical technical content, there is no need anymore to answer the problematic question whether a patent application perhaps relates to a business method. There are no objections against business method patents because they relate to business methods, but because they usually lack a vertical technical character.

Eventually we agree with the USPTO and the CAFC that business method patent applications – like applications for mathematical algorithms – should not be considered a separate category, but that they must be assessed using the same general criteria as other applications.[1035] Still we do not advocate business method patents: in our perception, these general criteria include the vertical technical character requirement, and that will effectively restrict the patentability of processes usually identified as business methods.[1036]

1033 *See* p. 147.

1034 Cooper Dreyfuss 2000, p. 275.

1035 CAFC 23 July 1998, no. 96-1327, 149 *F.3d* 1368, 1375 (*State Street Bank & Trust v. Signature Financial Group*).

1036 *See also* section III.4.1, "Does the new technology concept cover the old?", p. 163.

IV.2.7. Computer programs

According to the EPC "programs for computers as such" are no inventions, and therefore can not be patented.[1037] Software patentability in the US used to be governed by restrictions on the patenting of algorithms.[1038]

Again, the EPC apparently requires two questions to be answered: does the application relate to a computer program,[1039] and: is it perhaps a "computer program as such"?[1040]

At first sight, the exclusion of computer programs in European patent law serves the purpose to prevent duplication with copyright. While there is some debate whether software really fits into the system of copyright,[1041] legislators nowadays leave no doubt that it is protected by copyright law.[1042] Still there is a demand for software patent protection because copyright law only protects "expressions", not ideas, as becomes apparent from various regulations. The TRIPS Agreement provides: "[c]opyright protection shall extend to expressions and not to ideas, procedures, methods of operation or mathematical concepts as such",[1043] and a nearly identical provision is included in the WIPO Copyright Treaty.[1044] The European software copyright directive excludes "ideas and principles which underlie any element of a computer program, including those which underlie its

---

1037 Art. 52(2c) in conjunction with subsection 3 EPC.

1038 *See* p. 186.

1039 Art. 52(2c) EPC.

1040 Art. 52(3) EPC.

1041 *See for instance* Soltysinski 1990.

1042 E.g. Art. 10(1) TRIPS, Art. 10(1) sub 12° Dutch Copyright Act, § 2(1) sub 1. UrhG, Council Directive 91/250/EEC of 14 May 1991 on the legal protection of computer programs (*OJEC* L 122/42), superseded by Directive 2009/24/EC. 23 April 2009 (*OJ* EC L 111/16). While the American Copyright Act does not explicitly mention software in the (non-limitative) enumeration of copyright-protected subject-matter (17 USC § 102(a)), various other provisions in this Act explicitly refer to software.

1043 Art. 9(2) TRIPS.

1044 Art. 2 WIPO Copyright Treaty.

interfaces".[1045] The German legislator has adopted this provision in its copyright act,[1046] but the Dutch legislator refrained from doing so, because it considered it just obvious that copyright never protects ideas etcetera.[1047] American copyright law does not protect ideas and the like either: "[i]n no case does copyright protection for an original work of authorship extend to any idea, procedure, process, system, method of operation, concept, principle, or discovery [...]".[1048]

This limitation of copyright law does not mean that there is a gap that necessarily must be filled by some other form of protection. On the contrary: generally speaking, ideas are free. Still we can conclude from the above provisions that at least there is no duplication of copyright *if* patent protection is provided for underlying "ideas and principles". The fact that the TRIPS Agreement obliges its member states to provide copyright protection for computer programs as "literary works"[1049] therefore does not imply *a contrario* that patent protection is inappropriate.[1050] Furthermore, TRIPS only sets minimum requirements to legislators, and does not prohibit them to provide more protection.[1051]

A "proof by contradiction" that software patents do not duplicate software copyright is that patents are granted after complicated and costly procedure for a maximum of twenty years from the application, while copyright is provided automatically and applies for

---

[1045] Art. 1(2) Directive 2009/24/EC (*OJEC* 2009 L111/16), formerly Art. 1(2) Directive 91/250/EEC (*OJEC* 1991 L 122/42).

[1046] § 69a(2) UrhG.

[1047] Explanatory Memorandum for the proposal to adapt the Dutch Copyright Act to the European Software Copyright Directive: Wijziging van de Auteurswet 1912 in verband met de rechtsbescherming van computerprogramma's. Memorie van Toelichting: *Kamerstukken II* 1991-1992, 22 531, nr. 3, p. 4.

[1048] 17 USC § 102(b).

[1049] Art. 10(1) TRIPS Agreement.

[1050] In case law this has been stated e.g. in TBA 1 July 1998, no. T 1173/97, 22 *OJ* 1999, p. 609-632, at 2.4 (*Computer Program Product I/IBM*).

[1051] Art 1(1) TRIPS Agreement.

seventy years after the death of the author, so that no one would resort to software patents if copyright would provide the same protection.

While the legal classification of software has always been controversial,[1052] the above analysis shows that so-called software patents do fit in the system of patent law. As always, a distinction must be made between the *invention* and its *realisation*.[1053] A software patent does not protect the programs themselves, but only knowledge that may be used to write programs (the "ideas and principles" in the legislation cited above). A study about the legal aspects of an open source software project notes that indeed software patents mostly deal with external functionality rather than software code implementation details.[1054]

Legislators and courts officially refer to patents on "computer-implemented inventions"[1055] or "computer-related inventions"[1056] rather than "software patents". At first sight, this terminology serves the purpose to make a distinction with "software as such", since that is not patentable under the European Patent Convention.[1057] But Americans use these terms too,[1058] although American patent law

---

1052 Kolle 1974a, p. 10. He gives thirteen perceptions on software, seven of which are a reason to allow patent protection and six are not.
1053 *See* p. 136.
1054 Sedlmaier & Gigerich 2005, Abs. 148.
1055 The term "computer-implemented invention" was introduced by the EPO, and since 2001 it is used in the EPO *Examination Guidelines*. *See* EPO Case Law 2010, Section 2.4, p. 16 and EPO Examination Guidelines 2010, Part C, Chapter IV, section 2.3.6. This term was also central to a – meanwhile rejected – European Directive proposal: Proposal for a Directive of the European Parliament and of the Council on the patentability of computer-implemented inventions, Brussels, 20 February 2002.
1056 *See* TBA 15 July 1986, no. T 208/84, 10 *OJ* 1987, p. 14 (*Computer-Related Invention/VICOM*).
1057 Art. 52(2c) and (3) EPC.
1058 USPTO, *Examination Guidelines For Computer-Related Inventions* http://www.uspto.gov/web/offices/pac/dapp/pdf/ciig.pdf.

usually refers to "algorithms" for subject-matter that would be designated as "software" in Europe.[1059]

The present president[1060] of the tenth civil panel of the German Federal Supreme Court, responsible for patents law also criticises the designation "software patent":[1061]

> The "software patent" concept, popular and often used in a polemical sense in the political debate, ought to be avoided. Frequently it does not properly reflect the substance. The patents thus designated usually do not involve the patenting of a program, but rather a technical teaching, that may be implemented with a computer program. Such a program usually is not even remotely the object of the patent claim however.

The designation "software patent" is also inappropriate for the reason that the inventive concept of such a patent nearly always can be implemented in hardware as well. And even in the exceptional case that only a realisation in software is possible,[1062] still the inventive concept must be distinguished from its implementation. So "software" is not a characteristic of a category of patented subject-matter, but just a possible means for realisation. Consequently it is incorrect to consider a hardware and a software realisation of the same inventive concept separate inventions, let alone to judge their patentability differently. Otherwise a hardware patent might be

---

[1059] *See* p. 83.

[1060] Peter Meier-Beck was appointed in September 2010 as the President of the 10th Civil Panel ("Senat") of the German Federal Supreme Court (BGH).

[1061] Meier-Beck 2007, footnote 1. Translated by the author of this study from the German: „Den in der politischen Diskussion beliebten und häufig in polemischer Absicht verwendeten Begriff der "Softwarepatente" sollte man vermeiden. Er trifft regelmäßig die Sache nicht. Bei den so bezeichneten Patenten geht es typischerweise nicht darum, dass ein Computerprogramm patentiert würde, sondern vielmehr um eine technische Lehre, die mit Hilfe eines Computerprogramms ausgeführt werden kann. Ein solches Programm ist aber in aller Regel auch nicht ansatzweise Gegenstand des Patentanspruchs."

[1062] Think of a programming language element. *See* Bergstra & Klint 2007.

circumvented by a non-patentable software implementation of effectively the same invention.[1063]

Specifically in the European context the designation "computer-implemented invention" is also wrong for the reason that the "invention" concept in European terminology is reserved for patent-eligible subject-matter,[1064] which is patentable if it is novel and sufficiently inventive as well, while the term actually relates to a category of applications that still have to pass all assessment steps.

Particularly confusing was the following definition in the former European Directive proposal:[1065]

> "computer-implemented invention" means any invention the performance of which involves the use of a computer, computer network or other programmable apparatus and having one or more prima facie novel features which are realised wholly or partly by means of a computer program or computer programs;

This definition confuses applications and inventions too, and refers to an implementation choice which is irrelevant for the nature of the subject-matter of the application. Additionally, it makes the mistake to involve novelty aspects in the subject-matter qualification. Novelty is not a property but a factor dependent on the "state of the art".

In sum, designations such as "computer-implemented invention" or "computer-related invention" are just as incorrect as the designation "software patent", because they associate a property of the implementation with the invention, which is a different object.

[1063] TBA 15 July 1986, no. T 208/84, 10 *OJ* 1987, p. 14, at 16 (*Computer-Related Invention/VICOM*). *See* p. 61 for an example under Dutch law.

[1064] Patentable subject-matter under the EPC is subject-matter that not excluded by of Art. 52(2) and (3) EPC. *See also* Section II.1.4, "Terminology", p. 19.

[1065] Art. 2(a) of the Proposal for a Directive of the European Parliament and of the Council on the patentability of computer-implemented inventions, Brussels, 20 February 2002.

The fact that it is actually no distinct category also becomes apparent from the practical difficulties in recognising this type of patents. It might be in the interest of an applicant to draft his patent application in such a way that it is not associated with software, in view of software patentability limitations. Usually this strategy is legitimate: the description in a patent application does not have to reveal more details than needed by a "person skilled in the art" to make an implementation,[1066] and often it can be left to this person whether he prefers a software implementation, and how he programmes that implementation. Furthermore, due to technological developments the distinction between hardware and software is blurred in certain cases.[1067]

Writers who proposed a special regulation for software patents[1068] struggled with the problem how to recognise applications for these patents, and they solved the problem by proposing a reversal of the burden of proof: they proposed that the applicant of a "suspect" patent could only escape from the proposed specific obligations if he could make plausible that there is a technically and economically feasible hardware implementation alternative.[1069]

Economic researchers too face the problem that software patents are no clear category. The *International Patent Classification* system[1070] has been used to select "software patents" from patent databases,[1071] but most researchers feel a need to resort to the actual text of the

[1066] Art. 83 EPC. Similarly: Art. 25(1) ROW 1995, § 34(4) PatG, Section 14(3) UK Patents Act, 35 USC § 112, Art. 29(1) TRIPS.
[1067] E.g. there are "Field Programmable Gate Arrays", chips that are configured by the user (rather than the manufacturer) to perform the desired function using a "hardware description language". The tool is (special) software, the result is hardware. *See also e.g.* Wirth 1998.
[1068] In particular they advocated an obligation to supply the source code for software patent applications.
[1069] Weyand & Haase 2005, p. 661.
[1070] http://www.wipo.int/classifications/ipc/en.
[1071] Graham & Mowery 2003, p. 231-232.

patents.[1072] Even methods have been applied originally designed to filter "spam" e-mail (based on "Bayesian" statistics).[1073] According to literature "the act of defining areas of technology in today's world is as much art as it is science".[1074]

While the designation "programs for computers" is actually inappropriate in a patent law context, it is even harder to decide what the "programs for computers as such" are the EPC refers to. The legislative history gives no clue how should this designation should be understood,[1075] and we found that a literal interpretation in the sense of "as far as limited to" leads to contradictions,[1076] actually because the designation "programs for computers" is inappropriate here, as explained above.

For software too, the EPO considers "as such" the opposite of "technical", so the EPC excludes nontechnical software. With the classical "horizontal" technology concept this conception leads to a straight contradiction, because in the eyes of the EPO actually all software is technical, so nontechnical software does not exist.[1077] The EPO concluded that merely software with a "further technical effect" could be patentable.[1078] The BGH followed with a similar "peculiarity" requirement,[1079] which confirms that a contradiction is unavoidable with the chosen premises.

But actually the observed contradiction proves by contradiction the inappropriateness of the traditional "horizontal" technology concept in patent law. The theory of the vertical technology concept provides relief, because it acknowledges that *knowledge* about a technical

---

[1072] Bessen & Hunt 2007, p. 163-167 and 185.
[1073] *See e.g.* http://www.neurologic.se/gauss.
[1074] Allison & Lemley 2000, p. 2109.
[1075] *See* p. 34.
[1076] *See* p. 35.
[1077] Literature criticises the perception that software would ever be non-technical. *See for instance* Broy & Lehmann 1992, p. 423. Broy is a prominent German computer science professor.
[1078] *See* p. 56.
[1079] "Eigenheit" in German. *See* p.77.

product produced by technical *people* is not necessarily technical: an unelaborated idea[1080] insufficient for a programmer (as a "person skilled in the art") is not "vertically" technical, even if it is an idea to write a program that is undeniably technical.

In sum, "programs for computers as such" in the EPC should be interpreted as knowledge about software lacking a *vertical* technical character. This interpretation is consistent with the law of treaties, which requires treaty terms to be interpreted "in their context and in the light of its object and purpose".[1081]

This interpretation not only eliminates the contradiction caused by the traditional technology concept in an elegant way, it also prevents patents for mere unelaborated ideas, which is a problem for software in particular.[1082] The present "horizontal" technology requirement does not prevent such so-called "wish list patents".[1083] Note that a distinction must be made between qualitative and quantitative elaboration. Vertically technical knowledge is sufficiently elaborated for any "person skilled in the art" to be handled. The fact that he still may have years of work to do is something else. Only if the *nature* of the work still to be accomplished, using the knowledge recorded in the patent application, is such that it can not be left to an average person skilled in the art, that knowledge is not vertically technical, so in our perception it is not patentable.

Another problem is that a single product that uses software is often covered by numerous "software patents", which leads to the "tragedy of the anticommons",[1084] which enables undesired "strategic" use of these patents.[1085] As we explained, the theory of the vertical

---

[1080] *See* section III.2.2, "For what subject-matter patents are suitable?", p. 136.
[1081] Art. 31(1) VCLT.
[1082] Kiesewetter-Köbinger 2001, p. 191.
[1083] German: *Lastenheftpatente*. *See* http://www.patentverein.de/verein.php.
[1084] *See* Heller 1998. Do not confuse this concept with the more widely known "tragedy of the commons".
[1085] *See* Section III.3.4, "Reducing detrimental side-effects", p. 159.

technology concept gives reasons not to grant patents for parts of products that can not exist as independent products,[1086] like interfaces.[1087] So there is no reason to allow interfaces to be patented, even though they are not protected by copyright either.[1088] While this is perhaps an unexpected conclusion, limitation of interface patentability is definitely desirable from a social point of view.[1089] That may seem unjust towards inventors of interfaces, but one should acknowledge that interfaces often are by no means technologically advanced, but borrow their value solely from "network effects".[1090] Interfaces may even be "non-obvious" in a negative sense: due to these very network effects there is a hurdle to get improved interfaces accepted by a sufficient number of users, so that technically obsolete interfaces often remain in use for many years.[1091]

In sum, we conclude that also for subject-matter associated with computer programs[1092] a vertical technology test gives a desired result, which implies that the impossible question whether the patent application is perhaps "software-related" does not have to be answered.

IV.2.8. Aesthetic creations

According to Art. 52(2)b and (3) EPC, "aesthetic creations as such" are no inventions, and can not be patented therefore. In American patent law there is no comparable exclusion. Apparently it is rather the opposite: the American patent act contains provisions especially

[1086] *See* p. 149.
[1087] Interfaces are often mentioned in one breath with standards, but here interfaces are the essence, although a popular interface is (at least) a *de facto* standard.
[1088] Art 1.2 Directive 2009/24/EC on the legal protection of computer programs.
[1089] *See for instance* Patterson 2002. *See also* Mueller 2002.
[1090] Blind 2004 p. 28-37. *See also* Lemley & McGowan 1998.
[1091] A fine example are the commonly used internet e-mail protocols.
[1092] We refer to an association that is factually made, for instance in Art. 52(2) EPC, and do not give an opinion here whether this association is correct in view of the above criticisms on the "software patent" concept.

for "design patents",[1093] but actually this regulation protects industrial designs rather than inventions.[1094] Literature shows that in the United States art and entertainment are eligible for patent,[1095] not just for design patents but also for "genuine" invention patents.

Unlike the other exclusions of art. 52(2) EPC this exclusion has no long tradition. It is not included in the lists of exclusions associated with the PCT[1096] that otherwise were an important example for the EPC framers,[1097] and it is not mentioned either in the *Banks Report,* that does mention other subject-matter excluded by the EPC as unpatentable subject-matter.[1098] An exception is the report by the British *Patents Liaison Group* (PLG) that recommended to exclude "designs and arrangements in which the novelty resides solely in appeal to the eye", in order to prevent overlap with industrial design protection.[1099] Remarkably, there was never a similar exclusion in American patent law, while all other EPC exclusions have (or had) an American counterpart.

At first sight, the exclusion of "aesthetic creations (as such)" simply aims at delimiting patent law from other legal systems. While the above PLG Report referred to industrial design protection, an even more obvious alternative is copyright, which in particular protects aesthetics as artistic works.[1100] But – just like for software – it must be a fallacy that this subject-matter is excluded from patentability for that reason, because why would one go through the hassle of a patent application if copyright would automatically[1101] provide sufficient

[1093] 35 USC § 171-173.
[1094] The patents discussed in this study ought to be distinguished as *invention patents.*
[1095] *See* Aharonian & Stim 2004.
[1096] Rule 39 and 67 Regulations under the PCT.
[1097] *See* p. 33.
[1098] Banks 1970, p. 62, nr. 213.
[1099] PLG 1965, nr. 42(v), p. 13.
[1100] Art. 1 Berne Convention.
[1101] Art. 5(2) Berne Convention: copyright is recognised without any formalities.

protection, and for a much longer term?[1102] While a design model right is not obtained automatically, it is still obtained much easier than an (invention) patent, if only because the registration[1103] of a model does not involve a substantive assessment. The rule that "[a] design right shall not subsist in features of appearance of a product which are solely dictated by its technical function"[1104] prevents circumvention of the more strict requirements of patent law by means of design model law. So as far as a delimitation is needed it is rather in the opposite direction.

The exclusion of "aesthetic creations" is also peculiar, because the general rule is that the eventual field of use of a product is immaterial for patentability.[1105] Several EPO decisions[1106] depart from this principle by questioning the patentability if an aesthetic result is pursued, even if technical means are used, and understandably literature is critical.[1107] But the use of technical means is not a meaningful criterion either, because unmistakable works of art usually are realised with technical means too. A writer notes that even a *Rembrandt* can be considered a "technical" object, because it reaches its aesthetic effect using technical means: paint-brush, oil paint and linen.[1108] For a bronze statue, the roles of the sculptor as an artist and the bronze-founder as a technician still are separate, but an industrial

---

[1102] Copyright usually applies for 70 years from the death of the author, a patent is usually valid for 20 years at most from the moment of application.
[1103] Art. 3(1) European Directive 98/71/EC on the legal protection of designs.
[1104] Art. 7(1) European Directive 98/71/EC on the legal protection of designs.
[1105] *See* for instance p. 113 for German law. Likewise, a Dutch court decided that a recipe for a tomato-plum jam was patentable: Board of Appeal of the Dutch Patent Office, 9 January 1947, 15 *BIE* 1947, p. 169-170 (*Tomato-plum jam*).
[1106] *See* TBA 21 April 1993, no. T 962/91 (*Plattenförmige Informationsträger/ POLYGRAM*); TBA 25 April 1989, no. T 119/88, 13 *OJ* 1990, p. 395 (*Coloured Disk Jacket/FUJI*).
[1107] Melullis 2002, Art. 52, Rn. 174.
[1108] Nack 2002, p. 244.

designer or architect combine the qualities of a technician and an artist to the extent that no boundary can be drawn.

According to the theory of the vertical technology concept it is irrelevant for patent law whether the creativity of the inventor is technical or artistic, and whether the product is a work of art or a technical achievement. According to this theory, a design, whether technical, artistic or both, is only patentable if it can be realised by any relevant "person skilled in the art". This person may not be expected to be creative, while the inventor must be creative, perhaps in an artistic sense too.[1109] Seen from the other side, an artist is more an inventor than a "person skilled in the art".[1110] An artistic idea that still must be worked out by an artist is insufficiently technical in the vertical sense to be patented. Copyright only protects "expressions", no "ideas",[1111] and the theory of the vertical technology concept shows why patent law should not protect artistic ideas either.

As an example of artistic knowledge lacking a vertical technical character we mention the rather bizarre but still illustrative idea of an American patent attorney to patent storylines,[1112] i.e. plots at a level of abstraction beyond the reach of copyright law. The USPTO so far rejected these applications, but that was not as obvious as one might think, as becomes apparent from worried comments,[1113] even from abroad.[1114] The theory of the vertical technology concept clarifies that these patents should not be granted because a storyline is not technical in the vertical sense, since its elaboration requires artistic creativity again and cannot be left to any "person skilled in the art".

[1109] *See* p. 138.

[1110] *See* the scheme on p. 139.

[1111] *See* note 1005 on p. 199.

[1112] *See* Knight 2004, Knight 2007. The author promotes his services on http://www.plotpatents.com.

[1113] *See* 'Pure Fiction: the Attempt to Patent Plot' 2005, Manevitz 2006, Sawkar 2008.

[1114] *See* McEniery 2009.

In sum, we find that there is no need either to adopt specific rules for "aesthetic creations", as long as patent applications are consistently tested for vertical technical character.

IV.2.9. Presentations of information

According to Art. 52(2d) EPC "presentations of information"[1115] are no invention, but again only "as such" according to subsection 3 of this provision.

Literally, the words "presentations of information" have a very wide reach: apparently they encompass the entire realm of information and communication technology, from modulation techniques and encoding schemes to communication protocols, data formats and interface specifications. However, the intent of this exclusion was only to reflect the age-old conception that no patent should be granted for applications only containing novel information *content*.[1116] In American patent law, the conception is known as the *printed matter doctrine*.[1117] Germans consider this type subject-matter as one of the two forms of *directions to the human mind*,[1118] and a British committee simply noted that such subject-matter was "never" considered an invention.[1119]

The wording of this exclusion was borrowed again[1120] from provisions in the *Regulations* under the *Patent Cooperation Treaty* (PCT)[1121] that was adopted shortly before EPC.[1122] Already during the

---

[1115] The rather odd plural form is also used in the authentic text in French, but not in German.

[1116] Kolle 1974b, p. 152-153, with further references.

[1117] Nack 2002, p. 45-56.

[1118] Elben 1960. In Section IV.2.4, "Schemes, rules and methods for performing mental acts", p. 194 we saw that this designation is also used in a more literal sense for information content that may be executed.

[1119] Banks 1970, nr. 213, p. 62.

[1120] The same applies for the other exclusions. *See* p. 33.

[1121] Art. 39.1 sub (v) PCT rules excludes "mere presentations of information". *For details, see* p. 33.

[1122] Kolle 1974b, p. 152.

PCT negotiations there was a debate whether the designation "presentations of information" was sufficiently clear, and the British delegation proposed to use the following wording instead: "designs or arrangements which serve only to convey information and in which the novelty resides solely in the information conveyed or in the form in which the information is presented", but that proposal was rejected. When the EPC was negotiated, a British delegation again proposed to clarify the confusing designation "presentations of information",[1123] but that proposal was rejected too, this time with the argument that too precise a definition might look narrower than the PCT wording,[1124] and would exclude less than intended. Shortly before the EPO was adopted a German writer qualified this exclusion in the wordings chosen as "very questionable".[1125]

Indeed the EPO has fallen prey to the confusion the British feared for.[1126] The EPO still interpreted this exclusion in its literal meaning, and questioned the patentability in cases involving the presentation of information by various equipment rather than information contents itself.[1127] While these cases clearly relate to techniques, often doubts were raised whether these methods were sufficiently technical to be patentable. Another questionable rule is the exclusion of presentations targeted at *human people,*[1128] because that excludes all kinds of audiovisual equipment and measurement tools. Why should technical equipment be excluded that happens to be used for the presentation of information to people? Still one may question the patentability of a presentation method that is designed solely from an ergonomic or even aesthetic perspective, and involves no novel

---

[1123] Kolle 1974b, p. 153.
[1124] Pila 2005b, p. 765.
[1125] Zipse 1973, p. 188.
[1126] *For an overview of pertinent EPO case law see* EPO Case Law 2010, Section I.A.2.6, p. 33-35.
[1127] *See* TBA 14 March 1989, no. T 163/85, 13 *OJ* 1990, p. 379 (*Colour television signal/BBC*); TBA 15 March 2000, no. T 1194/97, 23 *OJ* 2000, p. 525 (*Data structure product/PHILIPS*).
[1128] Melullis 2002, Art. 52, Rn. 221.

technology. Then the application may be assessed as an aesthetic creation following the criteria as explained in the last section.[1129]

In the United States, the "printed matter doctrine" is understood in its original meaning: as an impediment to patent mere information content. For instance, no patent was granted for the "invention" to add new directions for use to an otherwise unaltered kit for biotechnological research,[1130] and the idea to add tips for a more effective use of an existing medicine suffered the same fate.[1131]

For an assessment according to the theory of the vertical technology concept the criterion is what kind of *knowledge* is involved. Any factory-worker "skilled in the art" may add directions for use to a product, but it is by no means a novel invention, even if the directions contain novel information. That information may be valuable and inventive, but it is carried out by the buyer of the product rather than the manufacturer. As far as industrially applicable knowledge is involved, it may be patented as an invention in its own right, rather than as a product containing the information.

In sum, the problem with "Presentations of information" is the confusion what they really are, rather than the question when they could be patentable. The theory of the vertical technology concept provides clarification by requiring the *knowledge* in the application to be identified and assessed, even if the application refers to a product.

IV.2.10. Conclusion on the non-inventions of Art. 52(2) EPC

In the preceding sections we found that the "vertical" technology test is sufficient to limit the patentability of the specific subject-matter that is currently submitted in Europe to a "horizontal" technology test. For that reason, and because the theory of the vertical technology concept implies that all applications should be tested for

---

[1129] *See* Section IV.2.8, "Aesthetic creations", p. 213.

[1130] *See* CAFC 13 May 2004, no. 03-1524, 367 *F.3d* 1336 (*In re Ngai*).

[1131] *See* CAFC 2 August 2010, no. 2009-1437, 2009-1438, 616 *F.3d* 1267 (*King Pharmaceuticals. v. Eon Labs*).

"vertical" technical content, there is no need anymore to decide first whether an application belongs to one of the categories the EPC excludes "as such", an assessment that is often difficult and occasionally fundamentally impossible.[1132]

That confirms[1133] that Art. 52 subsection 2 conjunction with subsection 3 EPC can be interpreted in the sense of a vertical technical character requirement. As suggested by the words "in particular" in its beginning, the subject-matter categories listed in subsection 2 are to be considered as examples: perhaps it is more likely that patent applications related to this kind of subject-matter are non-technical, but by itself such subject-matter is not necessarily non-technical, as was confirmed by our observations in the preceding sections.

Mutatis mutandis the situation in the United States is similar in many respects. American courts established late last century already that it makes no sense to decide whether an application relates to a mathematical algorithm or a business method, because this subject matter is not excluded *because*, but only *as far as* it is overly abstract, and that the assessment of this subject-matter too should be based on the *general* patentability criteria. The Americans made the mistake though to consider a "useful concrete and tangible result" the general criterion, because it proved to be much too broad. Now that the "machine and transformation test" was recently rejected by the U.S. Supreme Court, there is no clear alternative. Perhaps the vertical technology criterion can provide relief.

[1132] We remind the reader of the classification problems we met in the preceding sections e.g. for "computer-implemented inventions" and business methods.

[1133] *See* section III.4.4, "Interpretation of the present rules in the light of the findings", p. 167.

IV.3. The vertical technology concept in American patent law

If the patent law domain is *inherently* restricted to ("vertically") technical subject-matter, how could American courts categorically reject a "technological arts test"?

Still we found that the exclusion of "abstract ideas" in U.S. patent law is somehow comparable.[1134] Interestingly, American case law from the time that this exclusion was developed – the 19th and early 20th century – shows criteria remarkably similar to the vertical technical character requirement we developed. From the late 1960s, these criteria somehow fell into oblivion, and a cumbersome quest started for new criteria, in particular for the patentability of algorithms, and late last century also for business methods.[1135] Could a return to the 170 years old roots of the "abstract ideas" exclusion be helpful to bring a solution nearer?

An important source of inspiration for the 19th century case law of the Supreme Court of the then still young United States[1136] about the limits of patentable subject-matter was a British decision in 1841 about a blast furnace. In order to make the distinction between a mere principle and a true invention the court posed the question whether "the inventor has given sufficient information to the public by which the invention can, on the expiration of the term for which the patent is granted, be brought into public use without experiments or expense".[1137]

In 1854 the Supreme Court referred to this decision when it decided that *Samuel Morse*, the inventor of the Morse code, was not allowed to claim future applications of – what we would call nowadays – electronic data communication, because that would cause the patent

[1134] *See* p. 82.

[1135] *See in particular* p. 83.

[1136] Prior to 1836, patent applications were not substantially substantively examined in the U.S. *See* Risch 2012.

[1137] Court of Exchequer 26 June 1841, 151 E.R. 1266, 1272 *(Neilson v. Harford)*.

to cover more than what Morse had actually invented, and block future developments.[1138] The U.S. Supreme Court again referred to the above British decision when it invalidated a patent on a certain principle to joint lead pipes, saying that: "a principle is not patentable. A principle, in the abstract, is a fundamental truth; an original cause; a motive; these cannot be patented, as no one can claim in either of them an exclusive right".[1139] Similarly, mere ideas are not patentable, as became apparent when the U.S. Supreme Court decided that the idea to attach an india-rubber to the tip of a pencil was not patentable because "[a]n idea of itself is not patentable, but a new device by which it may be made practically useful is. The idea of this patentee was a good one, but his device to give it effect, though useful, was not new. Consequently he took nothing by his patent."[1140] The difference between an abstract principle and a patentable invention was further clarified by the decision that a particular hydrolysis method for the production of glycerine from fats was patentable, because a *specific* solution was elaborated in detail, leaving other solutions free.[1141]

An important decision from the last century about the difference between abstract ideas and patentable subject-matter notes that "[w]hile a scientific truth, or the mathematical expression of it, is not [a] patentable invention, a novel and useful structure created with the aid of knowledge of scientific truth may be."[1142] Decisive is – again – whether an application has been elaborated, in this case a specific antenna. Subsequently the court decided that a certain breeding method was not patentable because it was a trivial application of a natural phenomenon. Although the phenomenon was not known before, patentability was denied because "[h]e who discovers a hitherto unknown phenomenon of nature has no claim to a

[1138] U.S. Supreme Court 30 January 1854, 56 *U.S.* 62, 112 (*O'Reilly v. Morse*).
[1139] U.S. Supreme Court 10 January 1853, 55 *U.S.* 156, 175 (*Le Roy v. Tatham*).
[1140] U.S. Supreme Court 1874, 87 *U.S.* (20 Wall.) 498, 507 (*Rubber-Tip Pencil Company v. Howard*).
[1141] *See* U.S. Supreme Court 1880, 102 *U.S.* 707 (*Tilghman v. Proctor*).
[1142] U.S. Supreme Court 30 January 1939, no. 127, 306 *U.S.* 86, 94, 59 *S.Ct.* 427, 431 (*Mackay Radio v. RCA*).

monopoly of it which the law recognizes. If there is to be invention from such a discovery, it must come from the application of the law of nature to a new and useful end.".[1143]

Again and again, the pattern is the same: "a patent is not a hunting license", as the Supreme Court once summarised.[1144] Whatever is claimed, should be described in such a way that it can be carried out by every person skilled in the pertinent art.[1145] That excludes mere theories, ideas and facts that can not be described in such a manner at all. So actually the Americans applied a vertical technology criterion – in our terminology – from mid-nineteenth century.

That only changed when around 1970 confusion arose about the patentability of software, and the "mathematical algorithms" contained in software, which was exacerbated by the persistent misconception that the American legislator wanted "anything under the sun made by man" to be patentable, while Congress actually said the very opposite.[1146]

Still there is hope. Recently the Supreme Court decided[1147] unanimously that mere knowledge a physician may use to determine the optimum dose of certain medicines can not be patented, because mere scientific facts still are not patentable.[1148] This decision follows the above tradition, and it shows again that not all costly or valuable knowledge is susceptible for patent.

[1143] U.S. Supreme Court 16 February 1948, no. 280, 333 *U.S.* 127, 130, 68 *S.Ct.* 440, 441, 92 L. Ed. 588, 592 (*Funk v. Kalo*).

[1144] U.S. Supreme Court 21 March 1966, no. 58, 383 *U.S.* 519, 536, 86 *S.Ct.* 1033, 1042 (*Brenner v. Manson*).

[1145] 35 USC § 112.

[1146] U.S. Supreme Court 28 June 2010, no. 08-964, 130 *S.Ct.* 3218, 3248-49 (*Bilski v. Kappos*).

[1147] *See* U.S. Supreme Court 20 March 2012, no. 10-1150, 132 *S.Ct.* 1289 (*Mayo v. Prometheus*).

[1148] In particular it is knowledge about the blood level of certain transformation products ("metabolites") below which the medicine is ineffective and the blood level above which harmful side-effects may occur.

IV.4. Finally

In this chapter we found that indeed various traditional exceptions in patent law can be brought on the common denominator of the vertical technology criterion. Because this criterion is inherent to the system of patent law, it is a *general* criterion, so there is no need to investigate first whether an application relates to a "suspect" category, like the categories listed in Art. 52(2) EPC in Europe, and "mathematical algorithms" and business methods in the US.

Some writers argue that a *One Size Fits All* patent law system is no longer appropriate nowadays, in view of the increasing diversity in subject-matter.[1149] The results of this chapter indicate that a *One System Fits All* patent law is definitely feasible. Ever more complicated rules make it difficult to see the forest for the trees, so it helps to abstract from the details and to concentrate on *general* rules that are rooted in the system of patent law, like the vertical technology criterion. Furthermore, specific rules for specific subject-matter is often a remedy worse than the disease, since they require a qualification of patent applications that is often problematic if not outright impossible, as we have seen in this chapter.

[1149] *See for instance* Kahin 2007 and Burk & Lemley 2009, p. 37-92.

V. To conclude

V.1. Concluding summary

Broadly speaking, this study consists of three parts: a comparative investigation into the positive law related to the assessment of the technical content of patent applications,[1150] the development of a new technology criterion,[1151] and finally an investigation whether the new technology criterion is usable as a general criterion to delimit patentable subject-matter.[1152]

The present situation is unsatisfactory, both in Europe and the United States. While the technology requirement has been codified in Europe some years ago,[1153] it is still unclear how the technical content of patent applications should be assessed. Is common parlance decisive, if it is unambiguous at all, or is "technology" a legal concept here, and is the technology criterion meant to serve any underlying purpose? Subsequently the question must be answered how (allegedly) partially technical applications should be assessed: should these "mixed" applications be assessed as a whole, as required by a principal rule of patent law, or should the technical aspects of the application coincide with the novel aspects? While at first sight the latter approach seems preferable, the principal rule can not be ignored, and occasionally it even leads to more satisfactory results. Still both approaches cannot coexist. The result is opaque case law that often pays lip service to the one approach while actually applying the other, so complaints are rife, both from puzzled lawyers and from interested parties who complain about a patent policy that is too broad or rather too narrow.

1150 Chapter II: "Positive law", p. 11.
1151 Chapter III: "Towards a better technology criterion", p. 133.
1152 Chapter IV: 'The application of the "vertical" technology criterion', p. 177.
1153 Art. 52(1) EPC, since "EPC 2000" went into force on 13 December 2007. Whether the words "in all fields of technology" in this provision really codify the technology requirement has been discussed on p. 29. In any case that is their intent.

In the United States too the boundaries of the patent law domain are unclear. American courts reject a technology requirement, but they acknowledge an "abstract ideas" exclusion. But what is an abstract idea, given the fact that all inventions are teachings that are abstract to some extent? In course of time, courts have adopted various rules to distinguish "abstract ideas", and all of these interpretations were rejected sooner or later, lately the "machine or transformation test". And the Americans too struggle with the paradoxical question how to assess applications allegedly partially consisting of patentable subject-matter. Should the principal "whole contents" rule be maintained for those applications, or should a practical but obvious application of a by itself inventive "abstract idea" be considered "insignificant post-solution activity" and ignored for the assessment of this type of "mixed" invention?

Should one really choose between two evils? Is there perhaps an other possibility? We considered that often the suggestion is made that patent law is *naturally* limited to technology, and that likewise (overly) abstract ideas *naturally* are not susceptible for patent. What are the *inherent* limits of the patent system? Is there a logical relationship between the contents of the rights of a patentee and the object? And what is the economic function of patents? How does the idea of patent protection relate to the principle of freedom of competition, that rejects protective measures? Is it a shortcoming or rather an indication that patent law does protect coincidental inventions that did not require any investment, while it does not protect the results of multimillion basic research?

Answering these questions leads to the conclusion, that patent law is only suitable *and* needed for *knowledge ready to be carried out by any person skilled in the (pertinent) art*. In common parlance, this type of knowledge is called *technical* knowledge, in contrast to purely theoretical knowledge. Thus we find that indeed patent law should (and can) limit itself to technology, but that "technology" should be considered an attribute of a certain quality of *knowledge*, rather than a designation of certain *products* (or product features) or certain *disciplines*, as it is considered hitherto in patent law.

We denominated the new technology concept as "vertical", because technical knowledge elaborates theoretical knowledge, so there is a hierarchical relationship, while the traditional, "horizontal" technology concept relates to product features or disciplines on a peer level.

By focussing on the quality of knowledge, there is no more "mixed patent application" paradox. Of course, the "vertically" technical knowledge must suffice to carry out the invention *as a whole*. It is immaterial whether the inventor is a technician, artist, business person or perhaps combines all three skills. The only thing that matters is whether the inventor delivers knowledge any "person skilled in the art" can carry out in a straightforward manner, without further experimentation, and without a need for further creativity.

The inherent limits we found should match the limits presented as inherent in present law. That gives new insights for the interpretation of Art. 52 EPC, and 35 USC § 101. Thus we find, at last, how the European exclusions "as such" should be interpreted, and how the American exclusion of "abstract ideas" should be conceived. Although American courts always rejected a *technological arts test* in patent law, there is apparently still an inherent limitation related to technology somehow. Incidentally, the interpretation we derived here is fully in concert with existing statutes and treaties, while the traditional "horizontal" technology concept leads to a controversy between the European Patent Office and British courts in particular, and in its effects it is also criticised in literature, even in Germany, the country where the technology criterion originates.[1154]

In the third part of this study we found that the new technology criterion provides a sufficient requirement for the subject-matter listed in Art. 52(2) EPC. In the present interpretation, first an assessment must be made whether an application relates to one of the "suspect" categories, and if it does, an assessment must be made whether it is sufficiently technical, or relates to just the pertinent subject-matter "as such". Since the vertical technology requirement naturally applies to all

[1154] *See for instance* Von Hellfeld 2008 and Klaiber 2010. For further information, please refer to the preceding chapters.

patent applications, there is no need anymore for the former assessment. That is a major benefit, because in practice the former assessment often leads to confusion, and sometimes it is even outright impossible.

While American patent law has the reputation to be very different from European patent law, we noted that the U.S. Supreme Court actually applied some sort of vertical technology criterion since the nineteenth century. That only changed when software patents emerged around 1970, and business methods around the last turn of the century. Fortunately, in recent years there is a turn on the tide now that the U.S. Supreme Court interfered in the debate about the bounds of "patentable subject-matter", and refers to the historical precedents some of which are over 150 years old. The often repeated assertion that Congress had said that "anything under the sun made by man" should be patentable was only recently identified as a misconception by the U.S. Supreme Court: if this phrase is read in its context, it becomes apparent that Congress actually said the very opposite.[1155]

V.2. *The answer to the research question*

In the introduction of this study we phrased the following research question:[1156]

> *What are the inherent boundaries of the patent law domain, and are they related to "technology", in any meaning?*

In this study we established that inherent to the patent system there is only reason to grant patents for *knowledge any relevant "person skilled in the art" can carry out,* and that this type of knowledge is technical in common parlance, in contrast to theoretical knowledge, mere ideas and bare facts, that may be useful as well, but do not fit in a patent law system.

[1155] U.S. Supreme Court 28 June 2010, no. 08-964, 130 S.Ct. 3218, 3248-49 (*Bilski v. Kappos*).
[1156] Section I.2, p. 3.

At first sight, this conclusion merely confirms what was always considered self-evident in a German tradition: patents are only for technology. We found however that the usual distinction between technical and nontechnical *products*, or between technical and nontechnical *disciplines* leads to insurmountable problems, because products often consist of mixtures of technical and non-technical elements, and/or are the result of a multidisciplinary effort, apparently requiring a dissection irreconcilable with the basic rule that patent applications must always be assessed as a whole. The result is inconsistent case law that is an obstacle to European patent law harmonisation and even is said to violate the EPC.[1157] These problems are solved if a distinction is made between technical and nontechnical *knowledge* in the above sense.

The focus on *inherent* boundaries is a limitation of this study, but the benefit is that our findings logically follow from the system of patent law, so they can convince rational proponents of a broader or narrower patent law as well. Another benefit of concentrating on inherent boundaries is that consequently our findings naturally apply to all patent law systems, including the American patent law system. While U.S. Courts reject a "technological arts test", they recognise the exclusion of "abstract ideas", and such ideas are actually non-technical, in the above sense.

Obviously the technical character is still just a *necessary* condition. Patentability is further restricted by policy exclusions and in particular by the inventive step requirement. But a necessary condition implies that other subject-matter is not patent-eligible, however inventive it may be. In particular, our analysis shows that there is an *inherent* reason not to grant business method patents,[1158] irrespective of whether they are "trivial" or the result of a multimillion euro project.

[1157] *See for instance* Klaiber 2010.

[1158] In this conclusion paragraph we assume that the "business method" concept is appropriately defined, as discussed in the preceding chapters. *See in particular* Section IV.2.6, "Schemes, rules and methods for doing business", p. 200.

Patent law simply is not suited to appropriate all forms of costly or valuable knowledge. Granting patents for knowledge that is not "technical" in the above sense would be *insufficiently determinate,* probably *disproportionate,* presumably *unneeded* and occasionally *insufficient.*[1159] There are useful alternatives for appropriation, and too much appropriation may hurt innovation.

V.3. The benefits of the proposed approach

The table below summarises the main differences between the traditional approach based on a "horizontal" technology concept, and the proposed approach based on a "vertical" technology concept, and for each aspect it gives the benefit of the "vertical" technology criterion.

	technology criterion		
aspect	**traditional "horizontal"**	**proposed "vertical"**	**benefit**
Applied to:	Product features, or disciplines.	Category of knowledge.	Suited for "mixed" applications.
Compliance	Violates EPC and TRIPS.	Follows statutes precisely.	Legitimacy.
Discrimi-nation	Only subject-matter listed in Art. 52(2) is tested for technical content.	All applications are tested for technical content.	Simplification, no discrimination.
Foundation	Tradition.	System of patent law.	Helps interpretation.
Constancy	"Dynamic" technology concept.	Fixed "future-proof" rule.	Legal certainty.
"Mixed" applications	Various "contribution" approaches.	Natural solution.	Resolves paradox.
Scope	Specific European rule.	Could be applied in American law as well (to "abstract ideas" exclusion).	Opportunity for harmonisation.

1159 *See* p. 158.

There are benefits both on the level of principle and the practical level. For instance, discrimination of patent applications is not just forbidden, it is also laborious.

The only *disadvantage* of the proposed approach is that it is not yet commonly accepted.

V.4. Finally

This study leads to the conclusion that the legislation should be interpreted in a manner very different from today in order to achieve a consistent delimitation of the domain of patent law, and gives both proponents and opponents rational arguments why patents can or cannot be granted for certain controversial subject-matter, like software and business methods.

Isn't it an illusion that a so very different approach will ever become the state of the law? This question should be juxtaposed with the certainty that the present interpretations have so essential shortcomings that they can never lead to a satisfactory result, as we have seen. It may sound contradictory, but a break with the past will eventually improve legal certainty, because only a radical change can liberate patent law from its present paradoxes.

In any case, the proposed approach is realistic insofar that it does not need legislative changes. On the contrary, it follows legislation more closely than the present interpretations, that actually violate the European Patent Convention, and occasionally even Title 35 of the United States Code, the American patent statute.

If we consider famous nineteenth century U.S. Supreme Court decisions that still hold as precedents, then the approach we recommend appears no revolution but a return to age-old arguments that still a very convincing.

In 2010, both the EPO Enlarged Board of Appeal and the U.S. Supreme Court were found not to be able to clarify the boundaries of the patent law domain, for various reasons. Is it the legislator's turn again? The chaotic discussion about the eventually rejected proposal for a European Directive for "computer-implemented inventions" some years ago shows that a solution is far away if the problem is unclear.

Sooner or later, the stalemate will end. It is hoped that this study will contribute to a structural solution that serves both justice and legal certainty, and eventually promotes innovation.

Cited literature

Aharonian 2004

Greg Aharonian, 'More 'technical' nonsense from EPO heard at a London meeting', 33 *The Journal of the CIPA* 2004, p. 23-27.

Aharonian & Stim 2004

Gregory Aharonian & Richard Stim, *Patenting art and entertainment. New strategies for protecting creative ideas*, Berkeley (CA): Nolo 2004.

Allison & Lemley 2000

John R. Allison & Mark A. Lemley, 'Who's Patenting What? An Empirical Exploration of Patent Prosecution', 53 *Vand. L. Rev.* 2000, p. 2099-2174.

Allison & Tiller 2003

John R. Allison & Emerson H. Tiller, 'The Business Method Patent Myth', 18 *Berkeley Tech L.J.* 2003, p. 987-1084.

Ambrose 1981

Katharine P. Ambrose, 'The Mental Steps Doctrine', 48 *Tenn. L. Rev.* 1981, p. 903-917.

Anders 2001a

Wilfried Anders, 'Die Patentierbarkeit von Computerprogrammen und Geschäftsmethoden: Jüngere Entscheidungen des Bundesgerichtshofs und des Bundespatentgerichts/The patentability of computer programs and business methods: recent decisions of the Federal Court of Justice and the Federal Patent Court/La brevetabilité des programmes d'ordinateur et des méthodes dans le domaine des activités économiques: décisions récentes de la Cour fédérale de justice et du Tribunal fédéral des brevets', *EPO OJ Special Edition* 2, 2001, p. 130-149.

Anders 2001b

Wilfried Anders, 'Die unwesentlichen Merkmale im Patentanspruch - Die wesentlichen Merkmale der Erfindung', 103 *GRUR* 2001, p. 867-873.

Anders 2004

Wilfried Anders, 'Erfindungsgegenstand mit technischen und nichttechnischen Merkmalen', 106 *GRUR* 2004, p. 461-468.

Aplin 2008

Tanya Aplin, 'Patenting Computer Programs: a Glimmer of Convergence', 30 *EIPR* 2008, p. 379-382.

Arora 2005
Neeraj Arora, 'Disabling Patentability for Skill-Based Inventions: Aligning Patent Law With Competition Policy', 22 *Santa Clara Computer & High Tech. L.J.* 2005, p. 1-50.

Arundel & Patel 2003
Anthony Arundel & P. Patel, *Strategic Patenting*. Background report for the Trend Chart Policy Benchmarking Workshop New Trends in IPR Policy 2003. http://www.proinno-europe.eu/events/reports/documents/TCW15_background_paper.pdf.

Bacher/Melullis 2006
Klaus Bacher & Klaus-Jürgen Melullis, § 1, 1a in: *Benkard Patentgesetz, Gebrauchsmustergesetz*, Munich: Beck 2006.

Bakels 2003
Reinier B. Bakels, 'Software: werkwijze of voortbrengsel?', 71 *BIE* 2003, p. 428-434.

Bakels 2005
Reinier B. Bakels, 'A New Paradigm in Patent Law: The Vertical Concept of Technology', in: F. Willem Grosheide & Jan J. Brinkhof (eds), *Intellectual Property Law, Articles on Crossing Border between traditional and actual*. Antwerpen-Oxford: Intersentia 2005, p. 349-365.

Bakels 2008
Reinier B. Bakels, 'Should Only Technical Inventions be Patentable, Following the European Example?', 7 *Nw. J. Tech. & Intell. Prop.* 2008, p. 50-62.

Bakels 2009
Reinier B. Bakels, 'Software Patentability: What Are the Right Questions?', 31 *EIPR* 2009, p. 514-522.

Bakels 2010
Reinier B. Bakels, 'Why is there no end to the software patent debate?', in: Erich Schweighofer, Jens Gaster & Benjamin Farrand (eds.), *Knowledge Rights - Legal, Societal and Related Technological Aspects*. Vienna: Österreichische Computer Gesellschaft 2010, p. 63-72.

Bakels 2011
Reinier B. Bakels, 'Are software patents something special?', in: Emanuela Arezzo & Gustavo Ghidini (eds.), *Biotechnology and software patent law: a comparative review of new developments*. Cheltenham: Edward Elgar 2011, p. 131-152.

Bakels & Hugenholtz 2002
Reinier B. Bakels & P. Bernt Hugenholtz, *The patentability of computer programs. Discussion of European-level legislation in the field of patents for software*. Study commissioned by the European Parliament. 2002.
http://www.ivir.nl/publications/other/softwarepatent.pdf.

Bambauer 2005
Derek Bambauer, 'Legal Responses to the Challenges of Sports Patents', 18 *Harv. J. Law & Tec* 2005, p. 401-433.
http://jolt.law.harvard.edu/articles/pdf/v18/18HarvJLTech401.pdf.

Banks 1970
M.A.L. Banks, *The British patent system: report of the Committee to Examine the Patent System and Patent Law*, Londen: HMSO 1970.

Beier & Straus 1982
Friedrich-Karl Beier & Joseph Straus, *Der Schutz wissenschaftlicher Forschungsergebnisse: zugleich eine Würdigung des Genfer Vertrages über die internationale Eintragung wissenschaftlicher Entdeckungen*, Weinheim: Verlag Chemie 1982.

Bently et al. 2010
Lionel Bently, Brad Sherman, Denis Borges Barbosa (with Karin Grau-Kuntz), Shamnad Basheer (with Shashwat Purohit and Prashant Reddy), Coenraad Visser and Richard Gold (with Yann Joly), *Exclusions from Patentability and Exceptions and Limitations to Patentees.* Geneva: WIPO Standing Committee on the Law of Patents 2010.
http://www.wipo.int/edocs/mdocs/scp/en/scp_15/scp_15_3-annex1.pdf.

Beresford 2000
Keith Beresford, *Patenting Software under the European Patent Convention*, Londen: Sweet & Maxwell 2000. Several years ago the publisher announced a second edition of this book, but according to the author it is uncertain whether and when it will be published.

Van den Berg 1996
Paul Van Den Berg, 'Patentability of computer-software-related inventions', in: Members of the Enlarged Board of Appeal of the EPO (eds.), *The law and practice of the Enlarged Board of Appeal of the European Patent Office during its first ten years: a series of articles reviewing the development of jurisprudence under the European Patent Convention.* Cologne [etc.]: Carl Heymanns 1996, p. 29-47.

Bergstra & Klint 2007
Jan A. Bergstra & Paul Klint, 'About "trivial" software patents: The IsNot case', *Science of computer programming* 2007, p. 264-285.

Bessen 2003
James Bessen, 'Patent Thickets: Strategic Patenting of Complex Technologies', 2003. http://www.researchoninnovation.org/thicket.pdf.

Bessen & Hunt 2007
James Bessen & Robert M. Hunt, 'An Empirical Look at Software Patents', 16 *Journal of Economics & Management Strategy* 2007, p. 157-189.

Bessen & Meurer 2005
James Bessen & Michael J. Meurer, 'Lessons for Patent Policy From Empirical Research on Patent Litigation', 9 *Lewis & Clark L. Rev.* 2005, p. 1-27 http://www.researchoninnovation.org/lclr.pdf.

Betten 1988
Jürgen Betten, 'Patentschutz für software-bezogene Erfindungen', 90 *GRUR* 1988, p. 248-254.

Beyer 1986
Hans Beyer, 'Der Begriff der » technischen Erfindung « aus naturwissenschaftlich-technischer Sicht', in: Bundespatentgericht (red.), *25 Jahre Bundespatentgericht*. Köln, Berlin (etc.), Heymann 1986, p. 189-210.

Beyer 1990
Hans Beyer, 'Der Begriff der Information als Grundlage des technischen Charakters von programmbezogenen Erfindungen', 92 *GRUR* 1990, p. 399-410.

Biela 2007
Joseph A. Biela, 'Claim Interpretation: a Claim Indefiniteness Analysis Proposal', 47 *IDEA* 2007, p. 561-586 http://www.piercelaw.edu/assets/pdf/idea-vol47-no4-biela.pdf.

Blind 2004
Knut Blind, *The economics of standards*. Cheltenham, UK: Edward Elgar 2004.

Blind, Cremers & Mueller 2009
Knut Blind, Katrin Cremers & Elisabeth Mueller, 'The influence of strategic patenting on companies' patent portfolios', 38 *Research Policy* 2009, p. 428-436.

Blind, Edler, Nack & Straus 2003
Knut Blind, Jakob Edler, Ralph Nack & Josef Straus, *Software-Patente. Eine empirische Analyse aus ökonomischer und juristischer Perspektive*, Heidelberg: Physica Verlag 2003.

Blind, Edler & Friedewald 2005
Knut Blind, Jakob Edler & Michael Friedewald, *Software patents. Economic impacts and policy implications.* Cheltenham [etc.]: Elgar 2005.

Blum 1977
R.E. Blum, 'Zum Begriff der patentfähigen Erfindung nach dem Europäischen Patentübereinkommen', 79 *GRUR* 1977, p. 357-359.

Boettiger & Bennett 2005
Sara Boettiger & Alan B. Bennett, 'Bayh-Dole: if we knew then what we know now', 24 *Nature biotechnology* 2006, p. 320-324, with further sources; Clifton Leaf, 'The Law of Unintended Consequences', *Fortune* 2005. http://money.cnn.com/magazines/fortune/fortune_archive/2005/09/19/8272884.

Bostyn 2001
Sven J.R. Bostyn, 'Ik denk, dus ik krijg een octrooi. Octrooieerbaarheid van bedrijfsvoeringsmethodes en ideeën in Europa en de VS', 69 *BIE* 2001, p. 77-88.

Bostyn 2003
Sven J.R. Bostyn, 'The Prodigal Son: The Relationship Between Patent Law And Health Care', 11 *Med. L. Rev.* 2003, p. 67-120.

Bracha 2004
Oren Bracha, 'The Commodification of Patents 1600-1836: How Patents Became Rights and Why We Should Care', 38 *Loy. L. A. L. Rev.* 2004, p. 177-244.

Brinkhof 2004
Jan J. Brinkhof, 'Wish List in the Area of Patent Law', 35 *IIC* 2004, p. 407-416.

Brinkhof 2009
Jan Brinkhof, 'On Enforcement of European Patents and the "Desire for Harmonisation"-Factor', in: Christian Osterrieth (red.), Patentrecht. Festschrift für Thomas Reimann zum 65. Geburtstag. Köln: Heymann 2009, p. 25-36 of 37.

Brodeßer 1993
Otto Brodeßer, 'Die sogenannte "Aufgabe" der Erfindung, ein unergiebiger Rechtsbegriff', 95 *GRUR* 1993, p. 185-190.

Broy & Lehmann 1992
Manfred Broy & Michael Lehmann, 'Die Schutzfähigkeit von Computerprogrammen nach dem neuen europäischen und deutschen Urheberrecht - eine interdisziplinaire Stellungnahme', 94 *GRUR* 1992, p. 419-423.

De Bruijn 1944
A.J. de Bruijn, 'Octrooiering van gezagsuitoefening', 19 *NJB* 1944, p. 171-175.

Bruzga 1987
Charles E. Bruzga, 'A Review of the Benson-Flook-Diehr Trilogy: Can the "Subject Matter" Validity of Patent Claims Reciting Mathematical Formulae Be Determined Under 35 U.S.C. Section 112?', 69 *J. Pat. & Trademark Off. Soc'y* 1987, p. 197-216.

Bulling 2007
Alexander Bulling, 'Sind britische Erfindungen anders als europäische? - Die aktuelle Rechtssprechung der EPA-Beschwerdekammern und des britischen Court of Appeal (Civil Division) zu computerimplementierten Erfindungen', 98 *Mitt.* 2007, p. 1-5.

Bunke 2009
Holger Bunke, '40 Jahre "Rote Taube" - Die Entwicklung des Erfindungsbegriffs', 100 *Mitt.* 2009, p. 169-173.

Burk & Lemley 2009
Dan L. Burk & Mark A. Lemley, *The Patent Crisis and How the Courts Can Solve It*. Chicago etc.: University of Chicago Press, 2009.

Calabresi & Melamed 1972
Guido Calabresi & A. Douglas Melamed, 'Property Rules, Liability Rules, and Inalienability: one view of the cathedral', 85 *Harv. L. Rev.* 1972, p. 1089-1128.

Casalonga 1979
Axel Casalonga, 'The Concept of Inventive Step in the European Patent Convention', 10 *IIC* 1979, p. 412-432.

Cockburn & MacGarvie 2009
Iain M. Cockburn & Megan J. MacGarvie, 'Patents, Thickets and the Financing of Early-Stage Firms: Evidence from the Software Industry', 18 *Journal of economics & management strategy* 2009, p. 729-774.

Cohen & Lemley 2001
Julie E. Cohen & Mark A. Lemley, 'Patent Scope and Innovation in the Software Industry', 89 *Cal. L. Rev.* 2001, p. 4-56.

Cohen, Nelson & Walsh 2000
Wesley M. Cohen, Richard R. Nelson & John P. Walsh, *Protecting Their Intellectual Assets: Appropriability Conditions and Why U.S. Manufacturing Firms Patent (or Not).* National Bureau of Economic Research 2000. http://www.nber.org/papers/w7552.pdf.

Colyvas, Crow, Gelijns, Mazzoleni, Nelson, Rosenberg & Sampat 2002
Jeannette Colyvas, Michael Crow, Annetine Gelijns, Roberto Mazzoleni, Richard R.Nelson, Nathan Rosenberg & Bhaven N.Sampat, 'How Do University Inventions Get Into Practice?', 48 *Management Science* 2002, p. 61-72.

Cooper Dreyfuss 2000
Rochelle Cooper Dreyfuss, 'Are Business Method Patents bad for Business?', 16 *Santa Clara Computer & High Tech. L.J.* 2000, p. 263-280.

Cotropia 2006
Christopher Cotropia, 'Observations on Recent Patent Decisions: The Year in Review', 88 *J. Pat. Off. Soc'y* 2006, p. 46-72.

Crouch 2008
Dennis D. Crouch, 'The Patent Lottery: Exploiting Behavioral Economics for the Common Good', 16 *Geo. Mason L. Rev.* 2008, p. 141-172. http://ssrn.com/abstract=1314374.

Davies 2004
Simon Davies, 'A reply to Mr Aharonian', 33 *The Journal of the CIPA* 2004, p. 77-79.

Descartes 1637
René Descartes, *Discours de la méthode*, 1637. Republished under http://www.gutenberg.org/ebooks/13846. English translation: *Discourse on the Method of Rightly Conducting One's Reason and of Seeking Truth* http://www.gutenberg.org/ebooks/59.

Dickinson 2000
Q. Todd Dickinson, 'E-Commerce, Business Method Patents, and the USPTO: An Old Debate for a New Economy', 19 *Cardozo Arts & Ent. L.J.* 2000, p. 389-403.

Dölemeyer 1993
Barbara Dölemeyer, ,"Das Urheberrecht ist ein Weltrecht". Immaterialgüterrecht und Rechtsvergleichung bei Josef Kohler', in: Elmar Wadle (ed.), *Historische Studien zum Urheberrecht in Europa.* Berlin: Duncker & Humblot 1993, p. 139-150.

Drahos 1995
Peter Drahos, 'Global Property Rights in Information: The story of TRIPS at the GATT', 13 *Prometheus* 1995, p. 6-19.

Dreiss 1994
Uwe Dreiss, 'Der Durchschnittsfachmann als Maßstab für ausreichende Offenbarung, Patentfähigkeit und Patentauslegung', 96 *GRUR* 1994, p. 781-791.
Duffy 2002
John F. Duffy, 'Harmony and Diversity in Global Patent Law', 17 *Berkeley Tech. L.J.* 2002, p. 685-726.
Duffy et al. 2008
John F. Duffy, John A. Squires, Thomas S. Biemer, Steven I. Wallach & Philip J. Foret, Brief Of Amicus Curiae Regulatory Datacorp, Inc. In Support Of Neither Party. 2008. In re Bilski, 545 F.3d 943 (2008), (No. 07-1130), 2008 WL 1842273, 7 April 2008. http://www.patentlyo.com/patent/bilski.duffy.pdf.
Eisenberg 2012
Rebecca S. Eisenberg, 'Wisdom of the Ages or Dead-Hand Control? Patentable Subject Matter for Diagnostic Methods after in re Bilski', 3 *Case W. Res. J.L. Tech. & Internet* 2012, p. 1-65.
Elben 1960
Wilfried Elben, *Technische Lehre und Anweisung an den menschlichen Geist im Patent- und Gebrauchsmusterrecht* (diss. Frankfurt/Main), [no publisher specified] 1960.
Engel 1978
F.W. Engel, 'Zum Begriff der technischen Erfindung nach der Rechtsprechung des Bundesgerichtshofes', 80 *GRUR* 1978, p. 201-207.
EPO Examination Guidelines 2010
Guidelines for Examination in the European Patent Office, Munich: EPO 2010, http://www.epo.org/law-practice/legal-texts/guidelines.html. A new version will enter into force in June 2012.
EPO Case Law 2006
Albert Ballester Rodès e.a., *Case Law of the Boards of Appeal*, Munich: EPO 2006. Also available in German and French. http://www.epo.org/service-support/publications/procedure/case-law.html.
EPO Case Law 2010
EPO Legal Research Service for the Boards of Appeal, *Case Law of the Boards of Appeal of the European Patent Office*, 2010. Also available in German and French. http://www.epo.org/service-support/publications/procedure/case-law-2010.html.

European Patent Office 2007

European Patent Office, *Scenarios for the Future. How might IP regimes evolve by 2025? What global legitimacy might such regimes have?* Munich: European Patent Office 2007.

Ergenzinger 2006

Edward R. Ergenzinger Jr, 'The American Inventor's Protection Act: A Legislative History', 7 *Wake Forest Intell. Prop. L.J.* 2006, p. 145-172.

Faure, Hartlief & Philipsen 2006

M. Faure, T. Hartlief & N. Philipsen, *Resultaatgerelateerde beloningssystemen voor advocaten. Een vergelijkende beschrijving van beloningssystemen voor advocaten in een aantal landen van de Europese Unie en Hong Kong*, Maastricht: METRO, Universiteit Maastricht, Faculteit der Rechtsgeleerdheid 2006, http://www.wodc.nl/images/1347_volledige_tekst_tcm44-59425.pdf.

Fellas 1999

John Fellas, 'The Patentability of Software Related Inventions in the United States', 21 *EIPR* 1999, p. 330-333.

Ganahl 2003

Bernhard Ganahl, 'Ist die Kerntheorie wieder aktuell?', 94 *Mitt.* 2003, p. 537-543.

Gerbrandy 1946

Sjoerd Gerbrandy, *Industrieele Eigendom en Subjectief Recht*. (diss. Amsterdam VU 1946). Zwolle: W.E.J. Tjeenk Willink 1946.

Gerwinski 2010

Peter Gerwinski, 'Overhauling the Patent System in the US and the EU', in: Erich Schweighofer, Jens Gaster & Benjamin Farrand (eds.), *Knowledge Rights - Legal, Societal and Related Technological Aspects*. Vienna: Österreichische Computer Gesellschaft 2010, p. 63-72.

Ghosh 2009

Shubha Ghosh, 'Patenting Games: Or, Baker v. Selden Revisited', 11 *Vand. J. Ent. & Tech. L.* 2009, p. 871-898.

Graham & Mowery 2003

Stuart J.H. Graham & David C. Mowery, 'Intellectual Property Protection in the U. S. Software Industry', in: Wesley M. Cohen and Stephen A. Merrill, eds., *Patents in the knowledge-Based Economy*, National Research Council, Washington: National Academies Press 2003, p. 219-258.

Gramm 1984
Werner Gramm, 'Die gewerbliche Anwendbarkeit - Inhalt und Bedeutung für die Erteilungspraxis', 86 *GRUR* 1984, p. 761-769.

Granstrand 1999
Ove Granstrand, The Economics and Management of Intellectual Property: Towards Intellectual Capital. Cheltenham: Elgar 1999.

Haase 2003
Heiko Haase, *Die Patentierbarkeit von Computersoftware* (diss. TU Ilmenau), Hamburg: Kovac 2003.

Haertel 1981
Kurt Haertel, 'Die Harmonisierungswirkung des Europäischen Patentrechts', 30 *GRUR Int* 1981, p. 479-490.

Hall & Ham 2001
Bronwyn H. Hall & Rosemarie Ham Ziedonis, 'The Patent Paradox Revisited: An Empirical Study of Patenting in the U.S. Semiconductor Industry, 1979-1995', 32 *The RAND Journal of Economics* 2001, p. 101-128.

Hanneman 1985
H.W.A.M Hanneman, *The patentability of computer software: an international guide to the protection of computer-related inventions*, Deventer: Kluwer 1985.

Hanneman 1986
H.W. Hanneman, 'Octrooiering van computerprogramma's als voortbrengsel', 54 *BIE* 1986, p. 33-36.

Hardin 1968
Garrett Hardin, 'The Tragedy of the Commons', 162 *Science* 1968, p. 1243-1248.

Hart 1989
Robert J. Hart, 'Application of Patents to Computer Technology - UK and the EPO Harmonisation', 11 *EIPR* 1989, p. 42-46.

Hartlief 1997
T. Hartlief, *Ieder draagt zijn eigen schade* (inaugural lecture Leiden), Deventer: Kluwer 1997.

Heller 1998
Michael A. Heller, 'The Tragedy Of The Anticommons: Property In The Transition From Marx To Markets', 111 *Harvard L. Rev.* 1998, p. 621-688.

Heller & Eisenberg 1998
Michael A. Heller & Rebecca S. Eisenberg, 'Can Patents Deter Innovation? The Anticommons in Biomedical Research', 280 *Science* 1998, p. 698-701.

Von Hellfeld 1986
Axel von Hellfeld, 'Protection of Inventions Comprising Computer Programs by the European and German Patent Offices', 2 *Computer Law and Practice* 1986, p. 182-189.

Von Hellfeld 1989
Axel Von Hellfeld, 'Sind Algorithmen schutzfähig?', 91 *GRUR* 1989, p. 471-485.

Von Hellfeld 2008
Axel Von Hellfeld, 'Ist nur Technik Stand der Technik? - Zum neuen Neuheitsbegriff im Europäischen Patentamt und dessen Anwendung auf rechnergestützte Erfindungen', 57 *GRUR Int* 2008, p. 1007-1013.

Hesse 1981
Hans Gerd Hesse, 'Die Aufgabe - Begriff und Bedeutung im Patentrecht', 83 *GRUR* 1981, p. 853-864.

Horns 2000
Axel H. Horns, 'Der Patentschutz für softwarebezogene Erfindungen im Verhältnis zur "Open Source"-Software', *JurPC* 223/2000. http://www.jurpc.de/aufsatz/20000223.htm.

Hössle 2000
Markus Hössle, 'Der nicht-statische Technikbegriff. Zu den BGH-Beschlüssen "Logikverifikation" und "Sprachanalyseeinrichtung"', 91 *Mitt.* 2000, p. 343-346.

Hunter 2004
Starling David Hunter III, 'Have Business Method Patents Gotten a Bum Rap? Some Empirical Evidence'. *The Journal of Information Technology Theory and Application (JITTA)*, 6:1, 2004, 1-24.

Hutter 1997
J.J. Hutter, 'Octrooiering van software: een overzicht van omgekeerde tweede medische indicatie tot octrooiering van CD's', 65 *BIE* 1997, p. 315-319.

Huydecoper & Van Nispen 2002
J.L.R.A. Huydecoper & C.J.J.C. van Nispen, E.A. *van Nieuwenhoven Helbach. Industriële eigendom. Deel 1: Bescherming van technische innovatie*, Deventer: Kluwer 2002.

Janis 2012
Mark D. Janis, 'The False Allure of Patent Eligibility Restrictions in the U.S.', 43 *IIC* 2012, p. 1-3.
Jehan 2001
Robert Jehan, 'Economical with the law', 30 *The Journal of the CIPA* 2001, p. 78-84.
Jestaedt 2002
Berhhard Jestaedt, Art. 1-3, 56, 57, 64 in: *Benkard Europäisches Patentübereinkommen*, Munich: Beck 2002.
Kahin 2007
Brian Kahin, 'Patents and Diversity in Innovation', 13 *Mich. Telecomm. Tech. L. Rev.* 2007, p. 389-399. http://www.mttlr.org/volthirteen/kahin.pdf.
Kappos, Thomas & Bluestone 2008
David J. Kappos, John R. Thomas & Randall J. Bluestone, 'A Technological Contribution Requirement for Patentable Subject Matter: Supreme Court Precedent and Policy', 7 *Nw. J. Tech. & Intell. Prop.* 2008, p. 152-170.
Kiesewetter-Köbinger 2001
Swen Kiesewetter-Köbinger, 'Über die Patentprüfung von Programmen für Datenverarbeitungsanlagen', 103 *GRUR* 2001, p. 185-193.
Kieff, Kramer & Kunstadt 2009
F. Scott Kieff, Robert G. Kramer & Robert M. Kunstadt, 'It's Your Turn, But It's My Move: Intellectual Property Protection For Sports "Moves"', 25 *Santa Clara Computer & High Tech. L.J.* 2009, p. 765-785.
Klaiber 2010
Kilian Klaiber, 'Stellungnahme zur vor der großen Beschwerdekammer des EPA anhängigen Vorlage G3/08 betreffend die Patentierung von Computerprogrammen', 112 *GRUR* 2010, p. 561-566.
Klemens 2005
Ben Klemens, *Math You Can't Use*. Washington DC: Brookings Institution Press 2005.
Klunker & Waldeck Pyrmont 2006
Nina-Sophie Klunker & Wolrad Prinz zu Waldeck und Pyrmont, 'Diskussionsforum über den Entwurf des "Abkommens zur Harmonisierung materieller Fragen zum Patentrecht" (Substantive

Patent Law Treaty -- SPLT) vom 1.-3. März 2006 in Genf', 55 *GRUR Int* 2006, p. 577-584.

Knight 2004
Andrew F. Knight, 'A Potentially New IP: Storyline Patents', 86 *J. Pat. Off. Soc'y* 2004, p. 859-877.

Knight 2007
Andrew F. Knight, 'A Patently Novel Plot: Fiction, Information, and Patents in the 21st Century', 47 *IDEA* 2006, p. 203-234. http://www.piercelaw.edu/assets/pdf/idea-vol47-no2-knight.pdf.

Knuth 1994
Donald Knuth, *Letter to the Patent Office.* http://www.progfree.org/Patents/knuth-to-pto.txt.

Kohler 1880
Josef Kohler, *Das Autorrecht, eine zivilistische Abhandlung: zugleich ein Beitrag zur Lehre vom Eigenthum, vom Miteigenthum, vom Rechtsgeschäft und vom Individualrecht,* Jena: Gustav Fischer 1880.

Kohler 1908
Josef Kohler, *Lehrbuch des Patentrechts,* Mannheim [etc.]: Bensheimer 1908.

Kolle 1974a
Gert Kolle, 'Der Rechtsschutz von Computerprogramme aus nationaler und internationaler Sicht, 2. Teil', 76 *GRUR* 1974, p. 7-20.

Kolle 1974b
Gert Kolle, 'The Patentable Invention in the European Patent Convention', 5 *IIC* 1974, p. 140-156.

Kolle 1977
Gert Kolle, 'Technik, Datenverarbeitung und Patentrecht - Bemerkungen zur Dispositionsprogramm-Entscheidung des Bundesgerichtshofs', 79 *GRUR* 1977, p. 58-74.

Kraßer 2001
Rudolf Kraßer, 'Erweiterung des patentrechtlichen Erfindungsbegriffes?', 103 *GRUR* 2001, p. 959-965.

Kraßer 2004
Rudolf Kraßer, *Patentrecht: ein Lehr- und Handbuch zum deutschen Patent- und Gebrauchsmusterrecht, europäischen und internationalen Patentrecht,* Munich: Beck 2004.

Kraßer 2009
Rudolf Kraßer, *Patentrecht: ein Lehr- und Handbuch zum deutschen Patent- und Gebrauchsmusterrecht, europäischen und internationalen Patentrecht,* Munich: Beck 2009.

Kukkonen III 1998
Carl. A Kukkonen III, 'Be a Good Sport and Refrain from Using my Patented Putt: Intellectual Property Protection for Sports Related Movements', 80 *J. Pat. Off. Soc'y* 1998, p. 808-829.

Kumm 1963
Alfred W. Kumm, 'Die Erfindungen und ihre Kriterien - Untersuchung einiger patentrechtlicher Grundbegriffe in Hinblick auf die europäischen Vereinheitlichungsbestrebungen', 12 *GRUR Ausl* 1963, p. 289-297.

Lee 1997
Eric M. Lee, '35 USC 287(c) - The Physician Immunity Statute', 79 *J. Pat. Off. Soc'y* 1997, p. 701-720.

Lemley & McGowan 1998
Mark A. Lemley & David McGowan, 'Legal Implications of Network Economic Effects', 86 *Cal. L. Rev.* 1998, p. 479-545.

Lieberman & Montgomery 1988
Marvin B Lieberman & David B. Montgomery, 'First-Mover Advantages', 9 *Strategic Mgmt. J.* 1988, p. 41-58.

Locke 1690
John Locke, *Second Treatise of Government*, 1690. Available via http://www.gutenberg.org/ebooks/7370.

Lundgren 1996
Carl Lundgren, 'Using Relative Profit Incentives to Prevent Collusion', 11 *Review of industrial organization* 1996, p. 533-550.

Luginbühl 2011
Stefan Luginbuehl, *European patent law. towards a uniform interpretation*. Cheltenham [u.a.]: Edward Elgar 2011.

Machlup 1958
Fritz Machlup, *An Economic Review of the Patent System*, Washington: US Govt. Print. Office 1958.

Machlup & Penrose 1950
Fritz Machlup & Edith E.T. Penrose, 'The Patent Controversy in the Nineteenth Century', 10 *Journal of Economic History* 1950, p. 1-29.

McEniery 2009
Benjamin J. McEniery, '`Storyline patents': are plots patentable?', 33 *Melbourne University L. Rev.* 2009.

McMillan 1979
John McMillan, 'The Free-Rider Problem: A Survey', 55 *The economic record* 1979, p. 95-107.

Manevitz 2006
Ben Manevitz, 'What's the Story With Storyline Patents - an Argument Against the Allowance of Proposed Storyline Patents and for the Rejection of Currently Pending Storyline Patent Applications', 24 *Cardozo Arts & Ent LJ* 2006, p. 717-737. http://cardozoaelj.com/wp-content/uploads/Journal%20Issues/Volume%2024/Issue%202/Manevitz.pdf.

Martin 1987
M. Martin, 'The Patentability of Program-Related Inventions in the Netherlands', 18 *IIC* 1987, p. 621-626.

Meier-Beck 2007
Peter Meier-Beck, 'Die Rechtsprechung des Bundesgerichtshofs zum Patent- und Gebrauchsmusterrecht im Jahr 2005', 109 *GRUR* 2007, p. 11-17.

Melullis 2002
Klaus-Jürgen Melullis, Art. 52-55, 58-62 in: *Benkard Europäisches Patentübereinkommen*, Munich: Beck 2002.

Melullis 2007
Klaus-J. Melullis, 'Einige ausgewählte Probleme des Patentrechts aus deutscher Sicht'/ 'Some problems of patent law from a German viewpoint' / 'Le point de vue de l'Allemagne sur le droit des brevets à la lumière de quelques problèmes choisis', in: *EPO OJ Special Edition 2,* 2007, p. 184-199.

Merrill, Levin & Myers 2004
Stephen A. Merrill, Richard C. Levin & Mark B. Myers (eds.), *A Patent System for the 21st Century*. Washington: The National Academies Press 2004. http://books.nap.edu/html/patentsystem/0309089107.pdf.

Meurer 2002
Michael J. Meurer, 'Business Method Patents and Patent Floods', 8 *Wash. U. J.L. & Pol'y* 2002, p. 309-339.

Miles Prince 2010
Mary Miles Prince (red.), *The bluebook: a uniform system of citation.* Cambridge, MA: Harvard Law Review Association 2010.

Morsink 1999
Johannes Morsink, *The Universal declaration of human rights: origins, drafting, and intent*. Philadelphia, PA: University of Pennsylvania Press 1999.

Moorrees 1912

W. Moorrees, *Het octrooirecht. Deel 1: De octrooiwet, 1910*, Staatsblad 313, 's-Gravenhage: Mouton 1912.

Moufang 1993

Rainer Moufang, 'Methods of Medical Treatment Under Patent Law', 24 *IIC* 1993, p. 18-49.

Moufang 2005

Rainer Moufang, 'Softwarebezogene Erfindungen im Patentrecht', in: Annette Kur, Stefan Luginbühl & Eskil Waage (ed.), "... Und sie bewegt sich doch!": patent law on the move: Festschrift für Gert Kolle und Dieter Stauder zum 65. Geburtstag am 25. April 2005 und 20. Oktober 2005, Köln: Heymann 2005, p. 225-250.

Moy 1998

R. Carl Moy, 'Statutory Subject-matter and Hybrid Claiming', 17 *J. Marshall J. Computer & Info. L.* 1998, p. 277-309.

Moy & Erstling 2008

R. Carl Moy & Jay Erstling, Brief Of Amicus Curiae William Mitchell College Of Law Intellectual Property Institute In Support Of The United State Patent & Trademark Office, In re Bilski, 545 F.3d 943 (2008), (No. 07-1130), 2008 WL 1842269, 7 April 2008.

Müller 2006

Florian Müller, *No Lobbyists As Such. The War over Software Patents in the European Union*. Starnberg: SWM Software-Marketing GmbH, 2006. http://www.crashrecovery.org/NoLobbyistsAsSuch.pdf. In German published as: *Die Lobbyschlacht um Software-Patente*.

Mueller 2002

Janice M. Mueller, 'Patent Misuse Through the Capture of Industry Standards', 17 *Berkeley Tech L.J.* 2002, p. 623-684, http://www.btlj.org/data/articles/17_02_01.pdf.

Nack 2000

Ralph Nack, 'Sind jetzt computerimplementierte Geschäftsmethoden patentfähig? - Analyse der Bundesgerichtshof-Entscheidung "Sprachanalyseeinrichtung"', 49 *GRUR Int* 2000, p. 853-858.

Nack 2002

Ralph Nack, *Die patentierbare Erfindung unter den sich wandelnden Bedingungen von Wissenschaft und Technologie* (diss. Munich LMU), Köln [etc.]: Heymanns 2002.

Nack & Moufang 2005
Ralph Nack & Rainer Moufang, 'Kommentierung des Europäischen Patentübereinkommens: Artikel 52'. Part 28 of: Friedrich-Karl Beier, Kurt Haertel & Gerhard Schricker (ed.), *Europäisches Patentübereinkommen: Münchner Gemeinschaftskommentar*, Köln [etc.]: Heymann 2005.

Nelson 1959
Richard R. Nelson, 'The Simple Economics of Basic Scientific Research', 67 *The Journal of Political Economy* 1959, p. 297-306.

Neuperth 1975
Ernst Neuperth, 'Die Tätigkeit des Bundespatentgerichts im Jahr 1974', 77 *GRUR* 1975, p. 250-253.

Newton 1687
Isaac Newton, *Philosophiae Naturalis Principia Mathematica*, 1687. Cambridge: Cambridge University Press 1972.

Niedlich 2004
Wolfgang Niedlich, 'Anmerkungen zu Ganahl "Ist die Kerntheorie wieder aktuell?"', 95 *Mitt.* 2004, p. 291-292.

Nurton 2007
James Nurton, 'IBM Flies Soft-IP Community Patent Plan', *Managing Intellectual Property*, 31 July 2007, http://www.managingip.com/Article.aspx?ArticleID=1398998.

Ochmann 1992
Richard Ochmann, 'Zum Begriff der Erfindung als Patentvoraussetzung' in: Karl Bruchhausen et al. (eds.), *Festschrift für Rudolf Nirk zum 70. Geburtstag, am 11. Oktober 1992*. Munich: Beck 1992, p. 759-775.

Ostergard 1999
Robert L. Ostergard, 'Intellectual property: a universal human right? ', 21 *Hum. Rts. Q.* 1999, p. 156-178. http://74.220.219.58/~drafting/sites/default/files/paper_article/Robert%20L.%20Ostergard%20-%20Intellectual%20Property_%20A%20Universal%20Human%20Right.pdf.

Van Overwalle 2009
Geertrui Van Overwalle (red.), Gene *patents and collaborative licensing models: patent pools, clearinghouses, open source models and liability regimes*. Cambridge, UK: Cambridge University Press 2009.

Pagenberg 1984
Jochen Pagenberg, 'Kommentierung des Europäischen Patentübereinkommens: Art. 56 und 57'. Part 5 of: Friedrich-Karl

Beier, Kurt Haertel & Gerhard Schricker (ed.), *Europäisches Patentübereinkommen: Münchner Gemeinschaftskommentar*, Köln [etc.]: Heymann 1984.

Pagenberg 2002
Jochen Pagenberg, 'WIPO-Konferenz vom 6.-10. Mai 2002 zum Substantive Patent Law Treaty', 51 *GRUR Int* 2002, p. 736-737.

Parchomovsky & Wagner 2005
Gideon Parchomovsky & R. Polk Wagner, 'Patent Portfolios', 154 *U. Pa. L. Rev.* 2005, p. 1-77.

Patterson 2002
Mark R. Patterson, 'Inventions, Industry Standards, and Intellectual Property', 17 *Berkeley Tech L.J.* 2002, p. 1043-1083, http://www.btlj.org/data/articles/17_03_03.pdf.

Pila 2005a
Justine Pila, 'Dispute over the Meaning of "Invention" in Art. 52(2) EPC - The Patentability of Computer-Implemented Inventions in Europe', 36 *IIC* 2005, p. 173-191.

Pila 2005b
Justine Pila, 'Article 52(2) of the Convention on the Grant of European Patents: What Did the Framers Intend? A Study of the Travaux Preparatoires, 36 *IIC* 2005, p. 755-787. Note that in the original title there is no accent on "préparatoires".

Pila 2010a
Justine Pila, *The Requirement for an Invention in Patent Law*. Oxford: Oxford University Press 2010.

Pila 2010b
Justine Pila, 'On the European Requirement for an Invention', 41 *IIC* 2010, p. 906-926.

Pila 2011
Justine Pila, 'Software patents, separation of powers and failed syllogisms: a cornucopia from the Enlarged Board of Appeal of the European Patent Office', 70 *C.L.J.* 2011, p. 203-228. Also available as *Oxford Legal Studies Research Paper* No. 48/2010, http://ssrn.com/abstract=1612518.

Pires de Carvalho 2010
Nuño Pires de Carvalho, *The TRIPS Regime of Patent Rights*, The Hague: Kluwer Law International 2010.

PLG 1965
Patents Liaison Group, *United Kingdom patent law. The effects of the Strasbourg convention of 1963. Report on legislative changes which*

would be involved in the proposed ratification by the United Kingdom of the Strasbourg Convention on the unification of certain points of substantive law on patents for invention. London: H. M. S. O. 1965.

Popper 1963
Karl Raimund Popper, *Conjectures and refutations: the growth of scientific knowledge.* London: Routledge and Kegan Paul 1963.

Prasch 1987
Hermann Prasch, 'Technische Problemlösungen mit Datenverarbeitungssystemen aus patentrechtlicher Sicht', 3 *C&R* 1987, p. 337-347.

President's Committee on the Patent System 1966
President's Committee on the Patent System, *To promote the progress of ... useful arts, in an age of exploding technology.* Washington 1966.

'Pure Fiction: the Attempt to Patent Plot' 2005
'Pure Fiction: the Attempt to Patent Plot', 19 *Harv. J.L. & Tech.* 2005 p. 231-252, http://jolt.law.harvard.edu/articles/pdf/v19/19HarvJLTech231.pdf.

Van Raden 1996
Lutz Van Raden, 'Technology Dematerialized: Another Approach to Information-related Inventions', 18 *EIPR* 1996, p. 384-389.

Rahnasto 2003
Ilkka Rahnasto, *Intellectual Property Rights, External Effects and Anti-Trust Law*, Oxford: Oxford University Press 2003.

De Reede 1944
J.J. De Reede, 'Octrooi No. 50242 and de verordenende bevoegdheid der gemeenten', 19 *NJB* 1944, p. 249-253.

Rijlaarsdam 2005
Arie Rijlaarsdam, *Octrooi en dienstbetrekking: een voorstel tot verbetering van de positie van de werknemer-uitvinder* (diss. Delft), Delft: VSSD 2005.

Risch 2012
Michael Risch, 'America's First Patents'. Forthcoming 64 *Fla. L. Rev.* 2012, currently available at http://ssrn.com/abstract=2017275.

Rivette & Kline 2000a
Kevin G. Rivette & David Kline, 'Discovering New Value in Intellectual Property', 78 *Harv. Bus. Rev.* 2000, p. 54-67.

Rivette & Kline 2000b
Kevin G. Rivette & David Kline, *Rembrandts in the attic: unlocking the hidden value of patents.* Boston, MA: Harvard Business School Press 2000.

Rogge 2002

Rüdiger Rogge, Art. 66, 70, 99-101, 138-140 in: *Benkard Europäisches Patentübereinkommen*, Munich: Beck 2002.

Samuelson & Nordhaus 2010

Paul A. Samuelson & William D. Nordhaus, *Economics*, Boston: McGraw-Hill/Irwin, 2010.

Sawkar 2008

Anu R. Sawkar, 'Are Storylines Patentable? Testing the Boundaries of Patentable Subject Matter', 76 *Fordham L. Rev.* 2008, p. 3001-3064.

Schäfers 1992

Alfons Schäfers, 'Harmonisierung des Patentrechts: Perspektiven, Chancen und Hindernisse', in: Karl Bruchhausen (ed.), *Festschrift für Rudolf Nirk zum 70. Geburtstag*, Munich: Beck 1992.

Schar 1998

Markus Schar, 'Zum objektiven Technikbegriff im Lichte des Europäischen Patentübereinkommens', 89 *Mitt.* 1998, p. 322-339.

Scherer & Ross 1990

F.M. Scherer & David Ross, *Industrial market structure and economic performance*, Boston (MA) [etc.]: Houghton Mifflin, 1990.

Schiff 1971

Eric Schiff, *Industrialization without national patents: the Netherlands, 1869-1912, Switzerland, 1850-1907*, Princeton, N.J.: Princeton University Press 1971.

Schiuma 2000

Daniele Schiuma, 'TRIPS and the Exclusion of Software "as such" from Patentability', 31 *IIC* 2000, p. 36-51.

Schneider 2003

Michael Schneider, 'Achte Sitzung des Standing Committee on the Law of Patents der WIPO in Genf vom 25.-29. November 2002', 52 *GRUR Int* 2003, p. 350-353.

Schölch 2006

Günther Schölch, 'Patentschutz für computergestützte Entwurfsmethoden -- ein Kulturbruch?', 108 *GRUR* 2006, p. 969-976.

Schricker 2008

Gerhard Schricker, 'Urheberrechtsschutz für Spiele', 57 *GRUR Int* 2008.

Schumpeter 1942
Joseph A. Schumpeter, *Capitalism, socialism and democracy*. New York [etc.]: Harper & Row 1942.

Sedlmaier 2004
Roman Sedlmaier, *Die Patentierbarkeit von Computerprogrammen und ihre Folgeprobleme*, Munich: Herbert Utz Verlag 2004.

Sedlmaier & Gigerich 2005
Roman Sedlmaier & Jan Gigerich, 'Rechtliche Bedingungen und Risiken der Landeshauptstadt Munich für den Einsatz von Open-Source Software', *JurPC* 10/2005, p. Abs. 1-Abs. 192. http://www.jurpc.de/aufsatz/20050010.htm.

Silberstein 1961
Marcel Silberstein, *Erfindungsschutz und merkantilistische Gewerbeprivilegien* (diss. Basel 1951). Zürich: Polygraphischer Verlag 1961.

Smith 1999
Jeffrey A. Smith, 'It's Your Move - no it's not! the Application of Patent law to Sports Moves', 70 *U. Colo. L. Rev.* 1999, p. 1051-1087.

Soltysinski 1990
Stanislaw Soltysinski, 'Protection of Computer Programs: Comparative and International Aspects', 21 *IIC* 1990, p. 1-30.

Somaya & Teece 2000
Deepak Somaya & David J. Teece, *Combining Inventions in Multi-invention Products: Organizational Choices, Patents, and Public Policy*. Haas School of Business CCC Working Paper No. 99-4, 2000. http://ssrn.com/abstract=259889.

Spoor, Verkade & Visser 2005
J.H. Spoor, D.W.F. Verkade & D.J.G. Visser, *Auteursrecht, naburige rechten en databankenrecht*. Deventer: Kluwer 2005.

Van Staaij 1944
J.A.M. Van Staaij, 'Octrooiering van gezagsuitoefening', 19 *NJB* 1944, p. 205-206.

Stallman 2006
Richard M. Stallman, 'The Anatomy of a Trivial Patent', 2006, http://www.gnu.org/philosophy/trivial-patent.html.

Stobbs 2008
Gregory A. Stobbs, *Software Patents Worldwide*. Alphen aan den Rijn [etc.]: Kluwer Law International 2008. Loose-leaf edition, updated periodically.

Straus 1996

Joseph Straus, 'Implications of the TRIPs Agreement in the field of patent law', In: Friedrich-Karl Beier and Gerhard Schricker (ed.), *From GATT to TRIPs: the agreement on trade-related aspects of intellectual property rights*, Munich: Max Planck Institute for Foreign and International Patent, Copyright and Competition Law 1996, p. 160-215. Weinheim [u.a.]: Verlag VCH 1996.

Straus 2003

Joseph Straus, 'Der Beitrag Deutschlands zur Entwicklung des internationalen gewerblichen Rechtsschutzes', 52 *GRUR Int* 2003, p. 805-812.

Sutton 1970

Samuel J. Sutton, Jr., 'The "mental steps" doctrine: a critical analysis in the light of Prater and Wei', 52 *J. Pat. Off. Soc'y* 1970, p. 479-521.

Tauchert 1997a

Wolfgang Tauchert, 'Zur Beurteilung des technischen Characters von Patentanmeldungen aus dem Bereich der Datenverarbeitung unter Berücksichtigung der bisherigen Rechtsprechung', 99 *GRUR* 1997, p. 149-155.

Tauchert 1997b

Wolfgang Tauchert, 'Programm und Patent - Betrachtungen im Zusammenhang mit dem Technikbegriff', *JurPC* 36/1997, p. Abs. 1-Abs. 61. http://www.jurpc.de/aufsatz/19970036.htm.

Teece 2000

David J. Teece, *Managing intellectual capital: organizational, strategic, and policy dimensions*. Oxford: Oxford University Press 2000.

Telders 1946

B.M. Telders, Nederlandsch octrooirecht: handboek voor de praktijk, 's-Gravenhage: Nijhoff 1946.

Teufel 2008

Fritz Teufel, 'Aktuelle Entwicklungen im Bereich Softwarepatentierung Patentansprüche für computerimplementierte Erfindungen', 99 *Mitt.* 2008, p. 196-200.

Thomas 2000

John R. Thomas, 'An Epistemology Of Appropriation: Patentable Subject-Matter After State Street Bank', 4 *IPQ* 2000, p. 27-65.

Trimble 2012

Marketa Trimble, 'Injunctive Relief, Equity, and Misuse of Rights in U.S. Patent Law', 61 *GRUR Int* 2012, p. 514-522.

USPTO 2005a

United States Patent and Trademark Office, *Manual of Patent Examining Procedure*, Eighth Edition, Revision 3, 2005. This and other older editions of this manual are available via http://www.uspto.gov/web/offices/pac/mpep/indexold.htm.

USPTO 2005b

United States Patent and Trademark Office, *Interim Guidelines for Examination of Patent Applications for Patent Subject-matter Eligibility*, 20 October 2005, http://www.uspto.gov/web/offices/pac/dapp/opla/preognotice/guidelines101_20051026.pdf. These guidelines have also been published (without page numbers) in *Off. Gaz. Pat. Office*, week 47, nr. 13 (22 November 2005), http://www.uspto.gov/web/offices/com/sol/og/2005/week47/patgupa.htm.

USPTO 2006

United States Patent and Trademark Office, `Chapter 2100 Patentability', Revision 5, 2006, in: Manual of Patent Examining Procedure, Eighth Edition. http://www.uspto.gov/web/offices/pac/mpep/mpep_e8r5_2100.pdf

USPTO 2007

United States Patent and Trademark Office, `Chapter 2100 Patentability', Revision 6, 2007, in: *Manual of Patent Examining Procedure*, Eighth Edition. While new revisions of some chapters of this manual have appeared since, mid-2011 "Revision 6" still is the latest revision of this chapter. http://www.uspto.gov/web/offices/pac/mpep/mpep_e8r6_2100.pdf or http://www.uspto.gov/web/offices/pac/mpep/documents/2100.htm

Vacca 2011

Ryan Vacca, 'Acting Like an Administrative Agency: The Federal Circuit En Banc', 76 *Mo. L. Rev.* 2011, p. 733-762.

Vermont 2006

Samson Vermont, `Independent Invention as a Defense to Patent Infringement', 105 *Mich. L. Rev.*, p. 475-504.

Wank 1985

Rolf Wank, *Die juristische Begriffsbildung*, Munich: Beck 1985.

Weyand & Haase 2005

Joachim Weyand & Heiko Haase, 'Patenting Computer Programs: New Challenges', 36 *IIC* 2005, p. 647-663.

Wiebe 1994
Andreas Wiebe, 'Information als Naturkraft – Immaterialgüterrecht in der Informationsgesellschaft', 96 *GRUR* 1994, p. 233-246.
Williams-Jones 2002
Bryn Williams-Jones, 'History of a Gene Patent: Tracing the Development and Application of Commercial BRCA Testing', 10 *Health L.J.* 2002, p. 123-146.
Winischhofer 2000
Thomas Winischhofer, *Computersoftware und Patentrecht* (Dissertation Linz), 2000. http://www.winischhofer.net/other/patent.pdf.
WIPO 2002a
WIPO Standing Committee on the law of Patents, *Seventh Session. Report adopted by the Standing Committee*. Geneva, 25 November 2002, http://www.wipo.int/edocs/mdocs/scp/en/scp_7/scp_7_8.pdf.
WIPO 2002b
Standing Committee on the law of Patents. *Eighth Session. Summary by the Chair*. Geneva, 29 November 2002, http://www.wipo.int/edocs/mdocs/scp/en/scp_8/scp_8_8.pdf.
WIPO 2004
World Intellectual Property Organization (eds.), *WIPO intellectual property handbook. Policy, law and use*. Geneva: World Intellectual Property Organization 2004. http://www.wipo.int/about-ip/en/iprm.
WIPO 2009a
Standing Committee on the law of Patents. *Thirteenth Session. Exclusions From Patentable Subject Matter and Exceptions and Limitations To the Rights*. Geneva, 4 February 2009, http://www.wipo.int/edocs/mdocs/scp/en/scp_13/scp_13_3.pdf.
WIPO 2009b
Standing Committee on the law of Patents. *Twelfth session. Report adopted by the Standing Committee*. Geneva, 23 March 2009, http://www.wipo.int/edocs/mdocs/scp/en/scp_12/scp_12_5.pdf.
WIPO 2010
Standing Committee on the law of Patents. *Fourteenth Session. External Experts' Study Regarding Exclusions, Exceptions and Limitations for the Standing Committee on the Law of Patents* (SCP). Geneva, 26 January 2010, http://www.wipo.int/edocs/mdocs/scp/en/scp_14/scp_14_inf_2.pdf.

Wirth 1998

Niklaus Wirth, 'Hardware Compilation: Translating Programs into Circuits', 31 *Computer* 1998, nr. 6, p. 25-31.

Zipse 1973

Erich Zipse, 'Wird das künftige europäische Patenterteilungsverfahren den modernen, zukunftsintensiven Technologien gerecht?', 22 *GRUR Int* 1973, p. 182-190.

Zirn 2004

Frank Zirn, *Softwarerechtsschutz zwischen Urheberrecht und Patentrecht: aktuelle Entwicklungen vor historischem Hintergrund und internationaler Zusammenhang* (diss. Humboldt-Universität Berlin), Stuttgart: ibidem-Verlag 2004.

Zuse 1995

Konrad Zuse, *Der Computer - mein Lebenswerk; mit Geleitworten von F.L. Bauer und H. Zemanek*. Berlin [etc.]: Springer 1993. Also published in English translation, as *The computer-my life*, New York: Springer Verlag 1993.

Abbreviations

Entries in italics refer to the names of periodicals. Abbreviations in designations of parties in case law references are not included here (like "BBC"). The same applies for initials of annotators and other persons.

The names of American law reports have been abbreviated according to the rules of the "Bluebook".[1160]

Some of the abbreviations explained below are registered trademarks.[1161]

Abs.	Absatz (subsection of an article or paragraph in a German statute)
Anm.	Anmerkung: German comment of a court decision
Art.	Article
BGB	Bürgerliches Gesetzbuch: the German civil code
BGBl.	Bundesgesetzblatt: the German periodical for the formal announcement of new statutes
BGH	Bundesgerichtshof: the German Federal Court of Justice
BIE	Bijblad bij de Industriële Eigendom (periodical of the Dutch Patent Office)
BMLR	Butterworths' Medico Legal Reports
BNA	Bureau of National Affairs
BPAI	Board of Patent Appeals and Interferences (part of the USPTO)

1160 Miles Prince 2010, Table 13 "Periodicals", p. 445-467.

1161 These trademarks are used here in conformance with customary use in scientific publications. In The Netherlands, such a use of trademarks "anders dan ter onderscheiding van waren of diensten" is permitted, as there is a "geldige reden". Similarly, under German law this use is permitted as there is a "rechtfertigender Grund" in the sense of § 15(3) MarkenG, and under UK law, there is a "due cause" in the sense of S. 10(3) UK Trade Marks Act 1994.

BPatG	German Federal Patent Court („*Bundespatentgericht*“)
BPatGE	collected decisions of the German Federal Patent Court („Entscheidungen des Bundespatentgerichts“)
BRCA	breast cancer
BW	Burgerlijk Wetboek (Dutch civil code)
CAFC	United States Court of Appeal for the Federal Circuit, specialised court among other things for patent cases, from 1982.
CBE	Convention des Brevets Européens (French name for the EPC)
CCC	Consortium on Competitiveness and Cooperation
CCPA	United States Court of Customs and Patent Appeals, specialised court among other things for patent cases, from 1910-1982.
CD	Compact Disk
CIPA	Chartered Institute of Patent Attorneys (United Kingdom)
CIPA	The CIPA Journal
CR	Computerrecht
C&R	Computer und Recht (German)
DPMA	Deutsches Patent- und Markenamt (German patent and trademark office)
EC	European Community
EIPR	European Intellectual Property Review
EPO	European Patent Office
EPC	Convention on the Grant of European Patents (European Patent Convention)
EPC 1973	The original European Patent Convention
EPC 2000	The new version of the EPC that was agreed in 2000 (and went into force on 13 December 2007)
EP	European Parliament
EPA	Europäisches Patentamt (German name for the EPO)
EPO	European Patent Office or Organisation
EPÜ	Europäisches Patentübereinkommen (German name for the EPC)

E.R.	English Reports (case law from 1694-1873)
EU	European Union
ECHR	European Convention on Human Rights or European Court of Human Rights
EWCA	England & Wales Court of Appeal
EWHC	England & Wales High Court
F.	Federal Reporter (1880-1924)
F.2d	Federal Reporter, Second Series (1924-1993)
F.3d	Federal Reporter, Third Series (1993-today)
FSR	Fleet Street Reports
GATT	General Agreement on Tariffs and Trade
GPS	Global Positioning System
GRUR	Gewerblicher Rechtsschutz und Urheberrecht (German)
GRUR Int	Gewerblicher Rechtsschutz und Urheberrecht Internationaler Teil (German)
Gw	grondwet (Dutch constitution)
H.R.	House of Representatives
HMSO	Her Majesty's Stationery Office
HR	Hoge Raad der Nederlanden (Dutch Supreme Court)
IIC	International Review of Industrial Property and Copyright Law
IP	intellectual property
IPQ	Intellectual Property Quarterly
kWh	kilowatt hour (3,6 MJ)
MA	Massachusetts
METRO	Maastrichts Europees Instituut voor Transnationaal Rechtswetenschappelijk Onderzoek (research institute of the law faculty of Maastricht University)
Mitt.	Mitteilungen der deutschen Patentanwälte (German)
MJ	megajoule
MMR	Multimedia und Recht (German)
MPEP	Manual of Patent Examining Procedure (of the USPTO)
NJ	Nederlandse Jurisprudentie (Dutch case law)
NJB	Nederlands Juristenblad (Dutch)

NRDC	National Research Development Corporation
OJ	Official Journal (of the European Patent Office)
OJEC	Official Journal of the European Communities
p.	page
PatG	Patentgesetz: patent act in German speaking jurisdictions
PCT	Patent Cooperation Treaty
PLT	Patent Law Treaty (WIPO)
PMZ	(Blatt für) Patent-, Muster- und Zeichenwesen (German)
R.O.	(Wet op de) Rechterlijke Organisatie (Dutch law about the organisation of courts)
RG	Supreme Court of the German Reich (*Reichsgericht*, highest German court from 1879-1945)
Rn	Randnummer (number of paragraph in German legal publications)
ROW	Rijksoctrooiwet: Dutch patent act
RPC	Reports of Patent Cases (United Kingdom)
S.Ct.	United States Supreme Court
S.Ct.	United States Supreme Court Reporter
SCP	Standing Committee on the Law of Patents (WIPO)
SIM	Subscriber Identity Module (of mobile telephones)
SPLT	Substantive Patent Law Treaty (WIPO)
Stb.	Staatsblad (periodical for the formal announcement of new Dutch statutes)
TBA	Technical Board of Appeal (of the EPO)
Trb.	Tractatenblad (Dutch periodical for the announcement of treaties)
TRIPS	Trade Related Aspects of Intellectual Property Rights
UK	United Kingdom
UrhG	Urheberrechtsgesetz (German copyright act)
US	United States
US	United States Supreme Court Reports
USA	United States of America
USC	United States Code
USPQ2d	United States Patent Quarterly, Second Series
USPTO	United States Patent and Trademark Office

US	United States
VAT	value added tax
VU	Vrije Universiteit (Amsterdam)
WIPO	World Intellectual Property Organization
WTO	World Trade Organization

9 789058 508621